SLEEPING WIT]

SLEEPING WITH YOUR EARS OPEN

On patrol with the Australian SAS

GARY McKAY

ALLEN&UNWIN

First published in 2001

Allen & Unwin
83 Alexander Street
Crows Nest NSW 2065
Australia
Phone: (61 2) 8425 0100
Fax: (61 2) 9906 2218
Email: info@allenandunwin.com
Web: www.allenandunwin.com

National Library of Australia
Cataloguing-in-Publication entry:

McKay, Gary.
   Sleeping with your ears open: on patrol with the Australian SAS.

   Bibliography
   Includes index.
   ISBN 1 86508 297 X.

   1. Australia. Army. Special Air Service Regiment – Officers. 2. Australia.
   Army – Commando troops. 3. Australia. Army. Special Air Service Regiment.
   I. Title.

358.41310994

Printed by South Wind Production (S) Pte Ltd, Singapore

10 9 8 7 6 5

CONTENTS

v

GLOSSARY

Term	Explanation
AATTV	Australian Army Training Team Viet Nam
Albatross	RAAF callsign for 9 Squadron slick helicopter
Albatross Zero One	RAAF callsign for the leader's aircraft in an insertion
Albatross Zero Two	the slick that actually carries the SAS patrol on insertion guided by Albatross Zero One
ANPRC–25	very high frequency, man portable, radio set
AO	area of operations
APC	M113 armoured personnel carrier tracked vehicle
ARVN	Army of the Republic of South Viet Nam
Bird Dog	propeller-driven aircraft used by forward air controllers and for reconnaissance
BT	British tropical (rations)
Bushranger	RAAF callsign for the helicopter gunships armed with mini-guns and Zuni rockets
casevac	casualty evacuation
clacker	the firing device which generates the power to detonate the Claymore mine
Claymore (mine)	a shaped anti-personnel mine capable of devastating results fired singly or in banks

click	one kilometre
CMF	Citizen Military Forces
CO	Commanding Officer, in RAAF terms, the commander of the squadron
comms	communications
covert	an act conducted in secrecy or disguise
CP	command post
CS (gas)	a disabling explosive powered chemical agent designed to render the opposition incapable of resisting in a fire-fight. Causes coughing, weeping and runny noses. Can be lethal in a confined space such as a tunnel or bunker
CW	continuous wave
C4	composition explosive
DCM	Distinguished Conduct Medal
Digger	an Army soldier, rank indeterminate
DOBOP	Directorate of British Operations
EW	electronic warfare
exfil	exfiltrate, covertly depart an area
FAC	forward air controller, usually airborne
FARELF	Far East Region Land Forces
fleschette round	a shotgun type of round which fires steel darts instead of balls
GPMG–M60	general purpose machine-gun 7.62 mm
H&I	harassment and interdiction artillery or air strikes
HE	high explosive
HF	high frequency
humint	human intelligence (sources)
IA	immediate action
infil	infiltration, covertly enter an area
Int(el)	Intelligence (officer, staff, sources)
Intrep	intelligence report
J	jungle
jungle penetrator	a device lowered from a helicopter to extract people from the thick vegetation when landing was not possible
karabiner	a roping and climbing device designed to

	allow one to hook onto a rope for extraction purposes
Karex	a term used for karabiner extraction or rope extraction
LFT	light fire team, two gunship helicopters
locstat	(patrol) location state
LOH	light observation helicopter
LRRP	long range reconnaissance patrols, usually American forces
LUP	lying up position, any place used by the SAS for a halt of some time (see Notes to Chapter 3)
LZ	landing zone
M16	5.56 mm rifle used by Free World Forces in Viet Nam
M18A–1	the Claymore mine designation
M79	40 mm grenade launcher
M203	5.56 mm M16 rifle with a 40 mm grenade launcher mounted below the rifle barrel
MG	machine-gun
mini-gun, 7.62 mm	a gatling type weapon mounted on the side of the gunships capable of firing 4000 rounds per minute
NCO	non-commissioned officer
NVA	North Vietnamese Army
OC	Officer Commanding, usually a squadron or company sized unit
OKC	operator keyboard cipher
OKRC	operator keyboard radio cipher
OPSO	operations officer, the person responsible for the actual deployment of patrols
OTLP	one-time letter pad
Owen gun	9 mm, automatic machine carbine, designed as a jungle weapon
patrol	the basic group in a troop; can be any size from four-man to troop size
PE	plastic explosive
PIR	Pacific Islands Regiment (PNG)
pop (throw) smoke	request to detonate a smoke grenade for aircraft identification of patrol location

psyops	psychological operations
PW	prisoner of war
PZ	pick-up zone, for helicopter extraction
RAAF	Royal Australian Air Force
RAD	rope attachment device, the in-board device used to hold the ropes lowered to SAS patrols for rope extraction
RANHFV	Royal Australian Navy Helicopter Flight Viet Nam
rapell	to belay down a rope suspended from a helicopter
R&C	rest and convalescence (leave)
reconnaissance	the act of searching an area or location with the intent of determining who or what is at that site. Can be overt or covert.
RF/PF	Regional Force and Popular Force militia of the ARVN
RPG	rocket propelled grenade, the weapon called a B–40 or RPG–2 and larger RPG–7
RPKAD	Indonesian parachute commandos, akin to the SAS
RV	rendezvous point
SARBE 9	Search and Rescue Beacon (see also URC– 10)
SAS	Special Air Service
SASR	Special Air Service Regiment, comprises three Sabre squadrons each of about 120 men
sched	scheduled radio report time
SEAL	(US Navy) Sea Air and Land teams
SHQ	squadron headquarters
SI	senior instructor
sitrep	situation report
SLR	7.62 mm, self-loading rifle, semi-automatic (but usually converted by the SAS to fully automatic)
slick	slang term for troop-carrying helicopter
SOP	standard operating procedure; the norm
squadron	a company sized group consisting of three troops

SSM	squadron sergeant major, the senior NCO of the squadron
Sten gun	9 mm, automatic machine-gun
Stirling	9 mm, automatic machine-gun
surveillance	the act of observing a known location in order to determine exact numbers, activities and the routine of those enemy being observed. Usually covert.
Swiss seat	a rope belt designed as a body harness for rope extraction
tiger suit	camouflage uniform worn by ARVN Ranger units
troops	a platoon sized group consisting of at least four six-man patrols
UH–1H	the Utility Helicopter used by the RAAF; 1H is the model designation
UHF	ultra high frequency
under and over	the M16 Armalite rifle with a 40 mm grenade launcher under the rifle barrel, also known as the XM148 or the M203
URC–10, URC–68	a small UHF radio beacon, also capable of voice transmission
UW	unconventional warfare
UXB	unexploded bomb
VC	Viet Cong, the main fighting arm of the National Liberation Front
VC Main Force	enemy troops who were extremely well trained and equipped
VHF	very high frequency
VR	visual reconnaissance
WHAM	winning hearts and minds (program)
white phosphorus	usually in grenade form for identification or as a weapon to deter follow-up
XM148	the precursor to the M203 'under and over' a 5.56 mm rifle with 40 mm grenade launcher underneath the rifle barrel
Zuni, rocket, 2.75 inch	a rocket fired in pods of seven from the sides of the Bushranger gunship aircraft
2IC	Second-In-Command

Sabah, Sarawak and Brunei

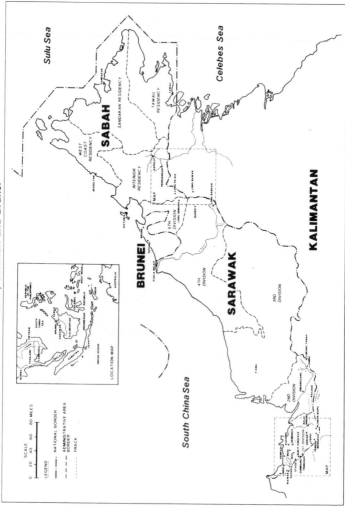

This map shows the two areas where the SAS served in Borneo. 1 SAS Squadron generally operated in the area marked as Map 2 in 1965, while 2 SAS Squadron operated in the area marked as Map 3 in 1966. (Map courtesy David Horner, author of *SAS: Phantoms of the Jungle*)

Indochina

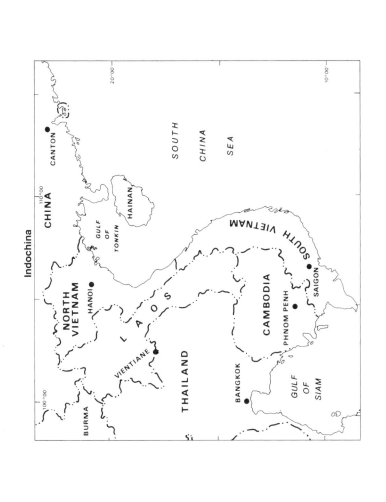

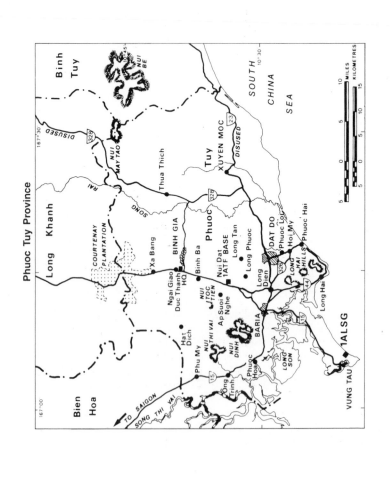

Phuoc Tuy Province

PREFACE

When I was approached by my publishers to write a book about the Australian Special Air Service (SAS) it was very clear right from the outset that it would not be a history of the SAS. That task had already been done most capably by the well-known historian and fellow author Dr David Horner, in his very highly regarded book *SAS: Phantoms of the Jungle*.[1] Indeed, I commend serious students of Australian Special Forces to read David Horner's book as it is a very faithful and complete work.

My intention in this book is to take you, the reader, on patrol with the SAS. The most recent operations which allow a look at what the SAS do on a patrol are those in Borneo and in South Viet Nam. The chapter headings will show you where we are going but, before we take this long patrol, it is important that we briefly look at the purpose and role of the SAS and quickly debunk a few myths, lies and legends about the men and the organisation.

When people use the phrase 'Special Air Service' many images immediately spring to mind of the men who are entitled to wear a sandy-coloured beret with the winged dagger emblem of the Special Air Service Regiment and its motto 'Who dares wins'. It is a badge of honour in the Australian Army and one coveted by many but only worn by a very select few.

Since 1957, when the regiment was formed, Australian SAS personnel have operated with the British SAS everywhere from

Northern Ireland to Bosnia. The Australian SAS was modelled on the British SAS Regiment formed in 1940 in the darkest days of World War II. Major Alf Garland, later to become a brigadier, led the SAS into its first operation on 16 February 1965 in Borneo.[2] During that deployment the regiment suffered one of its losses on active duty when Paul Denehey was gored to death by a rogue elephant. The squadron was involved in various operations during *Konfrontasi* with Indonesia, the most notable being cross-border operations into Indonesian territory known as 'Claret' operations and highly secretive for political reasons.

The Special Air Service Regiment (SASR) deployed a squadron to Viet Nam in June 1966. The role of the squadron was originally designed to be that of providing reconnaissance and surveillance for the 1st Australian Task Force. This role changed fairly dramatically later in the piece when the patrols were assigned harassing and other offensive tasks. The squadrons which deployed to the second Indochina war were most successful. During its Viet Nam experience it had 298 contacts with the enemy for 492 kills, 106 possible kills, 47 wounded, 10 possibly wounded and 11 prisoners. Australian and New Zealand SAS casualties in Viet Nam were one killed in action, one died of wounds, one killed in a grenade accident, two accidentally shot, one missing and one died of illness.[3]

Today the regiment is structured around 400 men in three sabre squadrons and one administration squadron. Each SAS squadron has three troops—a boat troop trained to operate off submarines, parachutists trained in high-opening, long-range drops and mobility specialists skilled in desert warfare and demolition. All members in the sabre squadrons are 'cross-trained' to cover other disciplines. Redundancy is a highly motivating factor in small group operations, as will be illustrated later in this book.

The SAS organisation is one based on skill and merit. The regiment is extremely self-critical of its members and its methods of operations. It never rests on its laurels. There is a deep and heavily ingrained desire to excel and to exceed previous levels of expertise. That is achieved through realistic and arduous training designed to take those who have never experienced combat as close to as humanly possible without mishap. But unfortunately, realism carries a high price and the regiment has lost almost 40 men in training incidents. Fatalities have included two killed in a 'killing house' practising counter-terrorism, four parachuting, two shot by colleagues, several drownings and fifteen in the Blackhawk tragedy in north Queensland in 1996.[4]

Many people might think that this elite force is composed of incredibly fit, competent, macho fighting men with incredibly high tolerance levels of pain and endurance. To a point that is correct; they are for the most part very fit, confident, competent and blessed with a sense of humour, but they are not all big, hairy-chested macho men with steely eyes and bulging biceps. Rather, they are fairly average in height and generally, I repeat generally, wiry in build. Most of them are under 183 cm in height and have a very good weight-to-strength ratio.

They very rarely talk about themselves or what they do. That is part of their training and part of the ethos of the SAS Regiment, which is based in Swanbourne Barracks in Perth, Western Australia. Braggarts have no place in this type of force, nor do men who cannot laugh at themselves. To use the term 'closed shop' is not too far from the truth, indeed, there were some members and ex-members of the SAS Regiment who were opposed to this book being written for fear that it might bring discredit to the regiment or cheapen the esteem and honour the SAS have worked so hard to attain. This was especially so as I have never been a member of this elite group. They spend much of their waking day training for their specialist roles—water operations, surveillance operations, parachute operations, long-range vehicle patrolling, counter-terrorism training, or a mix of all these activities.

The role of the SAS is not about raiding enemy positions or lurking behind enemy lines killing as many enemy as possible. In fact, it is the Australian Defence Force's information- and intelligence-gathering force, which relies on stealth to get in, get close and get out without being compromised or tipping off the enemy that they have been observed. That stealth is achieved through the use of small groups, which are easier to insert or infiltrate and can move faster and hide more easily than larger groups relying on massive support for their mission. Once the information on the enemy has been gained and then analysed to become intelligence, it then allows more conventional forces to deal with the enemy.

The fact that the SAS were sometimes used on harassing tasks in Borneo and in Viet Nam was simply a bonus. In the classic model of the creator of the British SAS forces, Lieutenant David Stirling, the attacks were 'based on the principle of the fullest exploitation of surprise and of making the minimum demands on manpower and equipment'.[5] To achieve this type of military operation requires men of a very high calibre who earn and deserve the clichéd title of 'elite'. They are that in the truest sense of the word, but not surprisingly do not like to use the term themselves.

The SAS deployed to Borneo and Viet Nam as squadrons which were roughly numbered at about six officers and 100 men. They deployed on four- or five-man patrols most of the time and their principal method of transport once they were in their area of operations was on foot. I asked one member of the SAS what he saw as the role of his squadron in Borneo and later in Viet Nam. His reply was:

> The policy was, with us, if you were compromised you came out. You only engaged the enemy if you had to, whereas later on they were encouraged that, if the patrol was almost over, whatever, have a go, give 'em a touch-up. But we were mainly reconnaissance, which is what SAS really was all about. One of the tasks was to carry out recon and surveillance and then either give enough information for conventional forces to go in or lead the conventional forces in. And in Borneo, Corporal John Robinson did the recce and conventional forces went in afterwards, and that's the classic employment of SAS.[6]

To gather the material for this book, I relied on first-hand accounts from the men who had 'been there and done that'. While I have some experience as an infantry officer, I am not of the SAS 'brotherhood'. Therefore I am especially and deeply indebted to those men who allowed me to interview them at length and to let me look inside the SAS organisation. This book could not have been written without the assistance of those men who appear in the bibliography and to a few others whose names I am unable to release for personal and security reasons.

Throughout this book I have spelt the country of Viet Nam as two words as it translates into 'people from the south of China' or 'the land south of China'. Western usage has combined the two words especially since the mid-1950s, however I feel that the more correct spelling should be used out of courtesy to that nation.

I must also thank my editor, Mark Evans, for turning my writing into English and readable prose and my publisher, Ian Bowring, for his continued support. My wife and two kids have once again stood by patiently while I banged away on the keyboard as they coped with university and Year 12 exams.

1

THE SAS TROOPER

A soldier who wants to be an SAS trooper can come from any corps in the army; some have even come into the regiment from the navy, especially diving personnel. A strong desire and personal commitment are required to enter this elite force, but there are some qualities that must exist within the individual which have proved essential to his meeting the very high standards and demands of SAS work. The role of the SAS requires that men must be capable of working in small teams, under very difficult and arduous conditions, and be capable of making difficult—and sometimes life-threatening—decisions under extremely stressful conditions.

Reconnaissance and surveillance of the enemy is not an activity that can be done from afar and in jungle warfare it can get very up-close and personal. This close proximity of the five-man patrol to the enemy, often out of supporting artillery or mortar range, calls for men who are not only physically capable of carrying heavy loads to support their mission, but also of carrying the enormous mental burden that such known immediate danger brings. To use the cliché of 'going deep' is not an understatement. Even though at times in Viet Nam the distances were not so great, the number of enemy in the area made up for the distance to be travelled to a likely target. An

SAS patrol launching into enemy territory must take everything it needs with it. The soldier will be carrying his house on his back—his ammunition, water and food—and this can be an awesome burden.

The trooper must be able to withstand a lot of pressures both physical and mental. To meet these demands the regimental selection board which preselects and then critically examines and tests the men on a formal selection course is looking for some indicators from aspirants who are seeking entry to the SAS. I spoke to several men who had spent decades in the regiment, like Major (later Colonel) Reg Beesley, who commanded a squadron in Viet Nam. Reg is one of many characters in the SAS who is affectionately referred to as 'The Beast'. He is typical in build to most of the SAS men I have met in my 30 years of military experience. He is a little shorter than average height, quietly spoken—unless riled—has a wiry and sinewy build, and when he was younger could run all day and all night if required. He said of the qualities he looked for in a trooper:

> In essence, there are three major qualities: intelligence, mental toughness and physical toughness. Other qualities are self-reliance, responsibility, reliability, confidence, loyalty, moral courage, unselfishness, a sense of humour, honesty, a high degree of integrity; together with an above-average ability to navigate by day and night, to communicate, possess a high level of endurance and leadership; have the ability to shoot accurately and to be able to march with heavy operational loads.[1]

That is quite a list but I found it was often repeated when seeking the basic qualities of a trooper. I asked another soldier who has spent most of his adult and military life in the SAS Regiment what he thought of Reg Beesley's list. Ian 'Connie' Conaghan, a trooper who saw action in Borneo and then on two tours of Viet Nam as a patrol sergeant, replied:

> I agree with all of them. I think all of those go hand in glove and I think it's very difficult to identify one as being the predominant one without the others being involved, but I do believe that mental toughness should take precedence over physical toughness.[2]

The mental toughness Conaghan refers to is that ability of an individual to put the physical hurt he is experiencing out of his mind and concentrate on the job at hand. It also refers to a soldier's need at times to make hard decisions to ensure that the task is carried out. Another Borneo veteran who went on to serve as a patrol and troop leader in Viet Nam, where he won a Military Cross, was Peter Schuman. He saw the basic ingredient of a trooper as requiring a lot of deep individual character and believed that:

> You've got to be able to drive yourself. You're the guy that can't sleep when you're tired. You're the guy that's got to keep his eyes open when you're absolutely buggered. So, it's that pushing yourself, it's that mental toughness. It's being able to adapt in changing circumstances. Don't get bogged down with doctrine, look at changing circumstances and apply new thought to it, take other people's advice, have an open mind.[3]

The types of operations that involve the SAS are more often than not going to be out-of-the-ordinary situations for what is considered conventional warfare. There is very rarely any such animal as a 'routine' patrol in the world of the SAS, otherwise they would not be doing it in the first place. Consequently, one former officer, Ron Dempsey, who served as a troop and patrol leader in Viet Nam, thought that a trooper should be someone who, when given a problem, will come up with a novel way of solving it.[4] Indeed, problem-solving is an essential part of the selection course and the ability to keep a clear head when all around you is turning to poop is absolutely vital.

Jim Hughes, a Military Cross winner from Korea, was a squadron commander in Borneo and later went on to command a rifle battalion in Viet Nam. This Royal Military College graduate had a very distinguished career and rose to the rank of major-general. He put together a list of soldierly qualities that he wanted from his troopers:

> A team player, physically and mentally fit, a man who grasps the initiative and is a lateral thinker. He has got self and corporate discipline, is efficient in all skills, infantry firstly and SAS specialist secondly.[5]

Hughes has raised a very important point about several issues in his 'wish list'. Many outsiders to the regiment believe that SAS types have to be 'loners' in the genre of men being able to withstand privation and able to maintain their focus when 'cut off' from support and other patrol members. However, there is a very heavy emphasis placed on a man's capacity to work in a team, especially a small team. Jim Hughes added that

> I had one of my men who had to operate that way as a loner when on operations with B Squadron 22 SAS, when he was separated, and he survived as a loner. He had enough initiative, enough knowhow to operate as a loner. But being a loner wasn't his basic training; he was a team player. His strengths were being with a team.[6]

The teamwork required in an SAS patrol is extremely critical, as there is no spare capacity to carry a bludger or someone who is not prepared to give his all. Everyone in an SAS patrol is vital to the success of a mission and everyone must be able to work competently with every other member of that patrol. There is no room for personal conflict or disharmony. The team has to work like a perfectly machined Swiss timepiece, and under extreme pressure and arduous conditions. One particular man I interviewed is one of the characters of the SAS Regiment and a Military Medal winner from his tour of Viet Nam as a patrol leader. Joe Van Droffelaar's thoughts were oriented towards the person being able to work in a team, but also:

> He must be determined to achieve a common goal. Secondly, he must show a high level of integrity, and thirdly, he must have strong self-discipline and the ability to command—if need be—to complete a mission. And fourthly, he is never to give up—even under adverse conditions, whether starving, cold, stuffed, even misplaced.[7]

So, what is the difference between your normal infantry-type soldier and this man who has been selected to be one of Australia's finest warriors? Often the tag 'Super Soldier' is placed on the SAS and it is highly detested by those within the organisation and is looked upon as almost derogatory by them.

Joe Van Droffelaar was fairly straightforward in his response to the question on the difference between a trained infantryman and an SAS trooper: 'I don't think there is much of a difference. The difference lies between the mental attitude and the will to succeed and never give up.'[8] Other troop leaders, like Bill Hindson, who completed one tour of duty with a regular rifle platoon and then a second tour as a patrol and troop leader—winning a Military Cross in the process—emphasised a slightly different aspect:

> You have got to have somebody who is really able to think for themselves, who has got all the attributes that make a good soldier. He is good at his infantry-craft; he's good with weapons; good with his fieldcraft; but, beyond that, and regardless of what rank he is, can think independently, can think laterally and can work as an individual and as part of a small group. He must really be able to fit in with a small group and cope with tasks which are both stressful and probably a bit terrifying at times.[9]

The slight understatement of Hindson's—'probably a bit terrifying at times'—sums it up succinctly. These men who venture out in four- or five-man patrols into what is basically the enemy's 'backyard' without the normal supporting agencies afforded regular combat units—apart from their long-range high frequency (HF) radio—definitely need a lot of confidence and an ability to control their fear. None of my respondents thought that there was anything wrong with being afraid; it was being able to control their fear that was critical. Jim Hughes offered the comment that an SAS trooper has to have controlled fear: 'I want him to be fearful but he has to be controlled.'[10] Strangely enough, while many regular infantrymen serving in Viet Nam conceded that the SAS in their opinion were 'absolutely insane'[11] because of the likely dangers they faced as a matter of routine, the SAS patrol members who became used to operating in small quiet groups where everyone could see everyone else and where everybody knew *exactly* what was going on—especially in a contact—had reciprocal misgivings, as Ian Conaghan explained:

> When I had been married up with infantry companies, where we were leading them into doing something or other, I was absolutely terrified because all of these people were around us and they're going to draw all the crabs! And I felt that we were going to get in the shit![12]

The officers in the Australian Special Air Service are trained and expected to lead patrols, unlike their counterparts in the British SAS who usually only command certain larger activities for which they might have the special skills required. The officers in the SAS undergo exactly the same type of training as their soldiers, which is understandable in such a small force which is quite egalitarian in nature. One officer, Dan McDaniel, who had commanded a squadron of the SAS when on counter-terrorist duties, sought something extra from the men who were likely to be troop leaders in the officer ranks:

> As far as the officers are concerned, I wouldn't have rated mental toughness as the most important characteristic. I would have been looking for creativity, flair, ability to think 'outside the square'. People skills are very important.[13]

One characteristic that everyone agreed was on their list of personal attributes required of an SAS soldier was a sense of humour. It might seem a strange quality to list but, as will be amply shown throughout this book, these men undergo such extreme pressures—both physical and mental—that there needs to be some kind of pressure-release mechanism and a sense of humour, no matter how macabre, will often allow that pressure to be eased. McDaniel was required to train men at a frenetic pace and under extremely demanding conditions for very hazardous 'real-life' operations in counter-terrorism and he thought:

> I think a sense of humour is critical and I say that with all sincerity—being able to release yourself from stress and pressure on operations which is fairly intense and a very, very difficult environment in which to work.[14]

Troop Leader Bill Hindson thought that, for a man to serve with the SAS, this sense of humour was absolutely essential. Especially when you're sitting out there in the middle of the wet season and it's night, it's pissing down rain and you've got nothing but a poncho so you wrapped yourself in it—we never put up tents. They were bloody hot inside and we would sweat. So we were wet no matter what happened. We had to cope with being wet all night, day after day, putting in ambushes and not seeing anybody—and you have really got to see the funny side of life.[15]

We can see from what has been said above, by the men who have been there and done it, that the type of soldiering the SAS are chosen to conduct requires a certain breed of soldier. To get into the SAS Regiment requires the successful completion of a very, very tough selection course, often referred to as 'the longest six weeks of their lives'. Why do they enlist to put themselves through the whole process? I asked these men who all went on to make the SAS and Special Forces their chosen military career path and the answers were often surprising. Indeed, it could be argued, after speaking to many of the men who made the SAS their life, that when they joined they were blessed with a great deal of ignorance about what they were letting themselves in for. Interestingly, despite that initial ignorance and the tremendous rigours and the ordeal of selection, they stayed and then themselves passed into SAS folklore and history.

A few chose the SAS because they wanted something different from normal infantry soldiering—like Ian Conaghan, who was serving in a rifle battalion and working at the Jungle Training Centre at Canungra in the Gold Coast hinterland when he made the leap into this different world of soldiering:

We were rehearsing for a company attack on this feature for a Staff College demonstration, and we attacked this same hill every day for about five days, and I was getting thoroughly pissed off at this stage of the game. I remember seeing an aircraft and thought, SAS would be beaut, wouldn't it, because they fly everywhere and just parachute in and don't have to do any of this walking crap![16]

The irony of Ian Conaghan's remarks should not be overlooked, as he then went on to serve with the SAS in Borneo, where he walked forever on several patrols across the Indonesian border carrying at least fourteen days' rations on his back and hardly ever saw an aeroplane except to take him to the point where he would start walking.

Another soldier who served with the SAS in Borneo and then did a couple of tours as a patrol leader with the SAS was another infantryman, Neville Farley. He was enticed by another SAS soldier who showed him a collection of photographs from the SAS training exercises. He recalled that they were

> blokes out in the desert in bloody jeeps, and wearing desert boots and shorts and bush hats. And I said, 'Do you do guards and all of that stuff?' and he said, 'Nah, none of that shit'. 'What about pickets out in the bush?' 'Nah, don't do any of that shit either.' And I thought well that sounds pretty cool, and he had all these photos and talking about being out in the desert and riding around in vehicles and all that and parachuting and I thought, 'Shit, I'll have a go at this.'[17]

Nev Farley's desire to get away from the tedium of everyday infantry soldiering was also the enticement that led another soldier who started his career as a Digger in the SAS and then went on to become an officer and troop leader in Viet Nam. Trevor Roderick had no hesitation in answering that it was

> just what they did—parachuting, diving, rock climbing; but probably more than that was the individuality and the small-group thing of the SAS which was the big attraction. Even now, when I think back on it, I liked being in small groups. The smaller the better. I think it was that that appealed.[18]

Some soldiers, however, are simply out-and-out mercenaries and are just in the 'game' for the booty. Men like Peter Schuman explained his motivation for enlisting into this elite force this way:

> After recruit training I was posted to the First Battalion, The Royal Australian Regiment, and the SAS was offering an extra 7s 6d [75 cents] per day for parachute allowance or specialist allowance and that appealed to me.[19]

Some men like Barry Standen had ulterior motives for signing up to have a crack at the selection course. Standen, who goes by the nickname of 'Muka', was a soldier in the Corps of Signals and serving in the eastern states in what was known as the Combat Ops Signal Squadron when his interest was aroused:

> It was from a flyer that came through which said someone was coming around to give a lecture. I attended the lecture and thought, well at least I can do some diving—which I was interested in—and it was a home posting. There was no romance about SAS sneaking through the boonies with a knife in my teeth or any of that. It was just a way to get back to Perth and do some diving, at the time.[20]

But in the end the realisation is that the men of the SAS are a breed apart and are employed to undertake military operations which are beyond the capabilities of normal infantry and combat arms soldiers. Bill Hindson recalled when he was attracted to sign up for the SAS, even though it would be some years and a tour of duty as a second lieutenant before he would be attempting his selection course and trying to 'cut the mustard' and become one of the elite:

> During Exercise NUTCRACKER in October–November 1962, the then SAS Company was involved and, as an infantry soldier at the time, I was impressed by a group of the SAS Company soldiers running around unburdened by all of the military paraphernalia that we had—and looking terribly fit and awesome.[21]

2

CUTTING THE MUSTARD

The soldiers who wish to join the Special Air Service Regiment must appear before a preselection board composed of officers and senior NCOs of the regiment seconded for recruiting duties. The aspirants must be recommended by their own unit commanding officers before they can apply to attempt the rigorous selection course. Once they have been interviewed by the selection board, they are told to report at a specified time, when the next selection course will be conducted. If a soldier is looked upon by the recruiting panel as likely material, he is asked to pass a basic fitness test and other specialty SAS barriers and then attend a selection course at Swanbourne Barracks in Perth, Western Australia. And so the screening and filtering process begins.

A selection course is conducted to ensure that only men with the 'right stuff' get through because the training demands and the nature of SAS operations are very demanding—and expensive. In days gone by, the selection courses were conducted in the eastern states by a cadre of men from the SASR and were commonly known as cadre courses. The men interviewed for this book attended a mix of courses, varying in nature, as the SAS grew from an SAS Company to a regiment of three sabre squadrons to meet the requirement for service in Borneo and later South Viet Nam.

When the SAS Company first came into existence, men like
Neville Farley signed up for what they thought was the chance
of a lifetime. Neville was serving with 3 RAR at Enoggera
Barracks close to Brisbane in Queensland when:

> They did this bloody selection—they made us climb the tower
> at the ABC studios on Coronation Drive to see if we were
> scared of heights. They made us climb up to the top and I
> was shit-scared of heights—I hated them. I had to climb up
> this ladder. I had my eyes closed and they said, 'Now take a
> look around and tell us what you can see.' I did a quick 360,
> told them, closed my eyes again and came back down.[1]

The aim of the selection courses was thought by many to
be a barrier test to see if aspirants had the physical stamina to
be able to partake in SAS operations. Others thought the course
was to see whether an individual's breaking point was high
enough. But Barry Standen, who was the Senior Instructor (SI)
for three years on selection courses conducted in Swanbourne
and other Western Australia environs, had a different perspective
and one supported by several other selection course SIs like Jim
Hughes and Reg Beesley:

> Principally it's not tied up with the physical side. What they're
> looking for to the greater degree is someone with a little bit
> of individuality; a bit of initiative; someone who can be relied
> upon in a tight spot; definitely a team player. Even though
> you're looking for individuality, it's got to be an individual
> who can fit into a team. And I guess you're looking for
> someone who is a bit of a misfit. Someone that doesn't want
> to polish his boots and march in line—but he wants to be a
> soldier. Someone with a little bit more flair, someone that's
> looking for something more in life than marching in line and
> perhaps going to war with a company or a battalion.[2]

One man who served as a troop and patrol commander in
Viet Nam vividly recalled his course and what he thought the
aim of the whole process was:

> I think it was two things. One was to push you to the
> limit—but not push you over the limit, just to see how much

you could take. And the other one was to see whether you had the ability to actually learn more about what the regiment did. Whether you could take it all in and use it or if that was your limit. If it was a certain level, and that wasn't the level they were looking for, then they didn't take you on. And I think it was more an exercise in actually establishing what level you were, so that they knew once you got into the regiment, what you needed to learn from there on.[3]

Another of the officers who conducted what was known as the Recondo Course and also ran many of the initial selection courses said that

during the selection course a number of objectives had to be met in determining suitability and unsuitability. Of course, a degree of subjectivity, or gut feeling if you like, had to be taken into account. This had to be recognised, monitored and controlled. Soldiers who failed the set objectives were normally returned to their units. For example: passing the swimming test in either warm or cold conditions was mandatory; likewise, the 9-miler in 90 minutes and the 20-miler in 5 hours (the former was done as a group whilst the latter was done as a measure of individual endurance). It should be noted that the staff were required to do these tests with the course.[4]

The officers who applied for service with the SAS were treated—for the most part—the same as the Diggers who were trying out for selection. This egalitarian approach has been the root cause for much concern over the years, most criticism stemming from the fact that, in the very early days of the regiment, officers did not have to attend a full selection course like the Diggers and consequently some officers were posted into the regiment who lacked some of the necessary qualities that the selection course was endeavouring to determine.

Reg Beesley, who commanded 3 Squadron in Viet Nam in 1969–70 was adamant that the same entry conditions should apply to all:

Unlike the Brit SAS, who rarely used their officers as patrol commanders, we expected our officers to have the capacity to lead a patrol, having completed both the selection and the patrol courses. Not only were they trained as patrol commanders but as troop commanders as well. Indeed, there was a great degree of pressure exerted on these young officers. They were required to do the selection course, for which an element of 'Digger recognition' was given.[5]

The Digger recognition which Reg Beesley talks about is essential for harmonious operations in a high-pressure environment where trust and reliance between patrol members are absolutely essential.

One man thought that teamwork was a big part of it because of that very factor on SAS operations of being a small group against the odds. He recalled one incident which he thought was significant for him from a personal perspective:

> I had a patrol down in the Collie area. I knew my guys were absolutely stuffed and I was too, but being the patrol commander I had things to do. So I let them sleep and I sort of kept my eyes and ears open, as much as I could anyway. I think to this day that it was probably something that helped me get through.[6]

Some of those who have attended the selection courses had different viewpoints on what they thought the course was seeking and had varying thoughts on what was hardest about the course, principally because everyone is different both physically and mentally. Dan McDaniel, who was over 30 years of age when he attended the course, thought:

> A lot of the stuff has nothing to do with what the regiment actually does. Patrolling was just purely a vehicle for testing and putting stress and pressure on the participants. The obvious things that they did were sleep deprivation, so you didn't get a lot of sleep. Very hard physical stuff, runs. And a bit of sensory deprivation in terms that you were never quite sure what was going to happen next. And there were deception plans involved, for example a copy of our course program was left lying around the night we had the alleged 'night off' and a couple of beers. We knew that there was probably a trick in there somewhere. It became 'them and us'.[7]

The adversarial nature of the courses often led to the 'them and us' attitude between the course staff and the soldiers vying for selection, but it also drew the aspirants together as a team.

The types of activities, tests and benchmarks will be covered in the barest detail in this book, principally for ethical reasons and to ensure that the element of the unknown is retained in the selection procedure, as that is one of the basic elements of the process. I asked everyone who volunteered to be interviewed for this book whether they thought the selection course was about physical or mental limits and capacity. Their responses were naturally varied and some were quite interesting. Most of the men who served in Borneo were imbued with a built-in requisite for physical stamina as a result of their experience in lugging very heavy operational loads across mountains and valleys in that campaign. But all those who saw operational service with the SAS agreed that a soldier in the SAS has to be very fit because:

> If you are fit, the mind is more active. The work is physically demanding—even normal infantry work is physically demanding and then you put an extra demand on the guy with extra weight on his back and being out on your own in a small group of fellows. If the body can take it, the mind has a chance of grappling with the problems. But when the body collapses, the mind collapses with it.[8]

Soldiers definitely do need to be fit for operational service because of the extreme demands made on their bodies as well as their mental state. They are subjected to long periods of work without rest and may be required to eat hard rations for long periods on end. For example, in Borneo, one of the SAS patrols led by Arch Foxley was out for a period of 89 days. The enemy rarely send you a copy of their planned activities and consequently the working hours are never set to a schedule. Long periods without sleep may have to be endured and, especially in the case of the SAS patrols, they are carrying everything they need on their backs as they are unable to take a resupply without compromising their position and their security.

Barry Standen did four operational tours of duty with the SAS—two in Borneo, back to back, and two tours in Viet Nam.

He conducted many selection courses and thought that it was primarily the mental attitude of men that would get them through the physical aspects of the course:

I would have to say that probably 80 per cent of the selection course is mental; because if you say to yourself, 'Shit, this nine-mile run is going to hurt'—well, it will hurt. But if you say, 'This nine-mile run is going to last 90 minutes', that's how long it will last. It's your focus and knowing your capabilities, and there is nothing superhuman about it. But it's hard; it's something that can be achieved with a little bit of effort. I think mental toughness and focus is very much the greater majority of a selection course. Being able to do your two-mile run, your nine-mile run, being able to do your chin the bars, and being able to get up and do bloody silly things in the water—swimming around with blacked-out face masks and all that sort of shit—it's all about being mentally tough and being focused on what you are doing—what you're here for, what the job is and how to achieve it—rather than, 'Shit, this is going to hurt'.[9]

Standen believes that if the mental attitude is right then half the battle is won. And it is a battle; there is nothing easy about the selection course because the selection board want to know what type of man they have out there. They want a bloke who will not quit, will think of the task before his own personal comfort and physical condition and, along with all of that, think of his team-mates as well.

Bill Hindson was a platoon commander on his first tour of duty in a rifle company and then returned to Viet Nam for a stint as a troop and patrol leader. His opinion is:

Certainly you need the fitness to assist in being able to be mentally alert and to be able to plan and carry out your operations under extreme conditions when you're physically just stuffed. You also need to be imbued with an inner driving force that compels you to maintain your own level of fitness. As we discovered later when we got up to Viet Nam where the demands of patrolling, contrasted with inactivity back in the camp, required you to constantly work at your own level of fitness to be able to stand up to the rigours of operations.[10]

PASS/FAIL?

The course is not a pass/fail course *per se*. But it is very hard not to think of it in those terms. For the men slogging their guts out when they are absolutely exhausted and have not had a decent sleep in two weeks, not graduating into the ranks of the SAS would hardly be called anything else than failing. Indeed, during the early 1960s, many officers who did not make the grade on the selection course resigned from the army rather than return to their units. Those who do not get selected for further training in the SAS are advised that they are 'not suitable', or not what the SAS is looking for. Barry Standen had to tell many men that they hadn't made the grade and in his words:

> What you have got to say is, 'Hey, the fact that you didn't make what we were looking for doesn't make you any less of a soldier. You can be an exceptionally good soldier at what you're doing, but you just didn't fit the mould that we are looking for.'[11]

One very real consequence of the selection course is opening a man's eyes to his own physical and mental limitations. As a Senior Instructor on the course, Barry Standen admitted that it really is something the instructors have to come to grips with because it is difficult to reject someone when they have tried so hard.[12]

So why do these men who know more or less what they are letting themselves in for not get accepted? What are the reasons for not making the grade? Trevor Roderick thought that in his day it was

> mainly on the physical side. Either they just couldn't hack the physical side of it, or they were so bloody tired they couldn't handle the thinking side of it. When I say 'physical', you know, the mind takes over, 'This is hurting too much; it's midnight; I can't handle this any more' and that's that. Farewell. So, it's a physical/mental thing.[13]

Naturally, other men had different experiences and one that was well remembered was by an officer who later went on to work as an interrogator on a selection course. His recollection was that moral courage, the courage of one's convictions, is an important facet of a man's character. He remembered one incident that led to a man's downfall:

> I was pulled out of bed about two o'clock in the morning, having been told we were having a night off—of course, part of the deception plan. And I was asked to give my personal position on females in the army, and then I had a team of interrogators who tried to change my mind. I sort of thought about it—and I can remember this reasonably clearly—I thought about it and put my position and I stuck to it. And I argued with them. But when I worked on a course later myself and I had a young officer, and we got him out of bed, and we got him to state his position on a subject, and later we got him to change his position, and then we got him to change it back to his original position. He didn't make it.[14]

The aspect of how strong a man's character is should not be treated too lightly. After all, these men are one day possibly going to be told that they are to be inserted deep into enemy territory with a radio as a lifeline and no other means of support, and that they are to accomplish a mission most normal units are incapable of completing. If a man did not have a strong belief in what he thought he was capable of and the mental nerve and moral courage to complete the task, then he would most likely become a weak link in a tenuous chain. When I asked Bill Hindson what he thought the selection process was about and why people didn't cut the mustard, he answered:

> Some people that you think are quite determined, quite capable and fit individuals, get to a point of stress where they just say, 'I don't need this bullshit' and want to give up. Of course in SAS you can't have any member of a small team, any individual who is going to do that, no matter what the case. So, it really is a matter of being able to push people along to get them beyond their perceived limits.[15]

Some men who do not make the grade are forced out because of injury suffered during the course. Those that are considered the type of man the SAS could use are asked to come back in twelve months and try again. In most cases it is two strikes and you're out, as those returning for a third try would have a decided advantage over those fronting up for the first time. However, one soldier was taken into the regiment after three courses. The startling thing about that fact is that this dedicated and driven man spent almost four months subjecting himself to the tough selection process![16]

THE LONGEST SIX WEEKS OF YOUR LIFE

The selection courses for most of SAS history have been conducted in Western Australia and in a typically perverse manner: 'If you're doing it in the warmer months they tend to put you in the areas that are going to be hot; if you're doing it in the colder months they put you in the areas that are going to be cold.'[17] The activities range from team to individual events, with the majority of the course conducted in normal patrol (five-man) groups. Locations range from Northam in Western Australia, where cross-graining patrol movement is done deliberately because it is pretty tough, particularly during the day. High temperatures—often exceeding 30°C—add to the difficulty of moving across the terrain going continually up and down hills. Some courses go down to the Stirling Ranges in the cooler south-west of the state and that is pretty rough country, hilly and cold—the ideal location in winter.

Basic instruction on SAS patrols is imparted in the environs of Swanbourne Barracks and then the patrols are tasked; leaders and patrol appointments are listed and the men venture forth to tackle the problems. The activities are designed to ensure that the soldier operates mostly at night, every night, under adverse conditions of weather and ground when the physical condition of the men at times approaches exhaustion.[18] The patrol will be harassed, chased, attacked, and if ever it looks like getting on top of the situation, one of the course-directing staff will factor in another problem—like a casualty to be carried—to take the men to their physical limits. One man who worked on many courses and was a very successful patrol leader in Viet Nam was concerned that his staff did not take the men too far in the quest for who could cut it:

I believe those that do possess the SAS criteria, the approach should be to push them beyond what he thinks his own limitations are—without setting a benchmark. Keep him in the dark, so to speak. I have pushed soldiers to a point where, if pushed any further, he will become psychologically affected. So there is a point where you must stop.[19]

The selection process starts from the moment these keen, bushy-tailed young men hit the front gate of Swanbourne Barracks. Ian Stiles was an eighteen-year-old private soldier serving with 2 RAR at Enoggera Barracks in Brisbane when he decided to do something different. He began learning lessons almost from the time he stepped off the bus.

I can remember the first morning after we arrived and the food was just great, and we just made pigs of ourselves. They had big urns of milk and lamb chops, eggs and stuff—all we could eat—and then we went out of the Mess bloated. And the sergeant says, 'Oh, we're going for a run now, take your shirts off'. So, we took our shirts off. I don't know how far it was, probably about three or four miles, but we were all spewing our guts out as a result of scoffing this huge big breakfast, so we only ever made that mistake once.[20]

The course sets very high standards of performance and the men seem to be continually running from one location to another. Trevor Roderick vividly recalled his time on the selection course when he arrived as a 22-year-old Digger from 1 RAR:

Nine-mile runs at about four o'clock in the morning—before breakfast. Unarmed combat where you took it easy on each other and then when one of the cadre staff realised you were taking it easy on each other, then they took you on themselves. Shit it used to hurt. Because they used to use a rubber knife, but if Ronnie Jarvis or 'Snow' Livock saw that you were taking it easy, they would pull out a bayonet—a real one—and they would come at you with a real one. And then it used to hurt, of course.[21]

SORTING OUT THE WHEAT FROM THE CHAFF

The course is unconventional in that what appears on the timetable or daily program can never be taken for granted. One officer, Dan McDaniel, who did the course thought that this uncertainty was necessary because of the need to determine just how the men would react. They need to be flexible in their approaches to solving problems because they will not always have the means to solve problems conventionally and they must also be adaptable to survive in a hostile environment and be capable of thinking 'outside the square'.[22] He also remembered

> the Northam exercise, and I had gone through the whole process of briefing my patrol for a patrol I thought we were doing. We got there and I was the first guy out of the chopper and they said, 'Yeah, you out, everybody else stays in.' Then you were on your own. And you went all day and all night, and you had to find an enemy camp, do a recce of it and then you had to make your way to an RV and it was a tough exercise, because you were on your own.[23]

Long distances to cover, very little rest and a continual climate of uncertainty take the men into situations they have mostly never experienced before. Many of the men recalled being almost asleep on their feet and experiences of imagining events or hallucinating were common. Nev Farley remembered:

> It was a case where you would be up all night bloody patrolling, come back, debrief, a couple of hours sleep, and they would wake you up again at four o'clock with a slab of PE [plastic explosive] or something. We would then go for a run and be briefed and do all our shakedown rehearsals and go out and patrol again all night. I've seen blokes asleep on a barbed-wire fence, literally. One bloke wandered off while we were walking, hit a fence and went to sleep over it. I remember seeing a bloke say, 'Watch out for that fella's hexy stove, you'll knock his brew over.' But there's no brew there! Or you would be standing behind a blackboy tree and saying, 'What's going on?' No answer. 'For fuck's sake what's going on?' and then realise, 'Oh shit, it's a blackboy.' The rest of the patrol

has gone and you race off after them trying to find out where they are.[24]

Sleep deprivation will test any man and take him to the point where he just simply wants to quit or go and have a lie-down and forget the consequences of his actions. This is where the men are watched most closely to see who has got the mental stamina, the resolve to go beyond normal limits. One man recollected that he got very good at sleeping with his eyes open and recalled one particular incident on an extremely arduous patrolling activity when he was leading a patrol as a scout:

> I was just out of it and I can remember walking along a track and hallucinating. I could see this great big tree lying across the track in front of us. We all sort of stopped and Reg Beesley was wandering along with us. It was about three o'clock in the morning with a bit of moonlight and people were saying, 'What's going on?' And I said, 'Well we've got to work out how we're going to get over this tree.' They looked up the track, then at me, and asked, 'What tree?' I mean, I saw some very strange things. I remember one guy seeing elephants.[25]

Another man mused over whether the fatigue and learning experiences weren't intertwined:

> I think probably the hardest was the Morse Code. I remember they used to put us in this room all day learning Morse Code and you had been up all night bloody playing around and suffered badly from lack of sleep. I don't know whether they were trying to teach us Morse Code or give us sleep deprivation.[26]

Other men took a different perspective on what was hard about the selection course. The men putting themselves through this ordeal are usually in their early twenties, sometimes younger, but they are confronted by a group of instructors who are all supremely fit, have been there and done it, and know exactly what is required to take the men to their limits. Peter Schuman was a nineteen-year-old private soldier when he was being pushed from pillar to post by men who had the battle skills that only time and experience can bring about. He thought that the hardest part of the course was

> being accepted. You had to make yourself like one of your instructors. You had to be smart. As a private soldier, you were expected to give orders that a corporal in a battalion would give.[27]

The staff on the selection courses also ensured that no 'bad' lessons were being learnt while the soldiers were attempting the course. When the men were given problems to solve or tasks to complete, it was always a race against the clock to give them a time and space problem to overcome but also to make sure that they were kept moving at a fast pace. There were rarely ever times when a task could be completed in the time allocated. Nev Farley was on a patrol exercise when his group came across a large obstacle which blocked their path. He recalled clearly what happened when his group tried to take a short cut:

> I remember one time we were doing this night patrolling exercise and we came to this big bloody opening. We looked across and said, 'We shouldn't go across this opening, we should go all the way around it. Ah, fuck it, nobody's going to see us.' We had a four-man patrol and here we are sneaking across this bloody opening and the staff waited until we got right into the middle of it and all of a sudden they had these signal flares and Very pistols and they opened up on us! And they're going whoosh and wham! And we're going for our quoits and they're still firing all these flares at us. At the debrief they said, 'We bet you pricks never go over open ground again.' I've never forgotten that lesson.[28]

Indeed, there were some things that were not forgotten and definitely not humorous. One man looked back on his experiences and recalled during the interrogation phase of the course when he was made to kneel on blue metal for quite an extended period.[29]

Other soldiers attending the selection course who have previous combat experience are often used as training aids by the staff to give a 'role model' example. One young officer, straight from a tour of Viet Nam in 1966, did a 'short' selection course with a fellow subaltern, Kevin Lunny. Bill Hindson recollected:

> We were both very enthusiastic and had a strong desire to prove ourselves. So we threw ourselves into the cadre course somewhat vigorously—which resulted in us both being taken off the course about two-thirds of the way through, because we were deemed to be too dangerous and setting bad examples to the other guys.
>
> The decision to 'advance' our graduation came about during a live firing exercise where they used Kevin Lunny and myself to demonstrate to the others how to do fire and movement. There were a couple of targets at the bottom of a hill and we were required to move a couple of times and then get into a position behind a log and throw a grenade. Well, we entered into that fairly energetically, covering one another, moving forward, firing and moving and got to the stage where I had to throw the grenade.
>
> So I pulled the pin, threw the grenade and took cover behind a log and as the grenade went 'bang!' I was up on my feet and moving and, in my enthusiasm, started firing. The first round hit the ground about two feet in front of my feet! The next one was closer to the target and the next one was in the target. But as far as the directing staff were concerned at the time, they perceived that I was actually up and moving before the grenade had gone off. And firing rather wildly as well.
>
> I think at that stage they said, 'Okay, you guys seem to have what it takes. Off you go and we'll get on with the business of training these other fellows. We were given our SAS berets and put straight into the regiment.[30]

As the course progresses, the men undergoing selection are coached, counselled and encouraged as they come to terms with situations they have probably never experienced before in their military careers. No-one is asked to withdraw from a course unless it is obvious to everyone except the subject himself that he has absolutely no way of being a suitable graduate of the course. Nev Farley recalled his time when he was attending a cadre course at Ingleburn in the SAS Company days:

To add to the tension, the staff had a course photo blown up in old 'Swampy' Skardon's office. [Captain] Geoff Skardon was running the course and every Friday you would front the 'green door'—because this building had a green door on it—and when you walked in, you had to march up to old Swampy's desk and you would look at the photo behind him and if your face had a big red cross through it, you knew that's it—you're on your way. But if the photo still had your face on it, all they did was give you a rev, and tell you you were a useless prick and if you didn't smarten up you will be out of here, and away you would go for another week.[31]

One of the prerequisites for SAS service is to be parachute qualified and after the men are selected for 'further training' they normally attend a basic parachute course at the Army Parachute School on the east coast of Australia. Bill Hindson attended his course after his abbreviated selection course and, still in the company of Kevin Lunny, again found himself being used as a training aid by one Sergeant O'Keefe, who was later to be Hindson's troop sergeant in Viet Nam. Bill Hindson recalled one particular day at Williamtown at the Army Parachute School:

When it came to harness release and drag training on the parachute, they tied the parachute on behind a Land Rover and drove up the strip between the married quarters and the towers while the poor trainee tried to release himself from the harness. They firstly put everybody through it, and then they asked for two volunteers to do it again and show how it *really* should be done. So, the instructors selected Lunny and myself and buckled us into the harness to drag behind the Land Rover and Sergeant John 'Slag' O'Keefe was driving it. I think he had it into second gear before I was out of the harness but Kevin Lunny couldn't release himself and didn't quite get out of it. And Slag managed to drag him the full length of the paddock. Kevin came back the worse for wear with cuts and abrasions, torn greens and everything.[32]

Asking men to jump out of perfectly serviceable aeroplanes has long been the subject for questioning the sanity of a person's mind. Ian Stiles thought the way they enticed him out of the aircraft was through sheer frustration:

They took us up in the aeroplane and we had our parachutes on, and they led us to the door and we looked down at the ground from the back of the Caribou. And we were all ready to go and then they would take us back and sit us back down and the plane would land. And then in the end you would be saying, 'Let me go, let me go, for fuck's sake!' We used to say we were that pissed off with the ground training, you just couldn't wait to get in an aeroplane and jump out of it![33]

ON PASSING

The day finally arrives when the men are standing on the grass parade ground at Swanbourne, accepted by the selection board and having passed their basic parachute course. The Commanding Officer of the SAS Regiment hands the soldier a sandy-coloured beret with the SAS winged dagger badge with attached motto of 'Who Dares Wins' and a blue lanyard for his left shoulder. They know they are the chosen ones. During the course some men have left of their own accord or have been injured and the casualty rate in drop-outs or non-acceptances is usually pretty high. Nev Farley recounted the pass rate from his course: of about 80 that went for selection, 22 made it to a cadre course and 11 graduated.[34] Pass rates vary depending on the calibre of those who have applied and there is definitely no hard and fast rule on a pass rate percentage. If you can cut the mustard, you get in. Passing a selection course as tough and demanding as the SAS selection course has an indelible effect on the men who made it through the crucible. Nev Farley recalled:

It was an incredible feeling because from my point of view I had never had to be tested before. To go through something like the selection course was the first time I had ever been really put to the test and to come out on top and to get that bloody beret and then to put on the para wings—I was on bloody Cloud Nine. Fantastic. My old man had an army background too, Second World War, CMF, so it was just fantastic to go home and say, 'I've done it.'[35]

Almost to a man the men interviewed for this book looked back with enormous pride and esteem on their achievement.

Peter Schuman recalled when he was told he had been accepted into the elite unit, but also intimated that it was just the beginning:

> It's the greatest day of your life. You become one of 'them', because you're always—you're never treated as an outsider—you were always looked upon as a candidate for getting into the regiment. You were never part of it until you passed all your tests and had been accepted and you were part of the mob. When I say part of it, it was a very low part; you had a long way to go before you got anywhere near full acceptance.[36]

Being accepted from the selection course is just the beginning for these men; they are on a very low rung on the ladder and have more hurdles to clear, but the course is always unforgettable:

> To this day, that course is sort of etched in my brain. It was one of life's great experiences but also one of life's most difficult experiences. You feel once you get that 'suitable' at the end of the course you are on top of the world. Nobody can do anything to you. 'I got through the SAS selection course.'[37]

Jim Hughes saw many men pass through the selection course and believes that most infantrymen are capable of making the grade but the primary difference between an infantryman and an SAS trooper is that:

> Additional selection criteria have been applied to him. Additionally, he has had additional training and practice at constant high standards. I believe that any good infantryman can become a good SAS trooper, subject to selection and additional training.[38]

Some older members of the regiment refer to the SAS as 'the brotherhood' and to a great degree it certainly is that. The experience of the selection course is a very strong adhesive that binds these men together. As one man put it:

> In hindsight, I think the course was the sort of experience where you learn a lot about yourself, your own shortcomings

and weaknesses as well as your strengths. A lot of the processes were purely designed to test you and if you didn't take it personally it wasn't too much of a drama. But if you did take it personally, you could make enemies there that would last you for the rest of your life. You basically learnt whether you were capable of responding to a challenge that you were absolutely frightened and shit-scared of, but been given as a challenge, and getting through it. And all the fears that you had before you did it were washed away with a sense of elation at the end. I think you know in your own mind that it's unlikely that you will ever have to do anything that hard again. I think when you come off that selection course, you have the same sort of feeling of power, and nothing can stop you. Whatever I have to do, I can do. It's a great confidence booster, and once you're in, you're in. You are one of the brotherhood and will be defended to the death by any other member around you.[39]

Bill Hindson echoed the sentiments expressed above when he said that:

In the end you almost came to believe that you had no limits. That you almost had to be totally exhausted—dead—before you could say, 'That's it, I can't do any more.'[40]

3

THE SAS PATROL

SIZE OF PATROLS

An SAS patrol for the campaigns fought in Borneo and South Viet Nam were drawn from a sabre squadron. The squadron was commanded by the Officer Commanding, a major, and he had three troops of about 21 men each. The troops were commanded by troop commanders, usually lieutenants, and the patrols that made up the troops were commanded in the main by sergeants. These men made up the backbone and the experience of the troops and squadrons who went on to serve so successfully in Viet Nam.

Usually four-man patrols operated in Borneo in 1965–66 and in Viet Nam from 1966 to 1971 they were usually five-man patrols. The army 'establishment document' that is the authority for the organisation of the SAS squadrons has the troops listed with six-man patrols. The reason for this anomaly most likely goes back to the days when the SAS had to be able to conduct unconventional warfare and the patrols were also to be employed as training teams in countries requiring Australian jungle exper-tise. Ian Conaghan was a young soldier when he first joined a patrol in Borneo and recalled:

The establishment strength was for a six-man patrol, but in
the light of 1 Squadron's and 22 SAS's experiences in Borneo,
it was modified a fair bit. I'm not really sure where the six-man
patrol actually came from, but it might have been from the
American Special Forces. You had a weapons instructor (in the
patrol) and it was more attuned to guerilla warfare rather than
straight recon.[1]

But as experience showed in Borneo it was more often than
not the capability of the agency tasked to insert a patrol which
dictated how many men would actually infiltrate into an area.
Many of the men who served in Borneo preferred the four-man
patrol if their task was purely reconnaissance—like Peter Schuman, who liked the idea of working in pairs:

I just got used to working with four. If I took five guys out,
then that was another set of eyes but it was another responsibility. When you looked around you could see your other two
blokes, because we were always in that one bound, and another
bound or another few metres and he's around a corner
somewhere. I just always felt uncomfortable with five guys.[2]

Men like Joe Van Droffelaar also expressed preference for
the four-man patrol in Viet Nam, where there were a hell of a
lot more enemy around than in Borneo. Van Droffelaar spent
most of his tour in Viet Nam on recce/ambush patrols and had
numerous contacts, which probably sways his opinion on the
'right' size for an SAS patrol:

Five was the normal size because it was part of the SOPs that
were laid down. I do not think that five-man was ideally suited
and I say that—not ideally suited—because the fifth man at
times became cumbersome in that patrol. The LUP was more
suited for four men.[3] When you had a five-man patrol, he was
just a pain in the backside. And six-man made it even worse,
but we had to have five men because—just in case one man
went down—at least you'd still have four men left to carry a
stretcher or some other means and to provide protection front
and rear. You were still capable of using two blokes to carry
that one bloke and you can then get yourself out of a contact.
But I would have preferred, particularly in close reconnaissance, to go with four men, it's more ideal.[4]

But as was experienced in Borneo and later in Viet Nam, if a patrol takes a casualty it really doesn't matter what size you are it will create a massive problem for a small group deep in enemy territory and out of range of normal fire support.

One of the squadron commanders from the SAS time in Borneo was Jim Hughes, who tried to answer the question on the optimum size for an SAS patrol:

> Our organisation allowed for six and I do recall we tried that at first, but it was a bit of a waste of manpower, because the organisation for an Australian troop were three patrols of six with a [troop] headquarters of three, being the troop commander, the troop sergeant and signaller. And what do you do with those three? You wouldn't send three out. So, then we experimented with five and four. We had done the same experiments in New Guinea and there we came up with the idea that five was probably the answer, because if you had a casualty, you could still get him out with five. If you have four you have problems getting one out. There was also a thought that your security was better facing out at night with five as opposed to four because you would have the sig transmitting and still have four points covered.
>
> We were flexible actually. I have to say for reconnaissance, we favoured four, but we tailored patrols when we thought they needed more for a particular task—if we thought they could run into an offensive situation. I think the biggest was probably seven. Patrols of four were not uncommon for certain tasks. What was the best? For pure reconnaissance, in a low-key thing, I would have to say that our organisation of six was an overkill; four worked.[5]

Some other patrol commanders actually preferred a five-man patrol, like Lieutenant Bill Hindson, who on his first tour of duty had patrolled with at least 30 men in a standard infantry platoon organisation. He liked the SAS concept of a five-man patrol:

> Five-man [patrols] were great; ten-man was starting to lose sight of part of the patrol. Strangely enough I started to have this feeling of being too unwieldy. Of course there were contacts where the people up the back were part of the action but couldn't see what was going on, so it just felt a little uneasy. It felt a lot better with five men.[6]

The key to the SAS is that it is a very flexible and very adaptable organisation. It can be moulded to suit whatever task is required owing to the plethora of skills and talent available in any troop or squadron. The military skills present in each patrol are quite staggering when compared to a normal infantry 'straight-leg' organisation. The numerous courses that Ian Conaghan completed during his time with the SAS and the range of skills he had mastered was fairly typical of an SAS soldier during the Borneo/Viet Nam War period.[7]

On occasion the SAS would be tasked to attempt to capture a prisoner and so two patrols would be linked and a ten-man patrol with considerably more firepower, including a GPMG–M60 machine-gun, would venture out after some unfortunate enemy soldier, but in the end it came down to doing what you were told.

Other men like Ian 'Bagza' Stiles liked the four-man patrol size because 'with four men you are quieter and it is easier to hide a smaller patrol'.[8] The SAS patrols are not out there to draw fire or create a ruckus. Their normal task is to insert, get close, find the enemy, observe him and withdraw. They report on their return on what they have found and then conventional forces go in and sort out the enemy. On occasion this would often mean that the patrols would take in an officer or someone from the conventional organisation to facilitate their later military operation. As with the captain of an aircraft, it doesn't matter who travels with an SAS patrol, the patrol commander is the man in charge, as Jim Hughes explained:

> If we took out one of the company commanders, I had to make him very much understand that my sergeant was in command, and he had to do what he said. There were no problems, but I felt I always had to make that point to them.[9]

THE JOBS

Squadron OC

The squadrons deployed to Borneo and Viet Nam were independent units attached to the brigade or the task force they were supporting. They are what is often called 'Army Troops' and do not fall into any set organisation, but are a specialist force to be employed as operations and political policies dictate. The squadron commander has the task of setting the tasks, briefing the patrols and maintaining his force in a combat-ready posture for whatever employment comes his way. In Borneo, Jim Hughes had a relatively easy task as his brigade commander was familiar with the role and tasks that SAS could or should perform, but he also thought that

> I had to protect Australia's interests. We were never asked to, say, cordon the local kampong, but if we had, of course, I would have had to throw up my hands and say, 'No way'. I was to report to the Commander of Australian Forces, FARELF. We don't do that sort of work. Because you have to be careful, every now and again, aid to the civil power gets out of hand. I had the standard sort of direction, a military paper, telling me that I could not do this or that and if I was invited to do it, then I had to report to the nearest Australian authority. I had a very good brigade commander who would never have asked Australians to operate outside of their charter.[10]

The squadron commander would not go out on patrol, as his job was to command the squadron which would never deploy as a squadron *per se* into the field. At any one time the squadron could have seven or eight patrols deployed and his job was to keep the overall operation under control and to ensure that resources were allotted and allocated as best as possible. Besides, as Jim Hughes himself explained,

> I would not have endangered a patrol, because their standard of personal training was well ahead of mine. But the cheek of me to usurp a sergeant or officer.[11]

Hughes saw his main role as the OC of 2 Squadron in Borneo as being quite simple. It was a twofold goal:

> Achieving our aims with the minimum loss of life itself. Leading the squadron and protecting its members. If we had been asked to go say twenty thousand metres in, I wouldn't have allowed them quite frankly without air and artillery

support. We were not allowed to have air at all. You couldn't get artillery support if you had a patrol cornered or cut off, but I would have asked.[12]

Another squadron commander was Reg Beesley, who served in Viet Nam as the OC of 3 Squadron in 1969–70. The Australian Task Force was of brigade size at that time and comprised three infantry battalions, a tank squadron, an APC squadron and the SAS squadron as the prime battlefield manoeuvre elements. Beesley's 3 SAS Squadron was commanded by the task force commander, a brigadier-general, and Reg Beesley explained his command and control relationship with the task force commander like this:

> Firstly, I established what the commander wanted. I would go away and look at the areas and so forth. I would then meet with him and we would discuss what he wanted from SAS, in other words—design for battle—regarding SAS. Fortunately, I had two good task force commanders, 'Sandy' Pearson, followed by 'Black Jack' Weir, and clear tasks were reconnaissance, reconnaissance/ambush. Primarily to find and gain information to allow the task force commander to work out in what area he was going to put his battalions. I would then do patrolling activities to achieve his mission. But also to maintain a presence of Australian Army in Phuoc Tuy Province when the battalions were sucked up into Long Binh [Province] and so forth, and that brought in the recon/ambush.[13]

In outline, then, the SAS squadron commander spent his time making sure his men were employed correctly, given the resources to do the job and not burnt out. His main aim in life was to ensure that the SAS were not used for tasks for which they were not suited, or were wasted on. Ignorance of what the SAS was and what they did or could do was their greatest problem, probably brought about by the fact that they lived in the west of the country, they were elite and had little contact with the rest of the army.

Troop commanders

The troop commanders were also patrol commanders in their own right as they led an ad hoc patrol containing their troop sergeant, the troop signaller and any troopers who were re-inforced into the squadron or left over from a patrol that was temporarily not functioning. Bill Hindson amplified the situation from the troop commander's perspective:

> Apart from being a troop commander in charge of a troop on operations, the troop commanders and patrol sergeants had a patrol and the main role of the troop commander in Viet Nam when off operations was to look after the administrative aspects and welfare needs of the troop and instil a sense of morale and efficiency amongst all of them. Because over time, with people being injured, and getting sick, reinforcements . . . the coming and going, the structure of the patrols changed.[14]

Second Lieutenant Ron Dempsey led a troop from 2 Squadron in Viet Nam in 1968–69 and saw his role as troop commander as being that of an overseer—fairly understandable in that he was a young officer with little experience leading a troop of 21 men, most with much more experience than himself. His role was

> just making sure I did the job properly, not to relax or overlook anything. You just had to make sure everything was well planned. There was a certain amount of standardisation, because you had to have it within the troop in case you had to swap guys over, so that if they went from one patrol to another one, they knew what the drills were rather than having to spend days and days going through new contact drills or new RV drills or new LUP drills and that sort of thing. However, in a lot of the other things, in the tactics that the guys used . . . it was left up to the patrol commander.[15]

In the SAS the patrol commanders have always been an entity unto themselves. The troop commanders do not task the patrols; that is done by the squadron commander, who then has a far greater asset at his disposal and far more flexibility.

He also has attached to the squadron a troop of signallers

from 152 Signal Squadron who are Royal Australian Signals Corps soldiers who are also beret-qualified as SAS troopers. The sigs are affectionately called 'chooks' because of the constant cackling and chattering away on the radio. At the same time they are held in the highest regard by their fellow SAS soldiers. This resource is invaluable to the squadron commander because each and every signaller was capable of deploying on patrol as Barry Standen, who did two tours of Borneo and two of Viet Nam with 152 Squadron amplifies:

> The chooks would come in on an 'as required' basis to replace someone sick, injured, on recreational leave. There might be a particular job on that needed more than a four-man patrol for a harassing job or an ambush job. There may be a patrol going to an area that was known to have very bad communications, so they would take someone—a more qualified person.[16]

The signal squadron was under command of the SAS squadron commander in all aspects and the rapport, the teamwork and the camaraderie between the two organisations was so close it was as if there was no difference between the two groups. The signallers were responsible for maintaining the communications link between the squadron headquarters and the patrols in the field. Barry Standen was the 152 Signal Squadron troop sergeant on his second tour of duty in Viet Nam and described their job:

> Principally the role—the rear role was to the Task Force Headquarters and you would just man a VHF link to the Task Force, and forward it was to troop and patrol level. And not only supporting communications from the base, but also deploying alongside. So, the chook was no better than an infantry soldier, but he was equal to the infantry soldier in that he had a patrol skill, but when the chooks weren't on patrol, they were operating the rear radios.[17]

Patrol commanders

Patrol commanders were normally sergeants with many years of experience in the SAS. Angelo 'Andy' Nucifora, who goes by the long nickname of 'Nuisance in the Foyer' saw the role of the patrol commander as being slightly different in base camp than when out bush. When he led his own patrol in Viet Nam when serving with 1 Squadron, he thought he had to

> make sure the lads were well briefed, make sure their weapons and their gear was always right, make sure they knew what was going on. It was important that you had to look after them. You've got your four Diggers, really look after them when they were in camp and make sure that everything is going all right—looking after their welfare. Make sure they've got their equipment, make sure they've got their pay and just generally mother them. But once you're out in the bush it was a case of making sure that they're doing the right thing and that they know what's going on at all times. So, that if anything happens, everybody knows their role that they're going to play regardless of whether they have moved or changed around in the patrol.[18]

Trevor Roderick was a young officer when he did his stint as a troop commander with 3 Squadron in Viet Nam in 1966–67. He had already seen active service in Borneo, where the four-man patrol dominated. Out in the bush and on patrol he saw his role as patrol commander as more a case of

> just keeping an eye on everything. Because there's only four people everyone—well not everyone navigates, two of us navigated—but because there's only four people, everyone is a forward scout, everyone is a machine-gunner even though they're not carrying a machine-gun, everyone is looking for information, everyone is listening. So in fact you weren't really the commander. You didn't command in the sense of a section, you know, 'machine-gun to the right' or the high ground. You were more part of a team really, you were just the boss of the bloody team. We knew. You didn't have to say anything because we knew what we were bloody doing.[19]

The scout

The patrol in a four-man team consists of the scout, the patrol commander, the 2IC and the signaller. The scout or 2IC doubled as a medic. In a five-man patrol the extra man is the medic.

The 2IC also carries the title of 'tail-end charlie' and watches the rear of the patrol. The medic will often act as a relief scout. In single file they also travel in roughly that order but it might change slightly between patrols. On one aspect most people agree that the two vital links in this chain are the leading two men, the scout and the patrol commander. Peter Schuman was a patrol commander in Borneo and then again in Viet Nam and he saw their relationship as:

The scout and the patrol commander always ran the patrol. There were three compasses in the patrol; the scout always carried one, I carried one and the tail-end charlie. I would set the bearing when we started the patrolling and then by hand I would point until the scout identified the same object that I did, whether it be a tree, a bamboo clump or whatever. He knew that's where he was going and where he had to finish up—but not his route. He would then use his instincts and start to meander. When he stopped, everyone stopped. He was the guy who was going to keep us in or out of danger. If he decided to stop for ten minutes no-one walked up to him and said, 'Hey listen, you know, let's get a move on mate'. If he went down on his knee, we all went down on our knee, we mimicked whatever the scout did. They were terrific those guys, they were just worth their weight in gold. I don't think you can train scouts, they're just natural hombres that can feel danger, they can smell danger, they can see danger even before you can think about it.[20]

Ian 'Bagza' Stiles was a patrol scout when he served in Viet Nam with 3 Squadron in 1966–67. He echoed Schuman's thoughts on the close work done between the two lead men and added:

The scout would walk along his compass route but the patrol commander, one back from the scout, he would be checking as well and also looking for signs of anything unusual—mainly tracks, any signs that people had chopped trees, or whatever. Your other senses also became finely tuned. You would listen a lot and use your sense of smell. You would move along and then possibly every half an hour the patrol commander would indicate 'Take five' (puts up five fingers), and the patrol would form an LUP—all facing outwards—a circle, and we would have a cigarette, a drink of water or whatever and we would listen and listen. Then we would be off again on our compass bearing.[21]

Movement in an SAS patrol is often painstakingly slow because the patrol cannot afford to be compromised before they complete their task. As one patrol scout said, 'We mightn't cover a lot of area in one day, but what we did cover was covered quite well.' The SAS patrols are most likely going to be outnumbered and must rely on stealth to achieve their primary mission. Ian Stiles thought the most important part of his job as a scout was

> making sure the rest of the patrol didn't bump into anybody. The hardest part was actually trying to pick tracks up because foot pads they are probably only a foot wide or 300 mm wide and of course if they're covered—with grass growing alongside of them—they were virtually impossible to see unless you were right on top of them before you would see them. And if someone is walking down a foot pad—and they can do this very quietly and quite fast as well. The first couple of contacts I ever had was VC coming down tracks and you virtually had them on top of you before you knew it.[22]

Another patrol commander, Sergeant Joe Van Droffelaar, led a patrol with 3 Squadron in 1969–70. He let his scout decide how fast the patrol would move because he was the eyes and ears of the patrol:

> I always used to maintain that the scout would pick the best tactical route, the scout would set the rate of advance. That is to say that he only moved as fast so he still had the ability to observe the enemy.[23]

The responsibility of being the scout is therefore somewhat daunting, with the constant mental pressure of looking, listening, waiting, smelling and ensuring that at any time he would be able to get the drop on any enemy before they got a drop on him. Strangely enough, as Ian Conaghan explained, the scouts would only give up their job if their legs were broken:

It therefore tends to be fairly nerve-racking, but interestingly enough, and it's not just me, but a lot of forward scouts really enjoyed being forward scout. Probably because, you're up front; you know everything that's going on; you're at the edge of it all. Whilst the patrol commander is ultimately responsible for navigation, it's the bloke up front going in the right direction—or not going in the right direction—that can cause a lot of stuff-ups. So your navigation has to be pretty good even though you are being guided by the patrol commander and the patrol commander is the bloke who is responsible for it, but yours has to be good.[24]

The patrol is only stretched over a maximum distance of 15 metres and everyone can see everyone else for the greater part. It is everyone's responsibility to ensure that they are constantly checking front and back for silent field signals or hand signals, as this would be the only form of communication while the patrol was actually upright and moving. Ian Conaghan explains that the halts to listen were one of the most important parts of patrolling for the SAS men:

Listening halts probably far exceed your movement. Quite often you would only move a few paces and as soon as the scout propped—you don't need any field signals—everybody else props. He would listen and normally before moving off again, just a quick glance back to the patrol commander to make sure he isn't frantically making hand signals and so on.[25]

Medic

Behind the patrol commander would travel the medic, or sometimes the signaller or the 'sig'. The medic was a trooper who had attended the special SAS patrol medics' course conducted at the School of Army Health, which qualified the soldier to attend to casualties better than a normal army medical assistant. The patrol needed this additional expertise because help might be a long time coming or might have to be delayed until the enemy were no longer a threat to the patrol's extraction with a casualty. Preference for which order people travelled in in this slow-moving caterpillar through the bush was the patrol commander's prerogative. Patrol commander Sergeant Joe Van Droffelaar explained why he had his medic at number three in the order of march:

> My medic was number three. Because if my scout goes down it's no good having the sig going forward and put a bloody wire down his throat. That's no good, you need a medic down there to fix him up. If contact was made then the medic would close up slightly on me. The medic wasn't that far behind me, he was only about three paces, then the sig would be about two paces behind the medic and then the 2IC would be about up to five paces behind the sig.[26]

The sig

The patrol signaller was an SAS trooper who had qualified on the SAS signallers' course and was capable of transmitting at least ten words per minute in Morse Code. The sig gets to carry the radio set, the spare battery and all the paraphernalia that goes with sending the messages in continuous wave (CW) on a high frequency (HF) radio. Sometimes the sigs from 152 Squadron would be co-opted into performing the role of patrol signaller on a patrol if the patrol sig was unable to go out. This would mean working that man into the detail of how the patrol operated and their drills and procedures. Ian Conaghan often had 152 Squadron chooks go out on his patrols.

> As a matter of principle, if I ever had someone from another patrol, like quite often a sig from our sig troop, come into the patrol, we would go right back to taws and start from the ground floor up through the whole nine yards of rehearsals, so that this guy knew everything at the end of it the way the rest of the patrol did.[27]

Many of the men from 152 Signals Squadron went on patrol. It was expected that they would go on patrol and it helped them appreciate just what the sig out in the bush was experiencing when trying to make a scheduled radio transmission. Because the operation of the radio equipment was their prime task, they were often sought after as replacements for patrol members, as Ian Conaghan recalled:

> In fact a lot of those guys chalked up more bush time than patrol members. Particularly the good ones, and there were some good ones amongst them. Because the good ones—every patrol wanted to take them if they were down a bloke. So, these poor guys ended up not getting to spend a lot of time in the radio shack because he was out on patrol.[28]

The patrol 2IC

The tail-end charlie or patrol second in command brought up the rear of the patrol and more or less operated as a scout but in reverse. He was also responsible for the administration of the patrol before they actually deployed into the field and made sure that everyone had all their supplies, their special equipment if required and the necessities of life like ammunition, food, water and whatever else was required to sustain the patrol in the field. As they moved through the bush, it was the 2IC's responsibility to make sure that they were safe from attack from the rear, much like a tail-gunner in a bomber aircraft. Andy Nucifora had been a 2IC on many patrols and said:

> I watched what was behind me and listened for sounds and covered up any tracks we might be making and try to keep the area as clear as possible and then follow up. Every now and then I would just stop and listen to see if we were getting followed up.[29]

If the patrol commander was hit it would not normally be the 2IC who would take over the patrol but the scout, as he was closest to where the action was and had been working most closely with the patrol commander. In some patrols, however, this would not happen. Andy Nucifora put it this way:

> Out in the bush you make sure you know who's got what and everybody else knows who's got what. And anything else for the admin of the patrol and the patrol commander tells you to do. So you're actually the admin guy for the patrol.[30]

COMBAT LOAD

What do these SAS patrol members carry when they head off on patrol? Lots. The patrol have to be able to maintain themselves for the period of the patrol and—with the exception of the Borneo patrols—without a resupply. That meant that in Viet Nam they had to carry everything they needed, including water, on their backs or on a belt around their waist. This all added up to a heavy load. Ron Dempsey remarked on how much he carried when he was in Viet Nam:

> I weighed it all up one day including pack, belt load and weapon and I think it came to around about 98 to 105 pounds [44.5–47.8 kg]. I was almost carrying myself around on my back at that stage. I think I was down to about 130 pounds [59 kg] anyway.[31]

The golden rule in the SAS is that one never removes or is ever more than an arm's length from one's basic webbing. The waist belt was more often than not a length of parachute harness webbing with an adjustable buckle that allowed the wearer to readily adjust the belt as he lost weight during a patrol. No-one ever gained weight.

Ian Stiles laughed when he remembered an incident after he was hospitalised and his waist-belt equipment was sitting on the floor in the field hospital:

> A medic tried to nonchalantly pick up my basic webbing. In it was twenty M16 magazines, a couple of water bottles, a couple of frag grenades, a WP [white phosphorus] grenade and a CS [gas] grenade.[32]

Stiles had about 10 to 12 kilograms of weight on his belt alone. The belt was the one piece of equipment that an SAS trooper never removed from his person when on patrol. This is the 'last ditch' survival belt. It was like Batman's utility belt in that it allowed the soldier to survive if he lost his back pack either through misadventure or in a need to shed weight during a withdrawal or hot extraction. He could lose his pack, but he couldn't lose his web belt. He always carried his emergency radio beacon, rifle ammunition, smoke grenades, fragmentary grenades, a secondary weapon such as a pistol, some water, emergency chocolate ration, first aid and survival kit including a knife on his belt.

Ammunition

The amount of ammunition carried by the SAS on patrol in Borneo was far less than they carried in Viet Nam, as the threat of enemy contact was far greater in the Viet Nam campaign. Because there was little chance of resupply once a contact started, the troopers used to carry whatever they thought they would need to get out of trouble. In a patrol the scout, patrol commander and sig would often carry the lighter 5.56 mm (the equivalent of .223 calibre) fully automatic M16 Armalite rifles. At least one of these M16 rifles would have a 40 mm grenade-launcher arrangement in what was known as the 'under and over'. This dual-barrelled weapon which could fire bullets, HE grenades, illumination, smoke, CS gas and a buckshot shotgun-type round, gave the patrol great flexibility in its firepower. The medic and 2IC would carry the harder hitting and larger calibre 7.62 mm (the equivalent of .308 calibre) self-loading rifles (SLR), but converted to fire on automatic instead of semi-automatic. All of these weapons carried a 30-round magazine and gave a very good initial burst of fire in a contact and gave the SAS patrol considerable firepower for a five-man group. An SAS contact drill often sounded like a 30-man platoon in contact when they opened fire instead of just five men.

Ian Stiles carried an SLR and an M16 at different times on his tours and his ammo load was:

I probably carried around about 240 to 250 SLR rounds—in magazines. When the M16 arrived, I used to carry about 400 M16 rounds. In fact the first patrol was a bit comical, in that we only had one hand grenade for the whole patrol. I remember we were all sort of laughing, 'Who is gonna carry this hand grenade?' But after a while, things got sorted and we had as much ammunition as we wanted. Hand grenades, white phos, frag. About twelve 40 mm M79 bombs; an escape kit; karabiner; Swiss seat; a knife and God knows what else.

You would probably carry about six smoke grenades in a patrol, but they might be say yellow and purple for one patrol, and another one would be green and red or whatever.[33]

Bill Hindson carried quite a few magazines for his rifle and when the M18A–1 Claymore mine came into service the SAS patrols also latched onto these devices, which were excellent for ambushing:

I used to have up to fourteen magazines. But to carry fourteen meant I would carry a couple on the weapon, taped back to back, and a big pouch that had most of them in it and a couple in my shirt pockets, in case you ever lost your webbing and so forth and a few grenades. Once we got Claymores, everybody carried at least one Claymore. Essentially it became every man's own choice and for special patrols you would take whatever weapons you might need. Like silenced Stirlings, when it was thought that we might be able to shoot people without alarming the rest of them immediately by the sound of being fired on.[34]

Other patrol commanders supplemented their ammo load with explosives after experience taught them some valuable lessons. Ian Conaghan recalled:

It was SOP in my patrol after a certain incident that everybody carried two slabs of C4 and initiation set except the sig. That came about because I came across a 750-pound UXB one day. There's a lot of explosive in a 750-pounder, probably 250–300 pounds of explosive, and you can make a lot of bombs out of that. Anyway, I positively marked the thing so eventually we or someone could blow it up or whatever. Lo and behold a month or so later, I was in the same area, and I came across exactly the same UXB. But Charlie [the Viet Cong] had been at it in the meantime and opened it up with a hacksaw and removed all of the explosive out of it. So, from there on in, as a matter of principle, I blew everything I ever found out there. I didn't worry about it compromising patrol security, because by whacking a charge on the thing if you were two or three hundred metres away by the time it goes off, explosions out in the J [jungle] up there were commonplace. So, there was no real compromising the patrol by doing it. But at

least, from my point of view, that was some explosive that the
enemy wasn't going to get their hands on.[35]

The golden rule in the SAS when it comes to a trooper's
personal combat load is that 'if you want to use it or wear it
you can, but you have to carry it'. As long as the weaponry
meets the patrol's requirements, he can carry almost anything he
likes as long as he understands that it is his responsibility to
maintain it.

Water

The one essential that weighed more than anything and was a
constant source of worry for the SAS patrol was water. Patrols
did not want to compromise their ability to remain undetected
by having to move to watercourses in the bush to resupply
themselves. Consequently on a five-day patrol they deployed
carrying their five days' worth of water. This led to some
ingenious methods of water carriage as Ron Dempsey recalled:

> I used to carry about seven or eight water bottles and I also
> carried a small plastic jerrycan. It was only a little one, but it
> took about a gallon, about four litres. And that just slid in the
> back of the pack.[36]

The amount of water carried by a patrol naturally varied
between the wet and the dry season and the types of rations the
patrol had to consume. Long Range Reconnaissance Patrol
(LRRP) rations were dehydrated and very light in weight but
required water to reconstitute them to avoid tasting like cardboard strips. The trade-off was always there and the weight that
patrols were forced to carry became incredible. Luckily they were
not moving great distances in Viet Nam. Bill Hindson reflected
on the combat load weight they had to endure:

> It varied considerably from the dry to wet season. The wet
> season was fine, you had very little; dry season was a huge
> problem because working across a three by three kilometre
> area, often you would have places were there was just no water
> at all. So, we used to carry a couple of water bottles on our

waist belt; you might have one strapped either side of your pack; you would have a collapsible bladder that was on top of the pack, and also had a plastic container. To do that in the dry though, along with the Claymores and all the other ammunition, you ended up with the loads being so great that in order to stand up once you were sitting down on the ground, you actually had to roll over onto your front and push yourself up by the arms and stand up.

We also had a problem that arose out of the amount of rations that we were eating on patrol. You would get towards the end of a patrol and guys were getting giddy when they were standing up and there was great concern that if we ever got into a fight and had to run that you would have people almost fainting from lack of decent nutrition. They were damned heavy, extremely heavy, particularly when you're in the position of being inserted and jumping off the helicopter. You stood a great chance of damaging your back or your legs, because you often had to jump down into long grass and stuff. But the good point was, I guess, it all lightened as you went along, although you still had the weight of the ammunition.[37]

Clothing

The normal issue greens worn by the Australian Army in Viet Nam lacked many things, including a disruptive pattern to break up the outline of the wearer. The pockets were too small to carry items like magazines or anything other than a map or a straight twenty-round box magazine. The SAS troopers scrounged their camouflage clothing from anyone who had a disruptive patterned uniform and became quite ingenious at modifying whatever clothing and equipment they had to use to carry the large heavy loads for a patrol. Bill Hindson reflected on the camouflage kit they 'acquired':

As people went off and met up with Rangers or were doing exchanges with a Ranger unit, or Long Range Reconnaissance Patrols or ultimately as they did with the SEAL teams, they were swapping their gear and coming back with camouflage gear of all types. Some of our first patrols we had straight-up Australian gear and it was quite a change to go from that sort of stuff to ultimately the camouflage gear. Whether it was real or not, the perception was there that the camouflage was better and they sort of behaved as though people couldn't see them.[38]

Radios

The patrol lifeline is the radio set and these changed between the time the SAS deployed to Borneo in 1965 and they returned from Viet Nam in 1971. Each patrol carried at least two rescue beacons called a SARBE 9 or an URC–10. These beacons emitted a high frequency distress call and when aircraft picked up the transmission they could close on the transmitter and find the patrol. That then allowed the patrols to talk ground-to-air and arrange their extraction or fire support. Barry Standen listed the radio load for a patrol in Viet Nam:

> You would normally carry two UHF ground–air communications, if you got in the shit you would just turn the beacon on and someone would hear it—sometimes it was a Pan Am aircraft—you would carry your HF [set] and batteries. Sometimes you would carry both HF and VHF but it depends principally on your task. For example if you were going out to marry up with or call in an infantry company or ready reaction. You couldn't do that with HF, you had to have VHF. But principally you would carry your UHF emergency beacons and your HF.[39]

Joe Van Droffelaar recalled that at one particular time in 1969 the whole requirement for communications got out of hand and every member of the patrol ended up carrying a radio of some kind:

> Communications within the patrol consisted of a 64 Set, Morse and voice capabilities, US-made; ground-to-air URC–10 241 and URC–10 243 radios (voice). These were the radios carried by the patrol during the first eight months of 1969 by 3 Squadron in South Viet Nam. The comms from patrol to SHQ and vice versa was good to very good on the 64 Set using Morse and signal strengths were at 4×5 or 5×5. Time spent on air was about ten to fifteen minutes.
> In the later period of 1969, breakdown of the crystal components in the 64 Set was a regular occurrence, thus

placing the entire communication within the patrol at doubt. Finally we were issued with a back-up patrol radio called the F1 Set with a Morse adapter and enough signal wire to make a patrol clothesline!

But because the F1 Set could not guarantee voice comms, they therefore issued us with a VHF 25 Set (ANPRC–25) for voice communications. So the five-man patrol finished up with a total of five radios: one 64 Set plus batteries, one F1 Set plus batteries plus equipment, one 25 Set plus batteries, two URC–10s.

So, from a situation of one 64 Set weighing 20 kg, we finished up with one and a half packs full of communication equipment. Time spent on the air setting up and then pulling down at times was $2\frac{1}{3}$ hours! It was a horse's arse, so to speak. The system somehow could not get new 64 Sets for the patrols.[40]

In 1971 the patrols were issued with the smaller PCR 68 set which had two UHF channels and two VHF channels plus a beacon capability. The set was half the size of an URC–10 and considered 'brilliant' by the likes of men like patrol commander Graham Brammer when it came to ground-to-air communications.

THE RIGHT MAN FOR THE JOB

The patrol members would sometimes swap their jobs to either gain experience in a slot or to give someone a break who might be getting tired or jaded in a certain patrol position. Ian Conaghan recalls his time when he was a lance-corporal and corporal as a patrol member:

> I did a number of scouting jobs and patrol 2IC. Quite often a lot of the jobs that you did weren't directly related to the rank that you had. Because you happened to be the available guy at the time. There were a few patrols that I had gone out on as a patrol commander's sergeant, as the 2IC to someone else, and a quick glance through those photos this morning and there's a picture of 'Slag' and myself going out, well Slag was my 2IC—even though he was my troop sergeant—he was my patrol 2IC for that particular patrol. We did some chopping and changing like that, but it was the exception rather than

norm as we tried to keep the patrol integrity as much as you could.[41]

Bill Hindson was asked to comment on the patrol composition and if it ever changed, as it could have fairly serious consequences on the personal dynamics of a small team in such dangerous assignments:

> The jobs within the patrol would change around. Some of our patrols would go to six [men] on occasions through illness of patrol members—the individuals would change around. In fact as we got into the wet season and people were catching colds and things the numbers changed quite considerably. As we went on, we had people getting injuries. Some were going on leave. You would be called on to patrol while members were away on leave so there was constant change. So, you weren't working necessarily with a full complement of the same patrol time and time again. Towards the end of the tour, we were actually swapping around so that instead of being patrol commander I was on a couple of occasions forward scout, the 2IC became the patrol commander, the forward scout became the tail-end charlie and so on.[42]

Military rank could therefore become irrelevant and it all came down to having the right man for the job and therein lies one of the unspoken rules in the SAS—everyone is important in a patrol regardless of their rank and their position. In a small team such as the SAS patrol, everyone must be a solid link in the chain or the consequences can be fatal.

4

BORNEO—THE PROVING GROUND

In 1962 the Indonesian President, Sukarno, began remonstrating that the formation of the newly created Federation of Malaysia which joined the states of Malaya, British North Borneo (Sabah), Brunei, Singapore and Sarawak was a neo-colonialist move and therefore a threat to Indonesia. Subsequent events such as the revolt in Brunei in December 1962 and some raids by Indonesian-backed forces into Sarawak and Sabah led to a general disquiet in Australia and the region regarding Indonesia's intentions.

The SAS Company was sent to Papua New Guinea on an exercise called LONG HOP in February 1963 with the aim of training in jungle but also with a political motive to have the SAS seen working in Australia's Territory. The region would soon have a common border with West New Guinea, where Indonesia was to assume control from the United Nations in May 1963. This training in New Guinea is covered in the next chapter, however it involved working as an Independent Company against the 1st Battalion of the Pacific Islands Regiment (1 PIR). The exercise was highly successful but more importantly highlighted some crucial shortfalls in SAS operations, especially in communications, which led to an SAS move to sky wave transmitters as opposed to ground wave transmitters and the use of continuous wave (CW) signals with Morse Code. This move to CW would ensure communications over long distances and would be a boon to operations which were soon to take place in Borneo.

The British SAS had been involved in the putting down of the rebellion in Borneo in December 1962 and when the Commanding Officer of 22 SAS Regiment visited Australia in July 1963, he intimated to the then Officer Commanding the Australian SAS, Major Alf Garland, that the overextended British SAS would welcome the Australian SAS to assist with reconnaissance and intelligence-gathering tasks along the 1100 kilometres of border with Indonesia on the island of Borneo. By 1964 Australia was looking north towards Asia and seeing increasing unrest and escalation of the civil war in Viet Nam; an increasingly hostile Indonesia adopting a policy of Confrontation (or *Konfrontasi*) with its immediate neighbours and the Federation of Malaysia; Communist terrorists operating in Malaysia; and security problems bubbling away in Thailand. The decision was made to increase the size of the SAS Company to a regiment, which was formed on 4 September 1964. At this time the Australian government was also about to introduce conscription for two years National Service for males aged 20 years. It was all happening.[1]

When Indonesian guerillas parachuted into Johore state in August and September 1964 and made a further abortive sea raid near Malacca in October that year, the Australian government was no longer able to remain detached as the threat of Indonesian forces crossing into Papua New Guinea was now quite real. Indonesia had the capability and had demonstrated physically the will to pursue an aggressive foreign policy. On 22 January 1965 the Malaysian government made a formal request for Australian assistance in the form of the SAS, the 3rd Battalion, The Royal Australian Regiment (3 RAR) and another battalion to go to Borneo. Australia did not have the capacity to deploy two infantry battalions, but agreed to send an SAS squadron and 3 RAR to Borneo. The SAS would be permitted to operate across the border into Indonesian territory. On 16 February, the SAS advance party arrived in Borneo and the remainder of the squadron arrived by sea from Singapore on 26 February. Operation TRUDGE was under way. The SAS squadron would deploy for six months and be the eyes and ears of the seven battalions situated along the Indonesian border with Kalimantan (see map, p. xii).

BORNEO—THE LAND

Situated just above the Equator and surrounded by the South China Sea and the Celebes Sea, the island of Borneo contained the three states of Sabah in the north, the tiny but very wealthy state of Brunei—which declined joining the Federation of Malaysia—and Sarawak in the south. All three states bordered Indonesian Kalimantan. In response to Indonesian confrontationist policy the Far East Region Land Forces (FARELF) deployed seven battalions into Sarawak. This was now a real war which was evidenced when the Malay Regiment suffered a mauling at the hands of the Indonesians on a raid in Sabah in late 1963.

The first SAS squadron, commanded by Major Alf Garland, deployed into Brunei. After a period of acclimatisation, the newly formed 1 SAS Squadron undertook specialist training with the British SAS troops. It was to prove a wise move as one of those soldiers recalled: 'The emphasis was on movement, close reconnaissance and surveillance. Long distances, but slow and careful movement, which is the way we ended up doing it.'[2] The training with their SAS hosts was conducted at Tutong, which is just south of Brunei. The British SAS took the fledgling Australian squadron under their wing. Trevor Roderick was a second lieutenant troop leader and continues:

> We had the basic stuff, and then when the British SAS got hold of us, we started the shooting and that's when the emphasis came on 'shoot and scoot'; the RV system, and the finer points of moving in the jungle. Bear in mind we did a fair bit of jungle training anyway. The company had been to Papua New Guinea on Exercise LONG HOP, we did the Kokoda Track and we learnt some very good lessons out of that.[3]

One of Roderick's close mates was another young officer Peter Schuman, and they had been in the SAS Company and then through the Officer Cadet School, Portsea, together. Schuman remembers the value of the time spent training with 22 SAS and how well they were prepared for their task ahead:

> We were hand-fed into the battle. We had some excellent instructors that came from 22 SAS. They taught us. They had been there—they had been fighting in the Radfan, Qatar, in Aden and also they had been in Borneo at that stage for a year and a bit on rotation. Their navigation in the jungle was superb. The techniques that they had of guiding scouts and then moving in bounds, their security in harbouring, their cooking techniques—all the little things for survival—we were taught down at Tutong. We were then sent off and we did field firing, we did live contact drills and we also had weapons and radios that we hadn't used. We tried out silenced Stirlings we hadn't handled before. It was about three weeks down at Tutong and it was almost like going to a small jungle training centre. Excellent instructors—you built confidence all the time, every facet of your training was tested, and you just continually built confidence.[4]

The troopers from 1 Squadron would need all the confidence they could get, because they were about to embark on patrols which would test all of their skills and their ability to operate as a small group over very long distances. The terrain they would traverse was tough. The border ran along a chain of mountainous ridges and in Schuman's words:

> It was absolutely horrendous. We would start our patrolling at a place called 'The Gap'. The maps were absolutely atrocious. Sometimes half the maps you had were just white with 'No reliable data because of cloud cover all year round'. Harry Butler would have loved the place as a naturalist. I travelled through moss forests, saw packs of orang-outangs in the wild and wild deer. It was just hard slogging—day after day of patrolling. That was what I called 'the loneliness time'. That was the first time that I was a million miles away from home, all by myself, in command—it was bloody lonely, it really was.[5]

The four-man SAS patrols were eventually allowed to operate up to 10 000 metres across the border. The patrols were a screen in front of the company outposts and were placed to detect any cross-border incursions. Often they would be out for a month and a half and then two months, resupplied by air every fortnight. But the trek just to get into some of the target areas was convoluted to say the least. The equipment used to ferry the patrols up to the border outposts was not really powerful enough or suited to the hot, humid conditions of the Borneo jungles. The patrols would have to be weighed before deploying as the British and Australian aircraft had great difficulty in coping with the tropical conditions. Barry 'Muka' Standen remembers quite clearly how much he weighed as a signaller setting off on patrol:

> I weighed in at 360 pounds [164 kg] on one particular patrol. We had to go forward from our base from 52 Brigade to a forward airstrip and then go by helicopter into an LZ. We used single and twin-pin [propeller] Pioneers, real old aircraft, and would have to weigh each guy individually and if you were over, they used to make an adjustment and say you're going to have to leave this behind or that behind.[6]

Depending on exactly where your patrol was heading, the insertions would vary but Peter Schuman recalled one of his insertions into an area up on the Indonesian border he became extremely familiar with during his six months with 1 Squadron:

> Our squadron was spread over hundreds of kilometres along the border doing surveillance and I was at a place called 'The Gap'. Four of us would get on an aircraft, a fixed wing, Twin Pioneer aircraft, flown by Brit Army [Air Corps] sergeants. We would fly from Brunei into a forward base called Pensiangan, which was a fairly large airstrip, and from there we would transfer into a single-engined short-take-off aircraft called a Beaver—a Canadian, high-wing aircraft—and then go into a place called Sapulot. That was the last forward airstrip before the border ridge with Kalimantan. And then we would fly in RAAF Wessex Whirlwinds up onto the border. Now, depending on the heat of the day when you arrived there, and depending on the load you were carrying in, whether you were carrying explosives to blast an LZ out of the hills or whatever, sometimes you used to be taken up to the border one at a time. So, as the patrol commander, I was the first one up with my pack and sat there for ten minutes while the helicopter disappeared down the valley and out of sight. Then

ten minutes later the chopper would return with another guy, and then there would be enough fuel to bring in the last two guys with some stores.[7]

Out there in Kalimantan as a four-man patrol with only a radio as a link to assistance, the concept of fire support was remote to say the least. The sheer difficulty of the terrain, coupled with the scarcity of resources over huge distances, led to artillery missions best described by Peter Schuman:

> Most of these border outposts had 105 mm pack howitzers, and in fact the Gurkhas used to take the pack howitzers apart and carry about six rounds of ammo and they would lug this into the jungle above some of these Indonesian fortresses which were usually on the other side of a river—they were hard to get to—and they would whack a few mortars into them and throw a few 105 shells at them and knock off any moving targets that were around the place and then come back across the other side.[8]

Before the cross-border reconnaissance and surveillance and then later offensive operations began, the Australian SAS patrols were deployed on what were referred to as 'WHAM' operations, or winning hearts and minds. This WHAM period lasted about a month and took place straight after the initial acclimatisation and training period. It was essential that the Australians knew as much about their area of operations (AO) and the people before they even got close to the enemy. With that in mind the patrols were sent to villages called kampongs to mingle with the locals and win them over to the British cause:

> Initially we did 'hearts and minds' where we were located in small AOs that included one or two kampongs and our medics looked after their health. We tried to get information out of them, learnt the language, and learnt their customs. We lived away from them but each day we would go in. We gave them kerosene and caught fish with them using explosives. We played cricket with them and played footy with them. We learnt more about living in the jungle ourselves, learnt more about them, and gained a lot of information on the areas. We went up to the border, but didn't go across it at this stage of

the game. It was good. I think it went a bit too long because we were all anxious to get stuck in, but it was good training, very good training.[9]

One of the reasons the men carried so much equipment when they went over the border into Kalimantan was that they had to cope with very cold nights when they were high up on the border ridge. The patrols would also have to carry in about fourteen days' rations because resupply was never certain owing to fickle weather conditions in the cloud-covered highland areas. There were other problems the patrols had to cope with, as patrol leader Peter Schuman explains:

> The search for water was always a problem. To get over the border ridge in The Gap area used to take three days. It was a day's patrolling to the top and then you knew you were in the badlands and if you hit a track it would take you another two days to get to water. So there was always a search for water and you always had this dilemma of leaving the low ground where there was plenty of water and going up. It never rained, it was always just this continual cloud.[10]

After a couple of months in Borneo the 1 Squadron patrols were unleashed to conduct operations across the Indonesian border. These were known as Claret operations and were kept highly secret for 30 years and only admitted publicly several years ago. It was important at the time that Indonesia not be aware of the fact that Australian and British SAS patrols were monitoring and recording the Indonesian patrols who were moving on targets in Sabah, Brunei and Sarawak. The initial patrols were to be covert and mainly reconnaissance and surveillance operations. The brigade commanders needed to know where the Indonesians were so they could deal with them with more conventional forces when required. Consequently, contacts with the Indonesians were infrequent, which is quite understandable given the huge tracts of land and relatively small numbers of troops that were involved. It was as Peter Schuman said: always scary because it was just like two trains in a tunnel that were silent going towards one another and you just never knew what you were going to hit.[11]

The Indonesian forces were a mixed bunch. The *Silawangi Division* used the rivers as their lines of communication. They were quite regularly sighted, observed, and patrols reported upon their boats and what they had in them and what protection they had. The Australian SAS thought they were below average. The *RPKAD*, who were the Indonesian equivalent of SAS, had the respect of the Australian SAS men. They were well trained—in fact their commanding officer was a friend of Jim Hughes from Staff College days. (Hughes would later command 2 Squadron following 1 Squadron, but in a different AO.) The last group were the Chinese Communist organisation. They were not considered by the SAS to be too much of a problem. They used the hinterland, high up on the Sarawak side of the border, and they were people who were taken across to Kalimantan, trained by the *RPKAD* and then sent back in.[12]

The patrols would target the rivers, as they were the principal method of movement in the thick, almost impenetrable jungle. The Indonesian patrols would be resupplied and reinforced in fortified camps set up along the major rivers inside Kalimantan. From those camps the Indonesian patrols could launch raids into the British zones. They were not all easy-beats as some people have suggested, as Trevor Roderick recounted when discussing an ambush patrol on a major river. Two other patrol leaders, Schuman and Petit, had already reconnoitred the location:

Peter Schuman and Johnny Petit had been in there, so we had had three patrols in there trying to ambush on this river, but obviously not the same place. They had seen two people in a boat and they were uncertain of what they were so they didn't shoot. We got in and it was a pretty big patrol of twelve men. We set up the ambush and it was one of those ambushes where you pull back at night, so there's lots of movement. On the second day a boat went underneath the ambush position, virtually underneath us, and one of our guys felt that the enemy had seen us. So we pulled back and the next day we shifted the killing ground and went back in again. About six or eight of the enemy came through so we hit them. We got them, but they reacted very quickly and we think they shot up our old ambush position. So they were sweating on us.[13]

Members of Trevor Roderick's patrol in Borneo at an insertion landing point on the border between Sarawak and Kalimantan. Note the steep terrain and heavy cloud. *Left to right:* Roderick, Pte Bruce English and Jack Gebhardt. *Photo courtesy of Trevor Roderick*

Not all things go as planned, even for the highly trained men of the SAS. Some tasks were purely surveillance where avoidance of the enemy or discovery of their presence was paramount for the security of further offensive operations. Trevor Roderick's patrol was sent into an area called Long Api and there was a good chance the enemy would be aware of their presence. They moved by foot across the border and began their reconnaissance task:

We were warned that the Indonesians were using locals to keep an eye open for us and we decided that we would cache our Bergen packs, our big packs, and we did all the normal stuff like walking on logs, down creeks, tippy-toeing over rocks. We then lowered our Bergens down a hole where a tree had fallen and then kept going down creeks, on logs, tippy-toeing and all this and set up an OP [observation post]

Trevor Roderick contemplating the loss of his socks to the Indonesians when his patrol cache was captured during a cross border operation into Indonesian territory in 1965. *Photo courtesy of Trevor Roderick*

within a couple of hundred metres of the target. Two men manned the OP and two stayed behind.

A fellow called Jack Gebhardt and I were in the observation post and we could see some Indonesian soldiers in uniform, some guys in civvies, who were obviously soldiers, and some locals. And I said to Jack Gebhardt that they had been out hunting because they had poles and things slung on the poles. Jack said, 'They look like our packs.' I said, 'Bullshit! It's animals, keep watching.'

They brought the packs into the village which is 200 metres below us and started ratting through our packs. I couldn't wear woollen army socks because they irritated my skin and my wife Helen used to buy socks and send them up to me. But here is this Indonesian soldier whose feet . . . were about bloody nine inches wide, pulling my socks on! Trying *my* socks on! Smiling all over his face and they were going through our tucker and all the rest of the stuff.

And then there was an almighty crash behind us and we thought it was a three-inch rocket-launcher but it was a mortar. So they had used these natives to find our cache. They then must have figured out roughly where we were—they knew we were observing them and they hit the ridgeline behind us. We said, feet get moving! It took us eight days to get in because we never moved on tracks, but we got out in 24 hours![14]

The patrol lost their Bergen packs with their rations and bedding but a standard operating procedure (SOP) was that the members always wore around their waist on their webbing belt some survival rations, a Sarbe beacon with which they could talk to aircraft, ammunition, fishing lines, medical supplies and water. But it was then a cold, hungry walk back out to their extraction point.

THE FIRST CASUALTY

In May 1965 one of the patrols commanded by Roy Weir was moving around an area about 35 kilometres south of Pensiangan to check on a known Indonesian infiltration route along the Selimulan River. The going was very difficult owing to torrential rain, sticky muddy ground and tough terrain. On 2 June the forward scout of the patrol came across an elephant track and in a sequence of terrifying and bizarre events, a rogue bull elephant, standing almost 3 metres tall, attacked the patrol that was trying to avoid the beast and the patrol signaller, Paul Denehy, was very seriously gored by the enraged animal. Despite being shot with nine 7.62 mm bullets, the elephant managed to strike the signaller seeking shelter behind a massive fallen log. The radio set was also badly damaged in the attack, which allowed the patrol to transmit but they were unable to confirm if the signal had been received.

The attack drove some salient points home to these SAS men who were operating deep in enemy territory. They had very little support in the way of aircraft and three men were going to find it very tough to extricate a stretcher case. Denehy was in considerable pain when he was moved. Two of his ribs had been torn away from his backbone and there was a puncture wound large enough to put a fist into. The bull elephant was still searching for the patrol, that somehow managed to move to high ground and send a message which was actually picked up in Swanbourne by a signaller on duty that night. Peter Schuman was one of the closest patrols to Weir and was sent airborne to try to establish communications with the distressed patrol, but to no avail. After some extremely frustrating forced evasive manoeuvres caused by the elephant, large red orang-outangs and very difficult terrain, two of the patrol were able to make contact with a Gurkha patrol sent to assist the extrication of the wounded soldier. On their return to the site where they had last seen their comrade alive with the patrol medic, he was found dead, having spent his last hours in considerable pain. The patrol medic had exhausted his supplies and when excessive time elapsed for the search party to return, he also set out for help and was in the process of leading another patrol to the dying Denehy when he was located.[15]

Paul Denehy was the first of the SAS men to die on active service. The soldiers had been together for a long time training for war, undergoing work-up training, exercises in PNG, treks through the forests south of Perth and now one of their own had been killed by an elephant. One of Paul Denehy's mates was Barry Standen and he felt:

It had a major impact on the squadron because when we were up there we were all romantic, we were invincible. We were the best there ever was. And we realised that it didn't have to be the baddies that got you. I mean who ever would have thought that you would get killed by a rogue elephant? After all the training, after all the psychological preparation, after the deployment to an active service area, who would have thought that is what could bring about your demise? I guess it was sobering, but it affected everyone and I think it made everyone realise that it is not all bloody beer and skittles. And it's not right and wrong. These sort of things happen and it doesn't have to be someone on a 12.7 mm. It can be something, I was going to say 'simple', but there was nothing simple about a rogue elephant, but it can be something like that. It affected the whole shebang, the whole organisation.[16]

THE SECOND TOUR

In August 1965 1 Squadron completed their tour of duty and were replaced by 2 Squadron, commanded by Jim Hughes. During the 1965 tour by 1 Squadron they mounted 23 recon-naissance, seven reconnaissance/ambush, two ambush, four surveillance, one special and thirteen hearts and minds patrols. Only six weeks of their three months on cross-border patrols were spent on offensive operations but they accounted for seventeen Indonesian enemy with their single loss of Paul Denehy to a non-battle freak accident.[17]

Compared to 1 Squadron, 2 Squadron operated in a totally different area of Borneo and in a different tactical environment. In September 1965 there had been an unsuccessful Communist coup in Indonesia and President Sukarno's authority was starting to wane, as was the enthusiasm for *Konfrontasi*. Although regular Indonesian activity was on the decrease in Borneo, there were now several paramilitary groups who were being trained by the Indonesian equivalent of the SAS called the *RPKAD*. These groups were now getting busier and the main SAS effort was now driven towards establishing the location and strength of these bases. The deployment to Borneo was a highlight for Hughes but when he arrived in theatre he received an indifferent welcome from the Australian staff on the FARELF headquarters.

> I always remember the indifference to our arrival shown by the staff of HQ Australian Army Force, FARELF. As if we were an embuggerance factor—you know, 'We got rid of 1 Squadron last year, now you buggers are here!' It was a genuine feeling that I had. I had a feeling I might have been interfering with their golf or something.[18]

However things got better for Hughes when he arrived in his final destination where the brigade commander was actually delighted to have the Australian SAS operating in front of his formation:

We went from HQ FARELF, who really couldn't have cared less, to the headquarters of the Directorate of British Operations (HQ DOBOPS). Now, the fact that the general was ex–22 SAS was by the side, but his whole staff, they couldn't have been more cooperative or thoughtful. Then we went down to West Brigade and they're a mixture of every regiment in the place. Headquartered at Kuching, with 300 kilometres of border and five battalions, and they couldn't be more helpful. And then we get down to B Squadron 22 SAS who we were replacing and again, they all bent over backwards. I can't think of any person who wasn't 101 per cent cooperative. The difference was chalk and cheese.[19]

The 2 Squadron soldiers travelling after Jim Hughes and his advance party flew into Singapore and then kitted out at Nee Soon Garrison on the island of Singapore before continuing on to Borneo. In Singapore they received briefings and acclimatised before arriving in Kuching. Ian Conaghan had his tongue firmly in his cheek when he described the deployment, which was supposed to be conducted with the utmost security:

The move to Borneo was a clandestine operation where we went in very secretly in civilian clothing, which meant that we all wore polyester trousers and white shirts—everybody was dressed exactly the same! We went on a chartered Qantas 707 and there were dependants on board for guys up at Terendak at Selarang. We flew into Singapore and the move was so successful in its secrecy and hiding our identity, it wasn't until the following day that the headlines in the *Straits Times* said, 'Aussie Bird Men Fly In'.[20]

Once again the men from the Australian SAS were given acclimatisation training and 22 SAS put them through their paces in the bush about 18 kilometres north-west of Kuching. Ian Conaghan recalled his training with the men from the British SAS Regiment:

We were introduced to Claymores there, did a tremendous amount of live firing and it was all in really good tropical rainforest. It was brilliant, and because it was under operational conditions, the normal safety limits were reduced to the absolute bare minimum. We had Iban Border Scouts attached who taught us tracking and they were very good. That was really invaluable training at Matang.[21]

The types of operations that 2 Squadron would see in their AO known as West Brigade would be substantially different from those conducted by 1 Squadron. The type and level of activity would be determined by what was happening on the political front in talks between the Indonesians and the Federation of Malaysian States and the British. Jim Hughes recalled what the main role for the squadron was to be:

> The aims in 1966 were different to '65 and '64—were firstly reconnaissance, secondly 'hearts and minds', thirdly the operations of border scouts for the Third Division, fourthly and last—air rescue. I was a bit worried about doing that because I found the parachutes were sitting on pallets on a dirt floor covered in dust and cobwebs in a shed.[22]

The terrain in front of Hughes' men was also different from the mountainous region of The Gap which 1 Squadron encountered. It was still jungle—hot, damp, humid and tough to negotiate—but not as high in altitude as the area to the north. There were more villages, occasional paddy fields and in the area close to the South China Sea large areas of swamp. Ian Conaghan has very vivid memories of the Borneo terrain he found himself trudging over:

> From swamp land to mountains. The border actually ran along a mountain chain and you crossed over the border and then went down into a fairly deep valley which was a major watershed for a huge river. It was about 10 000 metres across. That's where a lot of successful ambushes were fought.[23]

If the terrain was different, one thing remained unchanged: the maps that the patrols had to operate from were fairly ordinary. Not a lot of survey work had been conducted across the border and often the map would simply say 'Continuously Covered by Cloud' or simply be a blank space of white map. This lack of topographical detail made for interesting times, as Ian Conaghan explains:

Quite often we had no maps, so as the patrol commander was going through previous patrol reports from that area, the rest of the patrol would be allocated into the Int Section. We would have a blank sheet of paper and we would grid it. We might have a patrol report from D Squadron, 22 SAS, two years before or something. All the LZs were coded, because most of them were actually artificial, blown straight out of the primary jungle. From this previous patrol report would be, 'On a bearing of such and such there was an east–west flowing stream', so on the gridded sheet of paper we would whack that in and that was how we built our map. That was the going map for the patrol.

The maps weren't bad—up to the border. Generally over the border they were virtually non-existent, just blank sheets of paper. Your navigation had to be pretty well spot-on. One patrol I was on with Laurie Fraser, he was winding around a fair bit, and we had a hell of a lot of bouncing around, and we wound up getting a navfix by requesting an artillery star shell at a specific grid reference at a specific time so he could take a shot at it. That would give you a fair idea of where you were. We couldn't call fire missions or anything, because we didn't have the means.[24]

In preparation for a Borneo patrol, the OC of the squadron would attend briefings in the brigade headquarters and discussions would cover likely tasks for the SAS, as Jim Hughes recalls:

No two days were the same, but this is what I did most days. I checked the overnight sitreps and intelligence reports; I attended the commander West Brigade's morning prayers; there were discussions in committee, and then discussions one to one. So, often I would talk with the brigade commander in his office afterwards. I would come back to the SAS operations room and talk to the staff about what had happened that morning down at brigade headquarters.[25]

Hughes had to become something of a 'salesman' for the squadron, as the concept of Special Forces was relatively new to most western armies and had only been born out of operations during the Second World War. Getting the various battalion commanders in the 2 Squadron AO of West Brigade to use the

SAS in the manner for which they were designed was an ongoing task:

> I had to be a bit of a salesman. In the period from January to July probably ten battalions rotated through the five battalion positions. It didn't matter whether they were Malays, Brits or New Zealanders. They were only there for four months. I probably saw ten battalions, so it wasn't a case of selling our attributes once, I had to sell them twice. Every time a battalion changed, I had to start again.[26]

Once the squadron was given a task, Hughes would issue a warning order to the patrol commander on his likely task, prepare his own orders and when ready call the patrol commander in to the squadron headquarters. Jim Hughes remembers that the process was

> normally done in and around the squadron operations room. Sometimes it was supplemented at the departure point, not on the LZ but at a company base including our moving out through 4 RAR, or moving out through the Rangers, or moving out through the Argyll and Sutherland Highlanders. When we used their company base, it was an opportunity to get their latest local intelligence.[27]

The sources for operations in Borneo were primarily from human intelligence (humint). Ian Conaghan was asked to recount just what intelligence sources were at the disposal of the SAS patrol leaders preparing to go into Indonesia:

> Previous patrol reports, of course—our own and the Brits'; normal infantry reports where you had normal intreps from whatever sources; Special Branch used to run agents across the border—they were another source. The Border Scouts were also a very good source. They would actually go and live in the villages close to the border and any local gossip that was being picked up—they would get it. You couldn't get anything from photo recons or anything because the aircraft couldn't fly across the other side of the border. So, our electronic intel was zilch and most of it was humint of one description or another.[28]

The secrecy surrounding patrol activity in Borneo was absolute. Because the SAS Squadron headquarters was located in the town of Kuching, everyone was made to be acutely aware of their personal and unit security. It was no good training hard to infiltrate an area using various deception techniques if the enemy already knew the patrols were headed their way. Apart from the obvious physical danger, there was also a requirement that patrols only know what they really *had* to know. Ian Conaghan recalled that he didn't know where their own squadron patrols from the same troop were:

> One thing we did apply very, very strictly in Borneo was a total 'need to know' basis. You never knew where another patrol was and they didn't know where you were. Because the principle in Borneo being that if you went in the bag no way in the world could you compromise anybody else.[29]

The patrol leader would prepare his orders for the rest of the patrol and the process of packing and loading their personal equipment would begin. Owing to the tough terrain, the availability of aircraft for resupply and the time taken to get from one location to another, the SAS men had to carry fourteen days' rations on their backs. Hughes was concerned about the weights his men were forced to carry and attempted to limit their load to 90 pounds (40 kg). They would take a parachute or helicopter resupply every fourteen days, but this only applied if the patrol was on the friendly side of the border.

Carrying these extraordinary weights and living on hard rations had a significant effect on the personal body weights of the soldiers. It was not uncommon for the weight of men to fluctuate by up to 10 kg over several weeks. Barry Standen did both tours with the Australian SAS in Borneo and recalled that he would lose a stone to a stone and a half (6–9 kg) in four weeks. The rations the men carried were quite substantial and few had any complaints about the food apart from the weight of the stuff. Ian Conaghan remembered what his culinary load was like:

> We had a pretty good choice of rations, BT [British tropical] rations which were bloody awful, because they were mainly

big tins. We also had FARELF rations, which were mostly dehydrated stuff, not freeze-dried as we had in Viet Nam. And they used to have foil envelopes full of things like dried apple flakes. These things were really good because they would fit in pockets and so you could stick a lot of this stuff in your pockets. Even if you lost all of your other kit, at least you've still got some sustenance on you. We also had SAS rations, which were especially designed for 22 SAS for long-range patrols in the tropics and they were very good.[30]

Apart from the food, warm clothing, bedding and water, the men also had to carry ammunition, spare radio batteries and the like. Patrols also shared the load of carrying the Claymore mines, white phosphorus grenades, a medical set designed for 22 SAS and considered by most to be far better than the Australian medical pack, an explosive set when required for blowing things up if the patrol was tasked, and finally it was also normal to carry a mini-camera like the Minolta 1.[31]

The ground in the 1 Squadron AO was often wet or very steep so the men slept in hammocks unless it was likely that contact with the enemy was imminent. The soldiers carrying M16 Armalite rifles carried about 100 rounds which wasn't much compared to ammo loads carried later in the Viet Nam conflict. But their role in the Borneo campaign was not the same. They were there to observe and report and move in and out of Indonesia undetected.

Once they had packed their kit and received their orders, the patrol would commence the insertion procedure. Like 1 Squadron, the men again had to undergo a laborious procedure to finally get to their true infiltration point. One soldier remembered:

All of the air insertions I did were always split. Quite often we would take a fixed-wing aircraft from Kuching to a battalion strip quite a bit forward and then be airlifted from that battalion strip with a Whirlwind or a Scout, which was the army (Army Air Corps) aircraft. They were gutsy little aeroplanes, but it was a matter of space. In fact I think they could lift, in sheer weight terms, more than a Whirlwind. But of course it didn't have the space.[32]

A Borneo patrol awaiting insertion by helicopter. *Photo courtesy of J. Sexton*

Even though you could fit a four-man patrol on a RAF Whirlwind, they had a great deal of trouble lifting a fully laden patrol and it would have to be split while being inserted so the aircraft could burn off fuel and lift a bigger payload. There was a great deal of respect for the army sergeant pilots. In West Brigade, they also had Belvederes, a twin-rotor chopper called 'Widow-makers' by all and sundry associated with these unusual-looking aircraft. The insertions of patrols varied and were by every combination you could think of—foot, boat, helicopter, vehicle, fixed wing. For cross-border operations the preferred means, for security reasons more than anything else, was invariably by foot.[33] The patrols were generally brought to an LZ near, but not within sight of, the border so that it was about 1000 metres to cross, but some company bases were within two or three thousand metres of the border.

Fire support for the patrols was virtually non-existent and once across the border only exceptionally unusual circumstances could gain aircraft support. The artillery available to the

Commonwealth forces in Borneo was extremely limited and stretched to a point where unusual procedures for the application of supporting fire had to be implemented. Jim Hughes recalled that across the 300 kilometres of front in West Brigade they had a Brit battery of eight guns: 'So, you work that out, 300 kilometres divided by eight. That's only 37.5 clicks each and the range of the guns is about 10 kilometres.' So, the 105 mm guns were deployed as 'pistol guns' in a forward outpost supported by infantry but, owing to the ranges between them, they didn't even support each other. Occasionally the guns would come into action, as OC 2 Squadron recalled:

> Every now and again the Indonesians got aggressive and they would put one mortar shell or one artillery shell into Sarawak. I was doing an air reconnaissance with a patrol commander, in fact I had a company commander aboard too. Unbeknown to me the Army Air Corps pilot was an ex-gunner. He picked this enemy activity up on one of his nets, that a shell had arrived in a camp, and the next thing away he goes and he said, 'Oh, I've got approval to retaliate!' Now we were travelling at this stage at about 1000 feet, but the next minute we were at 8000 feet with this Brit clothing, freezing to bloody death with the doors off of course, and he is having the time of his life—single-ranging a gun there, then he would travel 10 kilometres down that way and single-range another gun in. An hour later we were just about having pneumonia and thank God we went down and landed.[34]

The patrol lifeline, whether in Borneo or in Viet Nam; was the radio. In Borneo the radios were not really suited to the environment in which they were being asked to perform. The patrols carried the British 128 radio set and a Mark Two Sarbe beacon, which was a more updated model than that used in Australia at that time. The radio communications out on patrol were always a trial for the signallers trying to get through on their scheduled report times (scheds). Barry Standen explains why is was always a drama getting comms:

> The radios we used were called 128 and 123s and they were designed for desert warfare in the Second World War. They weren't waterproofed at all and they were valve-driven. I

would have to say that more than 50 per cent of the times for a sched, you had to take the four retaining screws out, take the bloody radio apart and lay the guts in the sun for about ten minutes somewhere—very tactical! When dry, you would put it back together again and have your comms. And you did that every sched—you had to dry it out because it was designed for desert and there we were in the jungle using them.[35]

Not all the problems encountered by the patrols wore Indonesian uniforms. There were plenty of nasties in the Borneo jungle to keep the patrols on their toes. Ian Conaghan remembered:

Leeches were horrendous, unbelievable. I remember getting one in the groin, because with leeches you don't know you've had them and the stinging only starts at the very end before they drop off. And this thing was in my groin, and it must have tapped close to the femoral artery or something. We were covered in water and wet and our clothes were black, and I didn't realise how much blood had poured out of this wound until I actually pulled my daks down. My daks were not only soaking wet with water, but they were soaking wet with blood because there was this enormous tiger leech in my groin.

My patrol commander, Jimmy Stewart, was bitten on the arm by a scorpion, and honestly within just a few hours you would swear that someone had slipped a football under his skin. It was huge! It looked like he had elephantiasis.

There were lots and lots of snakes, orang-outang, lots of monkeys. Once I came across tiger spoor and you could actually smell the tiger, but we never actually saw one. We were coming across a really old track, and you tend to get little pools of water, where you can't exactly define the edge of the water and where the ground starts. There was this huge pad mark on the edge there and water was just seeping back into it. The hairs on the back of my neck went up and I had eyes like a mad cat because you knew there was big cat around the area. But logic tells you . . . here's a four-man patrol all with guns and so on and any chance of a tiger taking on something like that is pretty bloody remote—but still it made you sit up and take notice at the time.

The animals were a problem but not because of any physical threat to us, but because if we encroached on their territory they would make a lot of noise and it was just like having a jungle warning system. Anybody in the area would know that something has disturbed these guys.[36]

The patrols would move out of their LZs and into designated areas inside British North Borneo, or when authorised cross into Kalimantan. During 2 Squadron's tour they were not authorised to undertake offensive operations, which was exceptionally frustrating for these men who had honed their fighting skills to a very sharp edge and were unable to put them into practice. The squadron commander recalled with chagrin that from the end of February until the end of July they did 45 patrols. In March, April and May 1966 all 2 Squadron patrols were cross-border. In June and July they were mostly all on the friendly side:

> 1965 and 1966 were two entirely different years in Borneo. We patrolled, the Brits, the Australians and New Zealanders and Malays did what few cross-border operations they allowed in 1966, but chalk and cheese between 3 RAR in 1965, 4 RAR in 1966, and 1 Squadron in 1965 and 2 Squadron in 1966. I would have to say though that it was the stepping stone—without any doubt—for SAS in Viet Nam. Generally, the quality of the people we had in SAS in 1965 was very high. It took years of training, they were good but were never given their chance.[37]

Once a patrol had concluded its task and required extraction the reverse procedure of the infiltration would take place.

> Generally we made our way to an LZ. This is where navigation in Borneo was so critically important because the maps were pretty hopeless but the LZ truly was a pinpoint in primary jungle—it was a hole, like a vertical column that might be 50 to 75 metres wide. And you might be trying to get to it from 10 000 metres away through swamps and mountains and primary jungle without ever seeing a piece of open ground at all. You couldn't even see the stars at night it was that thick, and you have to find that little hole in the J. Because if you missed it you could still keep going for weeks on end before you got anywhere.
>
> So you get to the LZ and normally the day before, or maybe even a couple of days before, arrange for extraction at

a certain time. We had no ground–air communications. We carried a Sarbe, but that was beacon only. There was no voice communications, so you kind of hoped and prayed that everything worked okay and the airplane arrived at the scheduled hour . . . Normally he didn't have much endurance so we would fly to a forward base somewhere, get off there and catch a fixed-wing or another rotary-wing aircraft or maybe even a vehicle back to Kuching.[38]

Not all extractions are so carefully planned or go according to plan. Occasionally Murphy's Law is applied. Jim Hughes was involved in one extraction with the New Zealand SAS, who were attached to the Australian SAS and operated in the same AO:

On some occasions we had New Zealand patrols working for us and this four-man patrol had a member with a broken ankle. I recall that the patrol had at least two big Maoris. Somebody in the ops room told me there were four big men and that made it even worse. They missed the next sched on the radio next day. So, the next day, I'm going three days down the line now, with a RAF Whirlwind helicopter, we suddenly picked up their Sarbe signal. Now perhaps I was a bit naive, but also pleased to find them. I said to the pilot, 'Let's go.' We ended up going about two or three kilometres across the border!

We found them in a mangrove swamp area but we couldn't land and we got three—we got the wounded man up on a winch, we got the next two up on the winch and the bloody winch stopped dead. The line extended. The patrol commander, being a good man, last to get aboard. So by hand signals we had to say, 'Step on the hook and stay there' and the poor bugger had to be carried back at treetop height for two or three kilometres to the nearest company base. I don't think he was smiling and we had problems actually getting him to release.[39]

The Army Aviation Corps flew Scouts, which were ideal for a four-man patrol—a pilot and four. It was the aircraft mainly used for the squadron OC to attend meetings, and if he had to go and pick up a patrol or to drop a patrol off he would use the RAF Whirlwind. The Whirlwind took five plus crew. Patrols couldn't rappel out of a Scout very well, but could out of a Whirlwind.

The patrols would return to Kuching and be rested before their next task. The soldiers would experience an enormous loss of weight and also be suffering from the myriad of tropical illnesses that attack the human system when living rough in the tropical rainforest. Hughes was concerned about the condition of the men and tried to ensure that they were well fed when they returned to base from the arduous patrols:

> We fed our soldiers everything we could, probably overdid the protein and vitamins, but I was conscious over six months that their health, weight, even a layman could see was going downhill.[40]

Like 1 Squadron with their loss of Paul Denehy, 2 Squadron was to suffer when a patrol tried to cross a swiftly flowing, swollen river when operating deep in Indonesian territory. The patrol leader, Lieutenant Keith Hudson, was conducting surveillance of an Indonesian camp on the Sekayan River. While attempting to get closer to the camp, he and another trooper, Private Bob Moncrieff, were swept to their deaths. The patrol waited at the nominated RV for a day and eventually withdrew and were extracted back to Kuching.

The dilemma for the OC was that the men were missing in Indonesian territory and could still be alive. A search patrol was organised but was unable to locate the missing soldiers and no post-war search has ever found their remains or any trace of the missing men.[41] Jim Hughes was frustrated by the fact that the men had to be searched for covertly and the normal means of using helicopters and large ground parties would not be possible. It is one of the dangers of operating in small patrols and in clandestine conditions. Hughes felt it was one of the toughest times he experienced in his time in Borneo:

> The loss of Lieutenant Hudson and Trooper (Private) Moncrieff in March 1966, missing presumed drowned, was hard. Because you've got no say, no control, you just had to wear it. We had to try to minimise the results. Corporal (later Major) Geoff Ayles

made up a new patrol with the survivors and they went back that day. They searched for five days without success.[42]

In July 1966, 2 Squadron were relieved by a squadron of 22 SAS and returned to Australia. In August that year a peace agreement between the warring parties of Indonesia and Malaysia was signed, officially ending Confrontation. It had been a demanding, challenging but frustrating time for 2 Squadron, who were never let off the leash offensively, but still gained some valuable experience in jungle warfare, establishing a set of procedures that would stand them in good stead for the very near future.

THE EXPERIENCE

The deployment to Borneo proved a very valuable training ground for what was to become the SAS Regiment's greatest operational involvement since its genesis—the war in Viet Nam. One soldier who experienced the hardships of the Borneo campaign summed it up like this:

> I think there were a lot of things brought out from my experience in Borneo. The ability to navigate was certainly a biggy, there is no disputing that. Patrol routines, general bush skills, bushcraft squared away, which stood us in good stead, because six months later I was in Viet Nam. I remember coming back to Perth, doing another trip to New Guinea and then off to Viet Nam . . . The modus operandi in Viet Nam was quite different to what it was in Borneo—but I think those basic skills stood us in very good stead over there.[43]

5

PAPUA NEW GUINEA

After the initial success of 1 Squadron training in Papua New Guinea prior to their deployment to Borneo, it became a routine procedure that the SAS would train for jungle warfare in that country. Australia was still responsible for PNG security and while the threat of incursion from Indonesia across the West Irian border remained a possibility, it allowed the Australian government to kill two birds with one stone. The SAS got to play in the jungle and hone their skills against the Pacific Islands Regiment (PIR) soldiers, and there was a military presence—a 'showing the flag' exercise if you like—but not so large as to create a disproportionate response from Indonesia.

When a squadron was nominated to be the next one to deploy to Viet Nam, it became the norm that they would train in PNG rather than attend the Jungle Training Centre battle efficiency courses at Canungra in Queensland. Papua New Guinea gave the squadrons a better opportunity to train for their specialist role and was useful for the political reasons already mentioned. The squadrons deployed to PNG for a six- to seven-week training exercise and would practise their patrol procedures and drills for about two weeks in a typical rainforest jungle environment. The location of the training varied for several reasons. It would depend on which battalion of the PIR the exercise was with, and it could vary from around Lae up to the area near Wewak. If it was felt that a presence was required along the border with Indonesia, then that might become part of the 'long walk' part of the training activity. At the conclusion of two weeks acclimatisation and local area training, the squadron would deploy in their patrols of five- to six-man groups and walk from one part of PNG to another.

One of the squadron commanders, Reg Beesley, saw the training in PNG as an opportunity to train as close as possible to a real war environment, especially regarding safety distances for live firing and the employment of weapons such as Claymore mines, which were very strictly controlled back on the Australian mainland.

> Some of my blokes had never seen jungle, let alone fired a shot in it, so it allowed me some flexibility in regards to live firing. I didn't use *any* of the Claymores that were allocated to me in the twelve months back in Australia. I took them with me to New Guinea and I didn't have the confines, but it gave me a couple of grey hairs.[1]

As the squadrons deployed on their work-up training to PNG, it was also an opportunity for the squadron commanders to start selecting who was going to deploy to Viet Nam. The squadron organisation in Australia was based on four troops of about 21 men and the war establishment allowed in Viet Nam was one troop less. It was a quirk of military bureaucracy, but it allowed a competitive spirit to be introduced wherein only those patrols who performed at their peak would be allowed to deploy to Viet Nam. The squadron commander of 2 Squadron, Jim Hughes, was set this personnel jigsaw to solve before he went to Borneo in 1966 and he recalls:

> I had made the decision quite early in the piece that the four troops would be in competition. Whichever troops went, one would be left behind—knowing full well they would join the next squadron lined up. I didn't think it was right to break up the patrols, teamwork and all that and I'm very sorry for the troop that got left out. First-rate people got left behind, but collectively they weren't the best troop.[2]

Neville Farley and his forward scout Andy Nucifora in Papua New Guinea on a squadron training exercise before deploying to Viet Nam. *Photo courtesy of Nev Farley*

One of the troop commanders from 2 Squadron who toured Viet Nam in 1968–69 was Second Lieutenant Ron Dempsey. He was unaware of the political reasons behind the SAS presence in PNG, although back in 1965, earlier squadron OCs like Jim Hughes were actually placed on operational notice to deploy to either Borneo or PNG.[3] Dempsey was one of those troop officers who were under the microscope, as they knew that one of the troops would not be going to Viet Nam. He thought the training in PNG was multi-purpose:

The first aim was to give you actual acclimatisation in a tropical environment, experiencing the conditions, carrying the loads and so on. We had an exercise against the PIR guys there. Patrols would be scattered all over the place for their training. We would do collective training out of Lae, and the rest of it was getting out in your own little AO. A couple of patrols went up near the border, some went along the coast, others into the Highlands, and down to Wau, Bulolo, that area.[4]

Another troop commander was Lieutenant Bill Hindson, who would do his tour of Viet Nam in SAS with 1 Squadron in 1967–68. Hindson saw the whole exercise as being one of creating cohesion and patrol bonding more than anything else:

It was to get patrol cohesion, to get people working as members of teams. You could have done it probably anywhere else, but New Guinea gave us the difficult terrain, in places that put us into jungle, and it certainly gave us the humidity and heat similar to Viet Nam. At that stage we were allocated to the troops and the patrols that we thought we were going to operate in in Viet Nam.[5]

One of the troopers who served with 3 Squadron on both his tours of Viet Nam was Ian 'Bagza' Stiles. He saw the prime purpose in the PNG training as allowing the men who would one day be on patrol in a four- or five-man team, outnumbered and living off their wits, to build up intimate knowledge of each other:

We were operating in troops and as a squadron; we did water-borne operations and these long marches as a squadron, and walked for miles and miles and there was sort of really no relevance in patrol work—as a patrol. It was just more getting fit and working and keeping people together in troops. The patrol was the most important unit in SAS and after working and 'relaxing' with the other guys in the patrol you virtually didn't have to talk as you knew what the other person wanted—or was thinking.[6]

Stiles was eighteen the first time he went to PNG and was able to give some more down-to-earth reasons why the training in PNG was considered so useful for the squadrons working up in readiness for overseas active service:

I think the reason the SAS worked so well in Viet Nam was that they had this training program of going overseas to New Guinea where you were still subject to malaria and all the bugs and things of the jungle. It was also a psychological thing of going to a foreign place—hot and strange, but there were no bad guys over there. And of course there were no tigers or other things that would trouble you too much, whereas a guy in a battalion, he would have done training at Canungra and when he landed in Viet Nam he didn't have that psychological edge because it was his first time overseas. There's a lot of other things to worry about in the jungle besides the enemy— things like leeches, mosquitoes, ticks and diseases. It was a very good training exercise going to New Guinea; SAS people didn't land in Viet Nam completely 'green'.[7]

The patrols found that the long walks across the PNG countryside were more demanding than they had expected. Bill Hindson recalled his trek through PNG with his own patrol:

We worked up from small patrol activities to long-distance patrols. My patrol ultimately walked from Tsili Tsili in the Markham Valley, up and over the central range to Menyamya and then back over the central range to Bulolo (a straight-line distance of around 150 km). Although planned to take two ten-day treks, we managed to get through in a day or two less than that. People were weeded out through that demanding sort of training, but it was essential to get the patrol working together under very difficult conditions. I think eventually we came to respect one another. The training enabled everybody to test their communications over long distances, as well as getting the members of the patrol working together.[8]

Ian Conaghan remembered his long march when he was working up to go to Viet Nam with 1 Squadron, having just returned from a six-month stint with 2 Squadron in Borneo. His work in Borneo with incomplete or non-existent topographical maps stood him in good stead when his patrol set off:

We worked mostly in the Morobe district, off the end of the Eastern Highlands. Then the final exercise was called the LONG WALK—and it was! It was about a month or so and we had a parachute resupply in the middle of it. That was physically very, very demanding. Maps were absolutely bloody awful, half of it white paper saying 'covered in cloud'. The maps were put together by the US Air Force during World War II. I remember on one of them, you would come up to the edge of the map and the adjoining map was supposed to butt onto it. In reality there was a 20-mile gap between the two maps. Of course they were different scales too! It was all interesting stuff.[9]

Ian Conaghan agreed with Stiles when asked if he thought the training in PNG was valuable to SAS patrol work:

Very good, excellent. You really got to know your fellow patrol members because you were pretty isolated for a long period of time. We were working in a foreign country with people who speak a different language—primitive people. We all had a PNG constable with us on the LONG WALK and he was there more or less to show the flag, because he wore his dark blue shorts and blue shirt and .303 rifle over the shoulder and came along. He was essential, because our expertise in Pidgin you could inscribe on the head of a pin and leave a fair space left over. Plus, a lot of villagers didn't speak Pidgin, it was just 'place talk' or Motu, so the constable was always very handy. It was a really good exercise, worth its weight in gold actually.[10]

The long walks brought out the cunning of the SAS soldiers, who were faced with extremely arduous treks up and over the Highlands of New Guinea. Inclines of almost one in three were common and a traverse from one ridge to the other might only be 2000 metres but would take two days owing to the incredibly steep terrain. The devious troopers sought other ways to overcome these obstacles. Bill Hindson recalled when his troop members set out on their walk over the Central Highlands:

We all set out with great enthusiasm, then found that there were some very trying conditions. We found at times that we planned to get over the mountains and down into a valley where it was always warmer but we got caught out on one occasion on the top of a mountain and just froze our backsides off. We were kitted out for really hot, steamy jungle and we were up on top of this bloody hill and we just froze, absolutely froze. That's why on occasions we would go absolutely flat-chat to get across the top of a peak and down the other side, and that used to really push people along as well.

On a few occasions we used to cheat and hire native porters at a shilling a day [ten cents] to carry our heavy packs.

So some members of the patrol would be staggering along under the weight of a belt and compass, while the natives carried everything for them. Of course that had its drawbacks too. I remember on one occasion, just after we came out of Menyamya, the natives were somewhat reluctant to carry our packs up the hills. We badgered them and eventually we got a group of natives to carry our gear, so we set out and we had only been going an hour or so and the next thing the natives were some distance ahead of us and we were having difficulty just stumbling along and as we came around a corner all of our packs were in the middle of the track and the natives were gone. I don't think they even waited to get paid![11]

The SAS men weren't the only ones who could be devious, as Ron Dempsey discovered when his patrol was working on an exercise against the PIR battalion that he was trying to locate and attack:

Our enemy were across this big river and we couldn't get across the river because every time we got to a bridge, it had disappeared—they would just pull it up overnight. When we went back to where the last one was it would disappear, and then this one would appear and then disappear. The squadron commander was asking, 'Why haven't you got across the bloody river yet?' And we're saying, 'No, no, we can't find a bridge, because every time we get there—it's gone!' And he said, 'Oh, I flew over there yesterday and all the bridges were in place.' I said, 'Well yeah, but we were at this one and it wasn't there!' So, then he gave us an order to swim across and that was good because it was in the wet season and it was bucketing down, and the river would rise ten feet at night sort of thing. And you could hear it roaring. He said, 'Hook up your toggle lines and toggle ropes and swim across.' No thank you. There were huge logs going down and boulders crashing and so on. So, we never got across to close with the enemy at that stage—couldn't find the bridge![12]

Once the squadron had completed their six-week exercise in PNG they would return to Australia and begin the process of fine-tuning the troops who were selected to deploy to Viet Nam. There would only be about four months to go before they found themselves in Phuoc Tuy Province.

6

FINE-TUNING

TRAINING FOR OPERATIONS

As mentioned, there was always a 'thinning' or 'weeding out' process which created an atmosphere of competition as four troops worth of soldiers attempted to win a guernsey to deploy to Viet Nam. The process began with the testing and patrol-building exercises in PNG and continued back in Australia until the time came when the men would be warned for active service to allow final preparations to begin. Some of the squadron had to be left behind, as Jim Hughes reflected:

> When we returned from our New Guinea exercise, which was six or seven weeks at the end of '65, they were jumping out of their skin. They wanted to go. They had had a hard year, they had been pushed . . . I pushed them as hard as I could. I wanted to push but I didn't want to break. In fact they didn't break. I had a most regretful thing happen though, I had to leave one troop behind. There were four troops in the squadron and army headquarters had narrowed it down to three troops plus the additives like an additional technician to look after and repair the radio sets. So, I repeated exactly what 1 Squadron had done and was ordered to do and it was annoying to have to leave 21 men behind. That really hurt.[1]

Once the organisation had been chosen that would be deploying to Viet Nam, the process of ensuring that all patrols had their members trained in all facets of their craft—plus additional training—was undertaken so that every patrol had some redundancy when it came to vital specialist roles. For example, each patrol theoretically would have two men who were capable of operating the HF radio set in Morse Code. This was essential if the signaller was injured and a patrol needed to get extracted in a hurry. Jim Hughes detailed some of the additional training that was undertaken back in Australia before his squadron went to Borneo:

> We programmed people for external courses and internal courses for their individual training and specialist training. Everybody was a shallow water diver, everybody was a small craft handler, everybody was a rappeller or abseiler, everybody had to be a parachutist. The most important thing to do was the cross-training. Specialist training. A person had to be a pioneer, a medic, or a sig, or a linguist, but we had to cross-train them. We couldn't afford to have a patrol with only one medic or one sig—you had to have duplication.[2]

The squadron training was conducted in and around Swanbourne Barracks and for those troopers about to deploy to Borneo in 1965 and 1966, there was a deal of emphasis on water operations owing to the type of country they would have to operate in. Jim Hughes recalls that time and the drive for realism in training:

> We used both the sea and the river. We took some very, I think now, hazardous trips between Fremantle and Rottnest Island—how we survived I'll never know! In Zodiacs and things. Air training, Pearce and Bindoon. Land training was down near the river south of Perth called the Avon. We really kept to the south-west of Western Australia.[3]

Peter Schuman recalled his early days when water-borne operations were all the go in preparation for their deployment to either Borneo or PNG.

I can remember Rottnest and Garden Island were two of the big target areas we used to train on, knocking out the guns on Rottnest Island. They were mainly water-borne, shore-launched or boat-launched operations onto Rottnest and Garden Island, do the target over then back to Swanbourne.[4]

The dangers of hard, realistic training following the adage of 'train hard, fight easy' were driven home when Reg Beesley's 3 Squadron was preparing to deploy to Viet Nam in 1968.

Private [T. W.] Irwin drowned in the Collie River during a night river crossing. He drowned, he didn't have a heart attack. He was a Silver Star swimmer and all that sort of thing. The water was pretty cold. I was on the bank and he stepped into the water, did two breast strokes to take the string across—before you pulled the rope over to another guy on the other side. He took two strokes, yelled 'Help' and down he went. We couldn't find him until the next day when police divers went and got him. We still had to soldier on and that was the psyops I used at that stage.[5]

The 'psyops' that Beesley refers to is the need to maintain the focus on what the job ahead is all about. These soldiers are preparing for war. It is not a game, it is a deadly serious business and without being callous about it, you can't make an omelette without breaking eggs. No-one wants to lose soldiers in training or even in war, but it is a facet of soldiering that goes hand in hand with the grim reality that there will always be casualties in war. The SAS men have to train even harder than other combat soldiers and the training has to be realistic enough that the men will not falter when faced with that danger in combat.

The men are guided and encouraged as they prepare for their exposure to battle. Ian Stiles remembers what it was like as a young Digger, and says the reason he was so well prepared as a warrior was because the SAS organisation had a wealth of experience amongst their NCOs which was handed down to the younger members about to deploy to war for the first time:

When you look back on it, they were probably only about four or five years older than me—but they had been there and done that. And then there was the other older guys like Roy

Weir, Mick Wright and other World War II, Korea and Malaya veterans and they knew what was going on. When I look back on it, they were probably more like a father to me.[6]

This nurturing process extended outside of the formal on-the-job troop and patrol training and the younger members of the patrols were taken into the 'family' of the regiment, as Ian Stiles recalls:

> I was lucky. I had a guy named Tony Nolan as my first patrol sergeant and he had a lot of experience and he was also a very intelligent man—he wasn't just one of these gung-ho guys and he sort of mothered us a bit—Freddy Roberts[7] and myself—we were the two young guys in the patrol. The wives of the older patrol members 'mothered' us as well.[8]

The squadrons had to train in temperate forest in places like Collie in south-western Australia as a preparation for going to a jungle theatre, but the emphasis was on honing those patrol skills which had to be so natural that they were almost automatic. The forests simply provided the real estate where the men could use the ground and the vegetation to create the environment for contact drills, navigation training, moving and halting, and the myriad of other drills essential to battlecraft for the patrols.

> We did a fair bit locally in WA, places like Bindoon, Jarrah Dale, a lot down around Collie, then further south— Pemberton, through to Walpole. I remember doing the worst exercise of my life—it was called Exercise LANDSCAPE—we had to walk from Northcliffe which was just south of Pemberton to Walpole which was just near the coast, and we had a couple of weeks to do it. To the best of my knowledge, no-one made it. It was in the middle of winter and the forest down there is unbelievable with extremely thick undergrowth. We did a lot of trudging down there.[9]

Ian Stiles was, at eighteen and a half years old, one of the very young troopers who was sent to PNG as a reinforcement in case one of the men in the work-up squadron was injured or was removed from the organisation preparing to go to Viet Nam. He thought that training in New Guinea was worthwhile, but his views on training in Australia seem somewhat cynical:

That trip to New Guinea was a very good learning experience. And then we got back and we started on these squadron-sized exercises—which probably had no relevance to Viet Nam, but it probably gave the officers something to do.[10]

However one looked at it, the one thing that was paramount was the fact that the soldiers were being readied for the challenge of combat. The SAS had only been in existence a very short time before they were committed to operations against the Indonesians in Borneo and the training message was simple, as Peter Schuman recalls:

The training was always hard. It was always interesting but the guys who ran the training were fellows of the ilk of Ray Simpson, and these guys were heroes in their own right, heroes from Korea and Malaya. They just didn't tell bullshit stories, it was all real stuff: 'If you put your head up in these situations, you'll get it blown off. If you keep it down, you'll survive.' 'Don't be a hero, learn your sums well' and we were taught pretty well.[11]

BONDING THE PATROLS TOGETHER

It wasn't always hard slogging out in the training areas around Perth. The patrols had to learn their skills but they also had to get to know each other so well they could almost know what their fellow patrol member was thinking. This was essential for the type of work these men would be doing, because there is a great need for silence and stealth when doing reconnaissance and surveillance work in enemy territory. Sometimes the bonding process between the men got a little rugged. Bill Hindson recalled his times as a new boy on the block, especially as a young officer within an organisation with a preponderance of sergeants and warrant officers:

I had quite a few things to catch up including the usual bonding that was necessary. Some members of my troop used to go down to the OBH [Ocean Beach Hotel]—as everybody did. I don't think it was a recognised or a condoned practice, but I used to go down there with the sergeants and other members of the troop drinking on a Saturday. For lunch, they would wander around the corner to the fish and chip shop. Eventually the shouts of beer and the fish and chips got so big we got to the stage where we would order a banana box full of chips to take back to the hotel.

But they treated me with great respect. I can remember on one occasion being lifted up and bodily thrown out of the window into the courtyard and, having then stumbled around and abused everybody, I was promptly lifted up and thrown out the window again.

I suffered a similar fate when we had a squadron party on a chartered ferry on the Swan River. I got picked up and bodily thrown off the back of the ferry from the upper deck, which annoyed the captain of the ferry, of course. And having got back on the bloody thing, I was promptly thrown off again. The sergeants had a pretty warped sense of humour and a strange way of showing that they were bonding with you.[12]

While the men of the SAS were preparing for Viet Nam, the main support agency for when they would get to Viet Nam, 9 Squadron, Royal Australian Air Force (RAAF), were also going through the process of readying for war and they often trained with the SAS in Australia. RAAF Crewman Terry Pinkerton, who did two tours of Viet Nam, recalled some of his times with the men from the SAS:

We went to New Guinea with them. Our training was very detailed and the pads we used, some of them were very small and going to New Guinea we didn't have pads as such, sometimes you would go down into the trees and you would have to manoeuvre backwards and forwards to get under the canopy and all that sort of stuff to get down to them.[13]

This close working relationship between the SAS squadrons and 9 Squadron RAAF flying the Iroquois helicopters would reap enormous benefits later in Viet Nam when the choppers would be used extensively for inserting and extracting the five-man patrols.

Terry Pinkerton also had to practise resupplies for the SAS, who need security when operating so that their presence will not draw unwanted and dangerous attention from the enemy, who always outnumbered the SAS patrols. Pinkerton recalled one resupply from his helicopter with an SAS patrol which he completed in fifteen seconds—in all some 250 pounds (115 kg) of water, rations, ammunition, spare batteries and other items.[14]

Teamwork is essential in war and even more so when you only have a small group like a five-man SAS patrol. There is no slack for those who cannot work effectively within that small group. Each man is a vital part and must be acutely aware of how he believes his mates are going to react in certain situations. For survivability, the patrol must think and act like one. Neville Farley summed it up like this:

> You really do have to be a tight group; you have to know what each other is going to do; you have to know that if you say you're going to do something they think, 'Okay, I know what he's on about.' Like, 'Prop here, so and so and I are just going to have a bit of a shufty around here', you know that they are going to go straight into a bit of defence; they know which way you went, and the way they expect you to return. Not, 'They're going to wander off down the track 50 metres and set up a bloody ambush'. So you really do have to work as a team.[15]

7

VIET NAM

THE TRANSITION FROM BORNEO

Even as the Borneo campaign was drawing to a close, the SAS
Regiment was preparing to deploy to another theatre of war,
Viet Nam. The SAS squadron would become part of the 1st
Australian Task Force at Nui Dat. The SAS squadron was also
supplemented by a New Zealand SAS group who had to mesh
in with the way the Australians did business. They came under
command totally of the Australian SAS squadron commander in
much the same way the New Zealand rifle companies attached
to the Australian designated ANZAC battalions did in 2, 4 and
6 Battalions of The Royal Australian Regiment (RAR).

Many of the soldiers who formed 3 Squadron had served
with 1 Squadron in Borneo and had the experience of operating
in the true role of the SAS in surveillance mode. The Viet Nam
War was to be a whole new ball game. The role of the squadron
would develop from one of reconnaissance and surveillance to
more aggressive and offensive action. The Borneo campaign,
with its emphasis on solid navigational skills, hard physical slogs
over tough, rugged terrain in Indonesian territory, and good
communications skills was to stand the men of the Viet Nam
campaign in good stead, as Trevor Roderick recalled:

Borneo set the scene for Viet Nam. It was a different type of enemy in Viet Nam. The confidence was there, especially the confidence to operate in small groups, because that was the key to it all. It was felt that the distances wouldn't be the same and that there would be more camps, more booby traps, that things would slow down. Movement would be even slower, because in Borneo you had such a mass of bloody jungle and so few bloody places of habitation whereas in Viet Nam, even from maps that they showed us, we were likely to be running into more people, more baddies, more villagers. And so there was the emphasis on slowing everything down. It was continually evasive, as the CO, Bill Braithwaite, used to say, 'Softly, softly, catchee monkey'. The enemy were probably better and more determined and more tenacious than the Indonesians.[1]

Some soldiers went straight from one campaign to another with intensive training occupying their time between operations. Ian Conaghan was a private soldier (later to be called trooper) in 2 Squadron in mid-1966 when he was asked if he wanted to join 1 Squadron:

We got five days stand-down from Borneo and I went straight to 1 Squadron. I hadn't done a medic's course at that stage of the game so I was whipped over to Healesville in Victoria to do my medical training and that was about five or six weeks. I was back for less than a week, then whipped off to New Guinea for about six weeks. I then went on leave, came back from leave after about eight or ten days—and went off to Viet Nam for 12 or 13 months. They were sort of halcyon days! Your feet didn't touch the ground. It was all go. In the time we came back from leave we did manage to get a fairly solid weapons workout for a few days up at Bindoon, and then we were off to Viet Nam.[2]

TO NUI DAT

Second Lieutenant Peter Schuman was sent on the advance party with the first SAS squadron to deploy to the newly formed Australian Task Force. They disembarked in the coastal town of Vung Tau and trucked up to Nui Dat, about two hours convoy drive to the north and in the centre of Phuoc Tuy Province.

Peter Schuman, MC. A studio portrait of the patrol and troop commander after he was awarded a Military Cross for gallantry for his services in Viet Nam. He also served as a troop leader in Borneo as a second lieutenant. *Photo courtesy of AWM Neg. No. P1002/144/001*

We arrived there and it was just like out of an exercise in Australia. There was the chief engineer who was responsible for the defensive layout, I think his name was Major Leonard. I can remember arriving with myself and the five trucks and a Land Rover leading—which I was taught to do—and he said, 'Name?' and I said, 'Schuman'. 'Unit?' He asked, 'SAS?' I replied, 'Yes Sir', and he said, 'Drive down the road and you will see two star pickets and your perimeter goes from here to here on this map, get going.' I just couldn't believe my ears and I drove down this track and there it was! There was myself and four other guys and we had about 100 metres of perimeter and that was it and we started digging in! With five truckloads of stores to unload. We built a couple of bunkers and we had a dozen machine-guns all primed up and bloody boxes of grenades, got wire out and there we sat like stunned mullets and scared rabbits for five days until our mob arrived.[3]

While Peter Schuman and his trusty band of five Diggers were staring out into the bush beyond the Task Force perimeter, the main body was flying from Perth on a chartered Qantas 707 jet. Another troop commander, Trevor Roderick, recalled that they were not having too tough a time of it as the plane was catering for the thirsty troopers:

Drank it out in the first two hours. We went via Manila. They gave us the live ammo about an hour out of bloody Saigon. I'll never forget that. We weren't drinking on the second leg, but the live ammo came out just before Saigon.[4]

Once the SAS squadron had arrived, it was tasked to support the Task Force in clearing an area around the Task Force base. The initial SAS operations were a far cry from what became the modus operandi by the end of 1971. Peter Schuman went out on those initial patrols in 1966:

The battalions were clearing to gun range to about 17 000 metres and we were doing short patrols into sectors around Hoa Long to protect the area while the battalions were out doing a bit of the heavy stuff. That lasted for about a month, I guess, and then we started flogging out beyond gun range and that's when the baddies started to decide that they didn't really like us there and that's when the contacts started getting fairly heavy. We shot out beyond gun range then to start doing the long-range surveillance.[5]

The normal insertion of an SAS patrol was by helicopter, but in the beginning things were different:

Early days were foot, and it depended on the task. APCs, either an individual APC operation and we would get inside, be taken to an area, the APCs would kick up a cloud of dust, drop the ramp, we would get out and they would just drive away. Sometimes we would go in with a battalion as battalion members and after they finished their operation we would just stay there.[6]

Before long a standard type of patrol area for the SAS evolved which did not change too much from the first squadrons' tour until the last. The area designated for SAS patrols was based on the grid squares of a topographical map, which are 1000 metres square. Squadron commander Reg Beesley was responsible for tasking the patrols of his squadron and recalled the way the areas were laid out and why it was essential that everybody in the Task Force HQ coordinating air and artillery strikes knew where the patrols were:

> You had a patrol area two by four. I would put another buffer of 1000 metres around that. That was SAS territory and was 'no go' for H&I. It was up to us to keep the Fire Support Coordination Centre informed of where patrols were. On one occasion there was a stuff-up. Clem Dwyer took his patrol down to the Nui Thi Vais and was out there for three days on a ten-day patrol. He reported 30 to 50 enemy sighted, gave a grid reference and asked for an air strike. Well, an ARVN infantry company was in Baria, and a battalion adviser hadn't bothered to tell anyone that he was entering our area, and just by the grace of God, they didn't allow the air strike to go through, otherwise we would have lost a lot of friendlies. So, that's why we used to ensure that all interested agencies had an awareness of SAS patrols.[7]

TYPES OF PATROLS

The principal role of the SAS is surveillance and reconnaissance but as the war progressed an evolution in the way patrols reacted to the enemy in their area took place. It was decided that once a recon patrol had completed its mission, if it still had the capacity to do so it would conduct harassing type tasks such as ambush. The ambush was ideally suited to the five-man SAS patrol in Viet Nam as it was supplemented with the deadly M18A–1 Claymore directional anti-personnel mine. Reg Beesley discussed the type of patrols that he deployed with 3 Squadron:

> Two types of patrol evolved: recon and recon/ambush. Recon to gain info on an enemy's locations, logistics and movement. Recon/ambush to locate the enemy and destroy him—often conducted to maintain the presence of the Task Force in outlying areas and when the Task Force was engaged in ops outside the province. Some patrols were better at recon while others were more suited to recon/ambush.[8]

What Beesley refers to is the epitome of SAS operations. You planned and executed the tasks ensuring that you used the right man for the job. Some patrol commanders were far better at close-in recon and surveillance than others while some were extremely good at conducting more offensive patrols where guile and shooting with deadly accuracy were the principal requirements. Bill Hindson served with 1 Squadron in Viet Nam in 1967–68 and his squadron used ten-man patrols on occasion, but it came at a price:

> The aim usually was to be able to set up a bigger ambush; to be able to have more Claymores and more firepower. Five-man patrols were great, but with a ten-man patrol we lost sight of a substantial part of the patrol. Ten-man patrols were specialised patrols, mainly for ambush, and on occasions for capturing a prisoner.[9]

LOADED FOR BEAR

The greater enemy threat brought about another change for the SAS patrols—they needed to carry more ammunition as the enemy were more tenacious and were in greater numbers than they had experienced in Borneo. Ian Conaghan recalled that the ammo load

> varied depending on the mission and also between what squadrons considered SOP, but in Viet Nam what made a fair distinction on our weapon loads, if you were going out on an offensive op, you went loaded for bear; but if you were purely reconning, the ammo load that you carried was to keep you alive if you were sprung rather than getting in there and pouring in volumes of fire.[10]

As Conaghan explained in Chapter 3, he always carried explosives when on patrol. So did another patrol commander, Ian 'Bagza' Stiles, who had an ingenious method of deploying a time-delay device which was handy especially during an extraction:

> I used to carry detonators with safety fuse and dets. The Claymore shipping plugs were the same thread as the hand

On a marker panel is shown the belt survival kit as worn by Ian Stiles. His equipment includes a Beretta pistol, binoculars, a tin of chocolate, a smoke canister, a white phosphorus fragmentation grenade and an array of pencil flares and fuses with delay devices to allow a clean break from following enemy. *Photo courtesy of Ian Stiles*

grenades for white phos, and M26 grenades and you could unscrew the guts out of them and you could screw in the Claymore det or screw in the non-elec det with safety fuse. So, you had a delayed hand grenade or whatever and if you were being followed you could drop this and set it to go off in front of them or behind or whatever you wanted for a bit of confusion.[11]

Ammunition and the ammo load started to take on a greater importance as the patrols found themselves sometimes being pursued by a tenacious enemy. The Viet Cong, Viet Cong Main Force and North Vietnamese Army soldiers would often follow up patrols after contact and hound the SAS patrols desperately trying to break contact and extract. Nev Farley decided to take a psychological approach with his ammo load to ensure that he didn't blow it all away in the frenzy of a fire-fight:

I even used to carry bloody spare magazines in my pack—
working on the assumption that if I got into a real big shitfight
and I got careless, and I had to stop and get those spare
magazines out, which meant that you really had to calm down
and say, 'This is the last stand'. But normally if you were in
a fire-fight you would get out of it as quick as you can.[12]

THE AUTOMATIC 'LIGHT-BARRELLED' SLR

The SAS pride themselves on their individuality and this was
often expressed in the way they dressed for combat, their
weaponry and ammunition load. It all came down to—if you
want to carry it, it is your problem. The 7.62 mm Belgian-
designed FN semi-automatic (self-loading rifle—SLR) was often
favoured because it fired a very powerful .308 calibre bullet. The
standard issue rifle was carried by most riflemen in Viet Nam in
the infantry battalions but didn't fire fully automatic—that is,
when you pull the trigger the weapon fires until you release the
trigger. Normally it would fire only one shot every time you
pressed the trigger but would automatically chamber another
round so when you released the trigger and pressed again it
would repeat the firing cycle. However, soldiers—as is their wont
in combat zones—take extraordinary steps to try to give themselves greater firepower on the field of battle. One SAS patrol
scout on his first tour explained how he dealt with his weaponry
and ammunition load:

I carried a 'light-barrelled SLR', but it was fully automatic.
The SLR was actually designed with a holding open device
so that on the last shot of the magazine it held open and so
you could carry out an immediate action drill really easy, but
that's no good for a parade ground, you can't have people
messing around on the parade ground like this. So, the
hierarchy of the Australian army said remove the pin. Our
armourers put a pin where it was supposed to be in the
hold-open device so when the magazine was empty the
working parts were held to the rear—just like an M16. So we
would take the empty mag off, put it down your shirt, put
on a full mag, release the working parts by hitting the holding
open device, bang! Away you went again. So, that was a very

easy operation to change the SLR to fully auto—it was just inserting a filed change lever and jigging around with the return spring plunger on the trigger. I had a Claymore pouch with the 30-round magazines in them. It was quite a good set-up. When you look back it was cumbersome to be a scout with that weapon, but it was all right. It was good in a shitfight.[13]

The 'light-barrelled SLR' is an in-joke for the soldiers, as there was a heavy-barrelled SLR which went by the nomenclature of the L4A4 automatic rifle which was an SLR with a fully automatic firing mechanism and a heavier barrel to withstand the higher operating temperatures. It also came with folding bipod legs and could be used as a light machine-gun using 30-round box magazines. Another man who liked the hitting power of the SLR was Peter Schuman: 'I had seen a guy hit with an SLR through a rubber tree and I thought that was pretty impressive— so I liked that.'[14]

TAILORING THE LOAD

The patrols would not always carry exactly the same ammo load or weaponry for every patrol. Each patrol was different, with a different task, different area to operate in, different enemy threat and varying vegetation and topography. Nev Farley recalls the different weapons they carried on patrol:

Sometimes we went out to snatch a prisoner, so we would probably carry a silenced Stirling or a shotgun. A couple of times I carried a shotgun—the idea was to try and hit them around the legs and then patch them up and get them pulled out, so we could bring out a prisoner. But basically it was Armalites and SLRs.[15]

The SAS patrol is a long way from home when out from the Task Force base and if his weapon fails or becomes a casualty itself in a fire-fight, a second weapon would prove very handy. Consequently the troopers began arming themselves with second weapons as a back-up in case their primary weapon mal-functioned at a critical time. Bill Hindson was troop commander of B Troop, 1 SAS Squadron, and remembered his troop arming themselves during their tour:

> We managed to acquire a whole range of different pistols. We started out with the standard issue Brownings and ended up with a whole range of things. Neville [Farley] ended up with a little Beretta he used to carry around with him. I think, inevitably, a lot of people were concerned about the possibility of a weapon stoppage at a crucial time and wanted to carry multiple weapons. We also acquired all sorts of bayonets, starting out with whatever bayonet fitted the weapon you carried and then acquired other knives and various things. So in the end we had quite an outfit. At one stage when we were trying to capture a prisoner, I carried an automatic shotgun for a while and then went back to the Armalite.[16]

As the role changed for the patrols, especially to the recce/ambush patrol, the SAS began using the Claymore mines as the primary weapon in an ambush. The command-detonated mine gave the patrols an enormous amount of killing power with only a small physical outlay required. The high explosive content and spread of the mine pellets covered a good-sized killing area. If sighted correctly with overlapping arcs of fire, the mines were extremely deadly and had the added bonus of creating an enormous blast and accompanying shock to those unfortunates caught in the ambush killing ground. Ron Dempsey insisted that each patrol member carried a Claymore mine on his patrols, which were primarily recon in nature:

> Yes, every man carried a Claymore, because the patrols would be a recce patrol but if you came across something that looked interesting like a track, you could ambush it on the last day or the last two days of the op.[17]

THE COMMUNICATIONS

The SAS patrol relies on its radio to maintain the link to the squadron operations room and can call for help or to confirm their extraction details. The distances the patrols operated from base were greater than the limited range of the standard VHF

ANPRC–25 radio set and so a (relatively) lightweight HF radio called the 64 Set was used with the capability of sending in continuous wave (CW) using Morse Code and a coding system with a one-time letter pad (OTLP) for constructing messages. This ensured speed and security in transmission. Chook and sig troop sergeant Barry Standen explained why they used Morse Code:

> Well, the reliability and the fact that we never send anything in clear apart from a contact or a sighting code word, so it was always in code and it's a lot easier to dit on your machine, 'Dit dah dit', rather than say 'Alpha'. It's quicker to go, 'Dit dah dit', and when you're sending at 10–15 words per minute. Patrol sigs were qualified at 10, Corps of Sigs were qualified at anywhere between 18 and 25 words per minute. So, when you've got someone sending ten five-letter groups of code, they can do it a lot faster—funnily enough—with a Morse key than they can with a bloody pressel switch and going, 'Alpha bravo charlie delta'. So, it was speed and obviously reliability because with CW you can get through a lot easier than you can with voice. And with HF voice you also could have atmospheric problems, and you've got a bloody Jock on the end or an Irishman who is saying whatever in a nice lilting tone but you can't understand him because there's hash and crap in there. So, it's a lot easier; there's no tonal inflection, there are no accents with CW, and it's just a lot easier and a lot tidier as well to do. It is also much quieter and secure to tap on a Morse key because there are no voice sounds.[18]

The radio sets are powered by replaceable batteries and the downside to this reliable Morse link was the fact that patrols had to carry spare batteries for the HF radio. On occasion the patrol might have to take a VHF set to be able to talk to an infantry organisation and also a second radio and its spare batteries. Barry Standen recalled the load of batteries that had to be carried by the patrol members:

> In Borneo each guy carried one battery and the sig carried two. In Viet Nam, for the 64 Set, everyone carried a battery. For the 25 Set for VHF, you would carry one in the set and one or two spares in the patrol.[19]

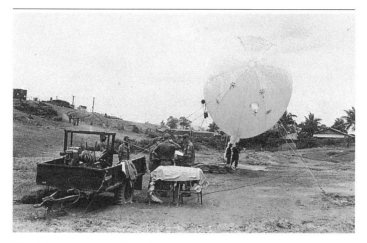

The balloon goes up. The Operational Research Section assisting the SAS to attain communications with distant patrols by VHF means in 1969. Later, SAS patrols would normally only use HF means to contact their base. *Photo courtesy of AWM Neg. No. P01892.030*

THE BALLOON GOES UP

To ensure communications with the patrols if they were carrying VHF sets, the squadron headquarters on SAS Hill inside the Nui Dat base rigged up a helium balloon connected to a remoted radio set and held down by a winch brake to take an aerial skyward to obtain better communications. But as Barry Standen explained, it also came in for some criticism from people inside the perimeter of the Task Force base when this large helium balloon was hovering above the base:

> If the patrol was in the shit, and we weren't getting real good HF comms and they happened to be carrying VHF, we would just hit the bloody winch brake, up would go the helium balloon and we would get much better comms. There was a lot of drama about having to put flags on it and so on. The pilots didn't like it; then you had the armchair military tacticians who said that it was a target for the bloody Charlie

to shoot at. I mean they didn't know there was a Task Force there at the time? So every time we put it up we were more likely to take mortar rounds or rocket rounds and all this crap. So we had a bit of flak from the Task Force Headquarters which we tended to ignore.

The switchboard [Ebony Switchboard] used to malfunction almost every time the winch brake came off! It was so coincidental. And we did carry a prototype of the Morse key—it was a modulator—so that you could send Morse over a 25 Set rather than speak because some of the patrols got into situations where you could send Morse but you wouldn't speak.[20]

152 SIGNAL SQUADRON DETACHMENT

The role of the signallers attached under command to the SAS squadrons is touched on in Chapter 3. The organisation for the Viet Nam conflict is detailed here to illustrate that the chooks were an integral part of the squadron make-up. Indeed, most of the RA Signal Corps soldiers who served in Viet Nam with one of the squadrons would say that they served with 1 Squadron or 3 Squadron rather than the signal troop attached. Barry Standen detailed the organisation as it existed during his two tours with SAS:

> The strength of that detachment was a lieutenant/second lieutenant, a troop sergeant and about twenty Diggers. You had one cipher, a couple of techs and the rest were operators. Of the operators you might have a couple of those who were cipher qualified, but you would have one guy who was in the position of a cipher corporal, OKC [operator keyboard cipher], and what was the norm if you could was that the OKC was an OKRC [operator keyboard radio cipher] so that . . . he had all those skills, and he was a pretty important man around the place.[21]

9 SQUADRON, ROYAL AUSTRALIAN AIR FORCE

One organisation which came to work very, very closely with the SAS was the helicopter-equipped 9 Squadron, RAAF. They used the Iroquois helicopter which was the aviation workhorse of the Viet Nam War. It was ideally suited for inserting and extracting the five-man SAS patrols as it could land them, hover and allow them to jump, or if required rappel by fixed ropes into a tight insertion landing point. It could winch the men out or if required drop ropes and do a multiple rope extraction. The RAAF maintained and based their helicopters in the safer logistical area at Vung Tau, which was only 25–30 minutes flying time from the 1 ATF base at Nui Dat where the SAS squadron lived.

One crewman who did two tours on the choppers was Sergeant Terry Pinkerton, who recalled the squadron organisation when he was in charge of allocating crewmen to aircraft for daily tasking: 'We had 48 pilots total, including the CO and I had 17 crewmen and 16 aircraft.'[22]

The RAAF squadron was also supplemented by New Zealand pilots from the RNZAF and at any one time had about seven or eight 'Kiwi' pilots flying with 9 Squadron. This gave the Officer Commanding 9 Squadron some flexibility and a chance to rest the pilots who were constantly flying in hazardous circumstances. One pilot who later went on to fly F–111s was then 25-year-old Pilot Officer Jack Lynch. He remembered the 9 Squadron organisation in 1969:

> It was about 25 or 30 crews. At one time it was less than 30 and there were more crews than there were aeroplanes. On any one day there would be three gunships available, and about a dozen slicks.[23]

A 'slick' is the slang term for an aircraft which can be used for a variety of tasks but primarily is only armed with GPMG–M60 machine-guns on the doors, one of which is manned by the aircraft crewman and the other by a door gunner. It is used mainly for battlefield transport of either troops or stores. Other Iroquois helicopters—also called 'Hueys' and 'choppers', because of the noise the rotor makes as it cuts through the air—would be specially set up as air-to-ground fire support platforms using 2.75 inch Zuni rockets, electronically fired high-volume machine-guns called mini-guns firing several thousand rounds per minute and twin M60 machine-guns on the doors. Others were set up for casualty evacuation and called dustoff choppers, with a stretcher ensemble and paramedic crewmen to provide resuscitation for badly wounded soldiers on their way to a medical facility.

In preparation for their tour in Viet Nam, the 9 Squadron pilots and crews were rigorously put through their paces before entering the war zone:

> We trained to operate the aircraft to its limits. Back in Australia, I can remember at Shoalwater Bay training area doing limited-power take-offs and approaches. We were actually winding the available power off and you would have absolute minimum amount of power and you would have to hover around in ground effect and pick the lowest point between the tops of the trees and get this aircraft out under a simulated operational circumstance identical to what you would find in Viet Nam. So, in terms of operating the aeroplane, absolutely no difference. You just learnt about the artillery and the live firing and

The tent lines that the SAS Squadron lived in on SAS Hill, Nui Dat. Pictured outside the tent is Sergeant Neville Farley and his tent mate, Sergeant John 'Slag' O'Keefe. *Photo courtesy of Nev Farley*

gunships, fighters and all that sort of stuff when you got in country.[24]

Unlike the SAS squadrons and the Australian infantry battalions, the RAAF used a 'trickle' reinforcement system to replace pilots and crewmen when their twelve-month tour of duty expired. This prevented a corporate loss of knowledge occurring all at the same time and allowed mentoring of newer men into the war zone. All new arrivals would be given a familiarisation tour of the province and would basically sit back and watch for a couple of missions before being thrown into the fray. This watching period was sometimes only one or two days and then they were into it.

SAS SQUADRON CHANGEOVERS

As the war progressed and the SAS squadrons rotated every twelve months, the squadron advance parties would arrive and be taken out on patrol to show the latest techniques developed

SAS Hill in Nui Dat. The troops' sand-bagged tent lines can be seen in the centre above the Mess with the white roof. *Photo courtesy of Terry Pinkerton*

in-theatre and to acclimatise and settle in the newly arrived patrol leaders. Nev Farley was a veteran of the Borneo campaign and arrived for his operational tour in 1967 but with the added responsibility of being a patrol commander:

> That was good value going out on that handover patrol. When the other blokes came up we did the same thing; this is how it goes, this is the way we are doing it, and everybody got briefed, and we had lectures and blokes were talking to each other. The Diggers down at the boozer were all talking to each other, everybody was sucking everybody's brains on how you did things.[25]

8

GETTING READY—PATROL PREPARATION

Once the SAS squadron commander is advised by the Task Force HQ of the information requirement from a patrol, he sets about briefing the squadron operations officer who is the 'patrol master' for the troop patrols. A system of advance warning to allow the patrols to prepare for their forthcoming patrols then swings into place. A Warning Order is issued to the patrol commander up to a week before a patrol is required to go out to allow several things to happen. The patrol commander must collect basic information on where he is going, decide where, how and when he will insert or infiltrate into his patrol's area of operations and make up a plan and set of orders to give to the other patrol members. Once they have done that they will then rehearse a variety of drills and actions to ensure that every member of the patrol is fully aware of his own requirements and that no mistakes are made at crucial times during the patrol.

INTELLIGENCE SUPPORT

The intelligence available to the SAS patrols was vastly different from the support provided in Borneo. Now there were intelligence collection agencies from all ranges of the intelligence spectrum. Besides human intelligence sources there were radio intercepts, aircraft recon missions, and chemical analysis from aircraft which overflew areas and analysed the air to pick up traces of ammonia and other human emissions. These were called 'sniffer' missions and were not always reliable as the author hunted a herd of barking deer for several days after an alleged 'hot sniffer report'. Peter Schuman recalled how he got his warning orders for a patrol and what it involved:

> You would get a briefing something like, 'You are to mount a four-man patrol into area X Y Z. The latest intelligence of the area is that back on such and such a day a patrol was fired at from grid square so and so. Lights have been observed on three occasions by so and so.' You didn't go out there and just hope that you might see something. You went out there on pretty reasonable intelligence. They might have got a Chieu Hoi, one of those surrendered enemy, who said, 'Yes, my unit used to always transit from point A to point B.' And we would see if we could interdict the track and then follow the track up to a camp or whatever.[1]

Every patrol that went out from the SAS squadron submitted a patrol report after the activity. They contained detailed information which later patrols found invaluable. Ian Conaghan recalled the sources he used in getting his patrol prepared:

> The intel was very, very heavy and there was much scouring of previous patrol reports, intelligence reports, air photos, electronic warfare reports, track overlays, LZ overlays, PW reports, special agent reports, the whole nine yards, until it was running out of your ears. Plus, we had a plethora of electronic intelligence in Viet Nam.[2]

The special agent reports were often from Vietnamese who were working with the Viet Cong as double agents. These men and women lived on the edge, as they could be attacked by the allied forces at any stage.

THE VR

Once an area had been designated for a patrol, the patrol commander would do a visual reconnaissance (VR) of the area to be searched or where his target was located. In planning his VR, he would be looking for several things:

> I would go and see the intelligence sergeant, George Gridley, and get the maps of the area and get a brief on what else was happening around there at the time from allied activity and our own Australian units. Then we would set about preparing and the first thing is having got the maps, air photos, picto maps, we would find where our patrol area would be—if it was to ambush a track we would work out where that track was. I would look for potential helicopter landing zones that were available in the patrol area or in the buffer area that was around the nine grid squares. I would organise with the operations officer for air reconnaissance, usually two days before the patrol was to go in. The helicopter would come up and land on the pad behind B Troop tents and I would go up there, brief the pilot, fly out over the area—trying to be as inconspicuous as possible. So you're not just focused on one particular area, I would fly around a number of other areas trying to look into the foliage to see the tracks to try to get an idea of whether they were well used or not. Look at the landing pads—the condition they were in, whether they were swampy or long grass, just how big they were and where we would need to land if it was a large one. The sorts of landing zones and the clear areas that we could be extracted from.[3]

Other patrol commanders utilised other assets when doing their VR, like Ian Stiles, who liked to record what he had seen to show the other members of the patrol:

> The squadron int guys would give me a camera, a big, long telephoto thing—a single lens reflex camera. I preferred to go in a rotary-wing Possum—a Bell 47. Sometimes they would send you in a fixed-wing Cessna or sometimes in a Pilatus Porter. I would fly over the area but wouldn't fly straight there, I would do a big circle, and I would actually take photographs of things that were relevant to our task, like LZs. Then I would

come back and give the camera to the intel people who had their own photographic processor and enlarger.[4]

The aircraft referred to by Ian Stiles were from the recce flight of the army's 161 Reconnaissance Squadron and a VR by the light observation helicopters (LOH) was the normal means of conducting a VR. Many patrol commanders believed the best intelligence reports emanated from the 161 Reconnaissance Squadron daily over-flys of the province as they were timely and accurate. The patrol commanders would usually conduct a VR with 161 Squadron to assist in the preparation of their orders.

Some patrols were luckier than others when it came to doing VRs of their area. During Ian Conaghan's second tour the whole patrol was able to view the AO:

> If it was possible, the entire patrol went up in a 9 Squadron Huey (Iroquois) with the bloke that was going to fly the Albatross Lead, in other words he was the mission commander for the insertion. So that you all were exactly on the same net and there were no screw-ups about LZs or the way the whole thing was going to work so that everybody had a fair idea of what it was like where you were going into.[5]

But this was for the most part a luxury and usually only the patrol commander would be able to see the actual infiltration (infil) and exfiltration (exfil) points. There were many air photographs of the areas plus an American-produced 'pictographic' map in 1:25 000 scale which had a monochromatic green photograph on the reverse side of a topographical map of the same scale. This showed all the vegetation and it was almost possible to tell which copse of trees one was sitting under if on the edge of a clearing.

THE RAAF

Some terms need to be explained before we proceed. Five helicopters would normally be assigned to insert an SAS patrol. The overall commander of the insertion operation flies in an aircraft called Albatross Lead. The 'Albatross' designation comes from the 9 Squadron emblem of the same species. The Albatross

Lead is the RAAF captain who commands the patrol insertion. His radio callsign is Albatross Zero One. Albatross Zero Two was the Huey slick which carried the patrol for insertion. Albatross Zero Three was a back-up aircraft in case Zero Two went unserviceable or was required for deception purposes. The helicopter gunships which came in two flying formations known as a Light Fire Team (two gunships) or a Heavy Fire Team (three gunships) were called Bushranger Seven One, Seven Two and so on. Normally only a light fire team (LFT) would accompany an insertion. RAAF crewman Sergeant Terry Pinkerton recalled the flying procedure when the confirmatory VR was conducted by Albatross Lead:

> It would be just a sole aircraft and you had to make it look like you weren't doing something that was going to infringe on the patrol security. The overfly would be at least a minimum of two clicks away, more if you can. If it's a large pad you went further away.
>
> We would go out and pass the area at 1500 feet, never below 1500 feet. You would get a feel for the position of the alternates: your actual insert pad; first alternate [pad]; second alternate and in some cases the third alternate. The patrol commander would have all the photographs, which would have been given to him prior to going out and we would go out and check them out and make sure there were no changes. You can see all that from 1500 feet quite comfortably. With a full load, maximum time airborne we had was an hour and a half. We might get two hours out on a VR because you're up at 1500 feet—we would probably be able to spread it out if we had full tanks.[6]

The landing zones or 'pads' are vitally important to the initial success of a quick, well executed insertion done with an absolute minimum of fuss. The helicopter pilots and crewmen would be able to say immediately to the patrol commander if the pad he wanted to use was suitable. Pinkerton reflected on pad sizes for a Huey insertion and said it was the width of a rotor disc and a bit to spare, or

> 48 foot. I can look up my book and tell you the exact allowance we were supposed to have, but whether that pertains

to what we actually used all the time was purely coincidental in some cases.[7]

While the patrol commander is off doing his recon, the patrol 2IC is getting the admin for the patrol squared away and following the requirements of what will need to be taken out from that section of the Warning Order. Nev Farley detailed his patrol's procedure when he was off on a VR:

> They would get themselves ready. Our gear was always 'stand-by ready', so most of them had their stuff ready anyhow. That just meant to go down to the Q store, get their rations, probably go down the range, test-fire weapons, use up the old ammo and make sure all the magazines worked. Because it wasn't a case of zeroing the weapons, because you very rarely fired a well aimed shot, but what you wanted to know was that every bloody magazine was going to work—that it hadn't been dented or anything.[8]

BRIEFINGS AND ORDERS

Once the VR had been completed, the patrol commander would go back to Nui Dat and start to do his appreciation and plan for the patrol. Patrol commander Joe Van Droffelaar talked about how he worked his way through his plan:

> I would study my map almost in a photographic sense and I planned out a number of routes in relation to my insertion point and for my possible extraction. I would work out the likely contact and ambush areas and I would rehearse those inside my brain and I would pick that up in a couple of days, and I would work it out. When I had that fixed in my mind that I would do this and I think I might be right, at that time the OC would then call me forward for the orders and I would then quickly brief the OC. Once he had finished with me on the likely route that I was going to go in and had given him a quick run-down on what action I would take in relation to contacts, once I had all those orders, I would generally then use a good day to write them up, get the blokes together and give a set of orders.[9]

The orders were given in the tent lines on SAS Hill and followed a set procedure used by the army so that everyone knew what was coming next and that no detail was overlooked. Once the formal orders were over, the patrol would then go through a detailed briefing of what to expect, as patrol commander Nev Farley explains:

> The blokes would all have their maps and we would mentally walk ourselves right through it, walk ourselves where we were going to go and what we were going to do. Know where all the LZs were, knowing where all the clearings were, that was pretty important because if the shit hit the fan you had to know where you had to go to get pulled out of it.[10]

REHEARSALS—THE SEVEN P'S

There is an adage used quite often by all sections of the army that 'prior preparation and planning prevents piss poor performance'. One of the procedures that the SAS takes great pride in and places great importance on is patrol briefing and preparation. One particular aspect of this preparation is the rehearsal. Like actors about to take to the stage, the SAS men would go down behind their tent lines at the bottom of SAS Hill and practise their various procedures and drills. If live firing was required for a special drill, they would go down to the small arms range area on the eastern side of the Task Force base facing towards the Long Tan battlefield rubber area and go through their procedures. Peter Schuman remembered what his patrol would do in the days between patrols:

> On the day of your brief, the dress was thongs and shorts and carrying your weapon. You relaxed as much as you could in those four days [between patrols]. Got the briefing and we then saddled up in all our gear, down to the range which was at the back of the engineers, where you would re-practise a couple of contact drills, test-firing, if you were going on an ambush—fire a few Claymores, get the wiring techniques right. Go through any drills that had been developed while you were out.[11]

Members of F Troop, 2 Squadron practising their 'shoot and scoot' drill down on the range at Nui Dat. *Photo courtesy of AWM Neg. No. P0966/97/37*

Ian Conaghan recalled the amount of ammunition the patrol might expend in getting their procedures right so that there would be no stuff-ups on the day:

> We would go through heaps of full-blown, live fire rehearsals, the whole lot. We might go through thousands of rounds of ammunition. I remember . . . on one patrol, I must have used anything between 30 and 40 Claymores rehearsing to get it right. But that wasn't a problem—we had more ammunition than you could poke a stick at! It was wonderful having 'The Land of the Free and the Home of the Brave' feeding us all this stuff, even though we paid for it in the long term.[12]

GETTING IT RIGHT

I have a calendar entitled 'Inspirations' and each month carries a photograph with a caption on topics such as motivation, leadership and opportunity. One month has a colour photograph of an eagle, giant wings spread, which has just claimed a fish out of a lake. The heading or particular inspiration is entitled 'Excellence' and the quotation for the month is, 'We are what we repeatedly do. Excellence, then, is not an act but a habit.'

The men of the SAS took this as their credo when fine-tuning for patrols. It never mattered how often they had been out together, they still carried out rehearsals to prepare themselves for action. A rehearsal also has another purpose. It focuses the mind, the body, the individual and the team. The lethargy of five or ten days off is instantly cast aside when men start detonating Claymores, carrying out contact drills or break contact drills, and the heavy staccato report of rifles spitting out automatic fire and orders being barked brings the patrol together as a fighting machine. The emphasis is on quick, violent reaction. On patrol it will come down to the quick and the dead. Bill Hindson detailed the sorts of things his patrol rehearsed:

> We did rehearse every aspect of the patrol—each member's position in the formation, the arcs that people would watch as we were going along, how we would set up communications and who would cover what areas when the antenna was being erected. How we would set the ambushes; how we would react to people in the ambush; how we would react if there were enemy that were out of the killing ground when the ambush was initiated and how to react if they became aggressive and returned fire. What actions we would take if we were contacted on the way to or whilst we were setting the ambush; what would happen if they hit us from behind or the flanks. We would rehearse what would happen if we contacted people while we were moving. When the forward scout saw somebody, he would stop and aim his weapon at the enemy, I would then move up beside him and the rest of the patrol would then peel off left and right and move up beside us so that we would have maximum firepower to direct at the enemy; or if we were caught and fired at, then we would try to do the same thing and then withdraw. So we had to practise all those different situations each and every time.[13]

Sometimes the rehearsals might involve the RAAF, as Peter Schuman recollected when his patrol was using 9 Squadron in the very early period of the Viet Nam War:

SAS and
9 Squadron
practising a double
hoist technique.
This procedure
was used prior to
rope extractions
being introduced.
*Photo courtesy of Ian
Conaghan*

In the early days, the helicopters used to land and we would climb in. Towards the end of the campaign, the choppers used to land and we would stand back to back—the four of us—and as the helicopters came in between us, we just fell back into the chopper. Because the baddies started to twig to the techniques that we had, and the longer you stayed on the ground, the better the target you made. So we had a few practices. Rappelling techniques were developed—they were mainly refinements to insertion techniques that we would go out and do a bit of training on. Hot extractions, roping using karabiners.[14]

The 9 Squadron choppers were always in Nui Dat awaiting tasking during the day and would often be used to perfect drills and procedures used in patrol insertions and extractions. Terry Pinkerton spoke about some of the drills they worked on:

> We would do a morning with them just to re-hash what they could do and what they couldn't do in terms of the aircraft embarkation, debarkation and all that sort of stuff. The main part of it was to do a double hoist to make sure we got it right.[15]

A double hoist drill is a procedure whereby the crewman drops a winch line to the patrol and hoists two men at a time up through the jungle canopy in case the helicopter is unable to land. This procedure was developed later on to include a multiple hoist extraction, which will be covered in Chapter 13.

Even though the patrols had been together for over twelve months and often longer, they still did rehearsals every time before they went out. Because of the constant changing in patrol personnel owing to leave, sickness and other duties, the requirement also existed to ensure that anyone not normally in that five-man patrol was fully up to speed with that patrol's drills. Even though the drills were fairly standard across the troop, it was still a normal routine to have rehearsals, as patrol commander Trevor Roderick explained:

> You always did rehearsals, it didn't matter how many times you had been out, we always rehearsed, always test-fired weapons, always re-zeroed weapons, and if you were carrying six mags you always fired some ammo—you test-fired each magazine just in case there was a hassle. All the way through SAS training, the emphasis is always on detailed planning and rehearsals. The emphasis is always on it. And even if it held up the start of an operation. But it was always drummed into us, all the way through, take your bloody time, prepare properly, you can have access to whatever information people had. We even used to go and visit the battalions and talk to the platoon commanders and company commanders who might have been in the area before. Now that could take half a day, so you might take three days to get ready.[16]

Once the orders were given to the patrol they followed a set routine of personal hygiene and sobriety that is best explained by Joe Van Droffelaar:

Once the orders were given, then there was no more boozing, no-one was to drink. All drinking would stop on completion of the orders. No more washing, no more shaving, and again the greens that they had on them at the orders—they would live in them. So by the time they go out in the scrub they smelt like dogs, and they looked like dogs. So, by that time we would still have a good three days left—roughly about 72 hours from the time we're given the Warning Order. Within that three days our primary function then was to receive our ammo, start making up our Claymore mines in ring mains and would put on delay fuse settings with igniters with delays from 5 seconds to 20 seconds. WPs [white phosphorus grenades] would all be rigged up with time delay.[17]

Patrols would go over their particular drills like contact drills and one scout, Andy Nucifora, details his patrol's drill to use if they took a casualty in a contact when he was a scout:

Depending if the forward guy was the scout or the patrol commander got hit, everyone went to ground and tried to find cover. Give covering fire and the next guy would go up and try and retrieve the body or drag him back and that's what we practised mainly. So they used to give covering fire and one of the guys would race up and grab me. And then we would scarper, and we would go into fire and movement and that's about all you could do normally. There's not much else you can do except throw a lot of fire about and keep anyone from following up until you could get free. We had our set RVs and alternate RVs and that sort of thing in case we did get in the shit.[18]

The drill that was normal SOP on a contact was to empty out a magazine in the direction of the enemy, reload and then start picking targets to conserve ammunition stocks. Nucifora recalled that the recovery drill was designed to get the enemy concentrating on their own survival and not on the SAS patrol. They would try to put

plenty of fire down initially, just to get the enemy to go to ground. Give yourself just a little bit of breathing space and then do your initial reaction—whatever it may be—whether it is to get him out or give him covering fire to get himself out if he was pinned down. Then selective targets and know which way you're going to bug out.[19]

Accurate shooting is an essential element of battlefield survival with a five-man patrol. Your shots must count as you do not have an endless supply of ammunition. As an example of how practice can lead to very good skill levels, Bill Hindson explained how his troop used to practise shooting and weapon handling:

> During test-firing preceding one of our patrols, Neville Farley and I had a competition firing from the hip at a can and although he didn't hit it with the first shot, he hit it within about two shots. Everybody was trained to move with their weapons held into the shoulder, and I think that patrolling with your weapon in your shoulder, and pointing it wherever you were looking, meant that as soon as you got the slightest feeling that there was enemy there, whether it was movement, sound, smell or whatever, the weapon was aimed and the only action required was to pull the trigger. We were able to immediately respond with aimed fire, so that we had the drop on the VC anyway. The VC on the other hand often had his weapon over his shoulder or in his arms and then had to work out where they were going to shoot and get the weapon into the shoulder or shoot from the waist and their fire was inaccurate. I think that's the reason why we were more successful and able to win—no matter who fired first.[20]

OOPS

Rehearsals didn't always go as planned—which is why you have rehearsals in the first place. The SAS Hill position dominated the Task Force base and was about 35 metres in height and above the Task Force HQ complex, a couple of hundred metres downwind from the hill. One particular rehearsal to try to snatch a prisoner using command-detonated CS gas by B Troop in 1967 could have gone better—as Neville Farley recalled:

> This was a rehearsal to see if it worked. And I remember 'Slag' O'Keefe and I—he was the troop sergeant—we got the boys all lined up with their gas masks on, and we put these two

bags of CS powder out and we fired them like Claymores. This bloody thing went off and we all went through the ambush drill and did a sweep through the spot. When it fired we were all sweating and carrying on and all this CS gas got up under our gas masks, and we were crying and bumping into trees and falling over and it was a total fuck-up! You know, you've got ten brave heroes all bloody smarting and bumping into things and falling over! Anyhow, that was fine, but we said, 'Fuck this, we're not going to do that because it could stuff up real bad.' The offshoot of this fiasco was that this big plume of CS gas went up and settled down on Task Force Headquarters and there was all shit to pay![21]

Eventually, after three to five days of preparation, the patrol is ready to go. The VR has confirmed the insertion point, the orders are all given, the briefings and rehearsals are all complete and the insertion day is tomorrow afternoon. The patrol members are unshaven, unwashed and ready to slip into the fetid, steamy jungle to execute their task. All they have to do now is get in.

9

GETTING IN

Infiltrating is the term applied by the SAS for getting a patrol into its area of operations and the whole idea is that the patrol is inserted into an area undetected so that the enemy are unaware of the presence of the five-man patrol. This secrecy is essential if the patrol is to have any chance of survival against a numerically superior force. During their time in Viet Nam, the patrols were inserted into their AOs by a variety of means.

When the Task Force was establishing itself at Nui Dat in 1966, the SAS patrols simply walked out through the perimeter wire, as the areas they were searching were within walking distance of the base. As the secure areas were broadened, initially out to mortar range and then out to artillery range, other agencies were used for insertion. Once the infantry battalions began moving out to search and clear areas in Phuoc Tuy Province, the SAS would tag along and stay behind in an area to observe any enemy movement, as Peter Schuman remembered with his patrol:

> Sometimes we would go over to 5 RAR and just jump on their trucks and go with them. Sit in on their briefings and you would get a one-liner—'and at the end of our deployment Patrol Juliet 34 will drop off'.[1]

Sometimes the insertions were quite unusual and related to supporting another military operation. Peter Schuman recalled one such insertion which had its moments:

There was a big operation around Long Son Island, which was down in the Baria area. It was a VC haven—they did training, it was an R&R centre. The Fifth Battalion (5 RAR) were doing an operation knocking over a few of those fishing villages on Route 15—cordon and search. I did a lot of training when I was in the regiment with water operations troop, so I was immediately the water operations expert. I deployed with five or six men. I'd arrived with a truck with assault craft on board, outboard motors, three assault craft actually, and the deal was when they assaulted village number three—which they had left alone because the baddies would go down through the tunnels and come up where there wasn't any danger and try and get away by boat—that was where we came in.

We were just about to launch the cordon and search and when I looked up, the entrance to this village number three and it had a great big stone entrance to it. And I thought, 'Shit! I wonder if my truck is going to fit through this entrance.' It was a big entrance made of huge sandstone blocks. So we took the measurement of the truck with a bit of rope and then, sort of whistling to ourselves, walked down the road, one guy stood at one side of the gate and I was at the other side of the gate and said, 'Shit, the truck'll fit', and went back. As soon as the cordon went in, I burst through the gates with the trucks and we launched the three boats. Our recognition sign—they had some gunships up to take out any boats trying to escape from the village area—recognition signs were red panels and I can recall getting on the air net as we launched the boats and I heard the gunship coming in. And it was coming in, and coming in and I heard this American voice say, 'Roger we see red panels'.

So we did that operation and we then left the coastline and then linked up with the rest of the squadron. It was 'Murphy's Navy' for about a week . . . The squadron sur-rounded Long Son Island and started knocking off boats that tried to escape from the island as the battalion assaulted later that afternoon from the mainland.[2]

Ian Conaghan did some boat insertions when he was attached on an exchange program the Special Forces people had going. He did not like it too much, probably because Ian is shorter than most people:

> We had one op when we went in by boat. Came in off the ocean off US destroyers out in the gulf. We would supply the coxswain and the bowman and so on for the Geminis. I did a lot of boat insertions when I was down in the Delta. I was seconded off to a SEAL team when I was there. Definitely up to your tits in mud and water for a long time.[3]

Occasionally the SAS patrols would be inserted using the armoured personnel carriers (APCs), which primarily transported the infantry platoons and companies in the Task Force. The infantry battalions wore a plain jungle green uniform throughout the war. The SAS wore camouflaged gear usually of an American pattern. It was important that the local villagers did not recognise the SAS men, as those locals sympathetic to the VC cause would soon get the word through to the enemy that the SAS were in an area. Ian Stiles deployed on a few patrols using the APCs:

> We only wore camouflage gear for patrolling—never around Nui Dat. If we were inserted by APC, and we were moving through a village like Binh Ba or wherever we had a green shirt on if you had your head sticking out of the APC, and then once you inserted, you put your camouflage shirt back on.[4]

Once the area around the Task Force base had been cleared and deemed reasonably secure, the SAS patrols were then sent further afield to discover where the enemy were located. The VC used the jungle to hide their formed units and also to train their new recruits and to rehearse for attacks and ambushes on the allied forces. Consequently, APC insertions were not feasible for the vast majority of SAS patrols simply because the areas to be searched were so far away from Nui Dat. Given the speed of the tracked vehicles, it would nearly take a day just to get to some of the more remote areas of Phuoc Tuy Province.

HELO INSERTIONS

For the greater part of their time in Viet Nam the SAS patrols were inserted by helicopters from 9 Squadron RAAF. A whole standard operating procedure (SOP) was developed by 9 Squadron for SAS operations.[5] The aim of a helo insertion was to get the patrol out of the chopper and then into the cover of the jungle as quickly as possible. Anyone on the ground in the bush finds it extremely difficult to determine where a helicopter actually is, the lower it is to the tree canopy. Even a slow-moving helicopter is hard to shoot at tree height through the vegetation. The higher the aircraft, the easier it is to see and to engage, unless it is above 1500 feet, when it is out of effective small arms range for most weaponry. Consequently the aircraft commanding and controlling the operation, Albatross Lead (radio callsign Albatross Zero One), flew at 1500 feet or higher, and when closing on the landing zone, Albatross Zero Two flew right down as close to the trees and as fast as the pilot could manage. This made it a difficult target and also hard to determine where it was heading or landing.

DOWN TO THE PAD

The SAS patrol moves from its tent lines down to the helicopter pad behind SAS Hill in jeeps and prepares to insert. More briefings are required to ensure that the RAAF know exactly what the SAS patrol is going to be doing and the SAS patrol understands how 9 Squadron will insert the patrol into its designated landing zone (LZ). Bill Hindson remembered the trip down to the chopper pad:

> On the day of the patrol insertion we would go down to Task Force Headquarters where we would have a special briefing in an area adjacent to the heli-pad. We would have a joint briefing during which we would be updated again by our own intelligence officer and we might have a special briefing by the Task Force intelligence officer. We would have the mission explained to the 9 Squadron pilots and crew and tell them our task and what we were going to do. How they were going

Ian Stiles' patrol preparing to move down to the Alert Hut to deploy on patrol. *Standing left to right:* Adrian Jones, Joe Rice and Ian Stiles. *Kneeling left to right:* Trevor McKenzie and Ted Ruska. Joe Rice is 'carbo loading' before he embarks on a patrol with less appetising dehydrated long-range patrol rations. *Photo courtesy of Ian Stiles*

to fly it would be explained and immediately before the patrol, we would hand any non-essential bits and pieces over to the SAS liaison officer who used to come down with us from SAS Hill. That would take the form of either handing in any last-minute letters or if some had taken cans of soft drink or water to drink on the way down—then that would be handed over so we weren't carrying any excess garbage around. We would then get on the helicopters, crank up and be gone.[6]

PRE-FLIGHT BRIEFINGS

The briefings were a very detailed run-through of what was to occur from the time the patrol took off from Kanga Pad next to the Alert Hut until they had got inside the treeline at their LZ. The briefings were given in the 9 Squadron Alert Hut where crews who were not on a task waited for a call from Task Force

The 9 Squadron briefing map in Vung Tau which every crewman was briefed on before assuming flying duties for the day. The briefing included all enemy and friendly movements in the last 24 hours. *Photo courtesy of Terry Pinkerton*

HQ for tasks in support of the ground troops, which could vary from a stores lift, an ammunition resupply, casualty evacuation or sometimes the extraction of an SAS patrol. The hut was a simple building with a tin roof, sort of semi-open sides with tiered wooden seats and a concrete floor. Many SAS men recall that it was similar to the ready room seen in World War II movies—minus the flying scarfs and Spitfires. The briefing map was a huge 1:25 000 scale map of the whole of Phuoc Tuy Province and the adjoining provinces. The aircrew flying the slicks supporting the insertion were brought up to speed prior to an infil, as crewman Terry Pinkerton recalls:

> We got our briefings along with the gunship crews. The SAS intelligence person would come down from the hill, he would give us an intelligence briefing from all the knowledge and stuff that he had been given about the area concerned. Movements, you name it right across the board, everything. Then

The helicopter crews awaiting tasking in the Alert Hut at Nui Dat. This is where the final briefings took place prior to a patrol insertion. *Photo courtesy of Terry Pinkerton*

we would get the patrol commander's brief. If he had anything to say he would have some special mentions about what he wanted to do; which directions he wanted to go when he got there, and any special requirements that he may have just on the landing to give him a better initiation to where he wanted to go.[7]

Which way the aircraft will be facing may seem trivial, but it allowed the patrol commander to set his compass prior to landing so that when they hit the ground they automatically knew which way they would be heading. This meant less time on the ground trying to orient the patrol and they would be in and under cover quickly. The patrols wanted to get into the bush with a minimum of time spent out on the open LZ, as Trevor Roderick reasoned:

As time went on, the enemy started to twig to likely LZs. They were doing the same types of appreciations that we did.

127

And in some cases they were starting to wait for us, they had a fair idea what LZs patrols were going to start using. You're really naked until you got in the bush. The bush was our home and the thicker the scrub the better, that was our home.[8]

The patrol commander and Albatross Lead talk in detail about the LZ for infil because of the need for coordinated action on everyone's part. On larger LZs it was necessary to detail *exactly* where on that pad Albatross Zero Two would put down. Nev Farley was a patrol commander who had to liaise closely with Albatross Lead prior to an insertion:

I would go down to 9 Squadron and go through the pilot's brief. He would have done his recce, mainly to look for the LZ that we were going in on and anything to pull us out. He would look at the LZ—at the way it was—and he used to draw on the windshield of his chopper the shape of it, and where north was and what direction we were coming in, so he could pick it up straight away. So you knew when you hit the ground and you came out that door and you went say, at ten o'clock, that you were pointed in a certain direction. So you virtually had your map oriented from the moment you stepped off that chopper, because if you did it arse about, you would run off and could be going in the opposite direction.[9]

The final insertion briefings for the aircrew and the SAS patrol would take at least 30 minutes. Albatross Lead ('Zero One') also has detailed discussions with the patrol commander, so they both agree before take-off exactly how the aircraft will insert the patrol onto the deck. Terry Pinkerton continues:

Then we would get a big briefing from Zero One about all emergencies, contingency plans, back-out plans, downed aircraft, unserviceabilities, wireless failures. Right across the board, every conceivable emergency that might happen on that trip in anybody's aeroplane; who was going to take whose place, slip, slide—even Zero One had a contingency plan for somebody to take over from him, which sometimes happened—with radio failures mainly, or sometimes even aircraft. Every last facet of emergencies would be taken into account and a question time and confirmation time. Everybody would go out and we would do your pre-flights and get ready.[10]

Everyone in the Alert Hut is listening intently to what is being said, as there can be no room for a mistake or a misunderstanding. The consequences of an error with a five-man patrol put in the wrong place could be fatal for the whole patrol. One of the 9 Squadron pilots, Jack Lynch, reflected on the atmosphere in the briefings prior to an insertion:

> It's usually pretty quiet, intense. Everyone is intent on picking up all the detail because no-one wants to screw up from their own point of view. And no-one wants to screw the thing up for the troops that are going into the scrub. There was always this great admiration for these blokes and I can remember time after time RAAF blokes saying, 'Jesus, I wouldn't do what these blokes are doing for all the tea in China.'[11]

THE FLY-IN—AIRBORNE

The aircrew and the patrol would leave the hut and get into the helicopters. Jack Lynch takes up the account:

> I would turn the radio on and then the mission commander would get everyone to check in, call everyone, 'Start engines'. Once we had started up and checked in on the radios again, he then just led you on out.[12]

The helicopters lift off from Kanga Pad with five heavily armed and heavily laden camouflaged SAS men as their cargo. The flight time to their infil pad could be twenty minutes or as long as forty minutes. RAAF crewman Sergeant Terry Pinkerton was the man in charge of the load space and the other door gunner and it was his responsibility to make sure that everything was in working order as they approached their LZ.

> Some cases we would go out far enough and we would check the weapons in a safe area, not always—depending on what our briefings had told us. It depended on briefing security, the risks and all that sort of stuff, what sort of reception we might get in the area. If we had the option we would check all weapons on the way out.[13]

An SAS patrol on board their 9 Squadron slick and about to infiltrate. SAS Hill is in the background. Note the bulky water bladder in the front of the trooper's shirt. This bladder would be the first water consumed in the immediate period after landing.
Photo courtesy of Terry Pinkerton

The aircraft group with Albatross Lead, the patrol slick and an LFT is all now at 1500 feet and heading towards a point on a map known as the gate. Terry Pinkerton recalls the procedure as the slick with the patrol on board starts its ingress to the LZ:

> Albatross Lead would tell us to start to descend at the appropriate 'gate' and then down we would go and if it was a single aircraft patrol we would go down as the insert aircraft with the gunships. The gunships would be along but they would be staggered way away from you, probably anything up to a click, a click and a half away behind us. No sense in having a whole bunch of targets in a small group. Besides they have a different job to perform. In the slick you would start getting ready for it and that's when you would start to get real serious. Albatross Lead is talking to you and you would be down at the weeds, right on at the trees and picking up bits of tree leaves and all that sort of stuff.[14]

From the pilot's perspective, Pilot Officer Jack Lynch describes the fly-in:

> Once Albatross Zero Two was airborne he was just directed, he would not see the pad until the crunch. He would be flying along at low level, right down on the trees basically. The mission commander would be up above 1500 feet, directing him off the map and maybe an aerial photograph and patches of jungle and clearings and all that sort of stuff. Directing 'Turn right, turn left' and he would actually tell him where to go, 'Hold that heading, maintain that heading, okay, the pad is now your right one o'clock, two hundred metres' . . . and then he would just call him into it and then depending on which way you're going to do it, you might say, 'Okay, pads out right one o'clock, do a right 180, now' and then he would just go in and flare and wouldn't see it until he was right on it.[15]

Being guided into the pad by Albatross Lead calls for a great deal of trust between the pilots because the captain flying Zero Two is concentrating on not filling his windshield with a large tree and maintaining the directions given to him by Zero One through his earphones. Jack Lynch said it made him feel

> a certain sense of uneasiness because you're not totally in control yourself. You trust the other fellow, but there's just a little uneasiness because you don't know what the pad is like. You haven't seen it, but you know from historical assessment that things are going to work out pretty well. The other bloke up there knows what he is doing and it's just this total trust between you.[16]

In the back of his chopper the patrol are told through the headsets that their LZ is approaching and they have a minute to get ready to deplane their slick. The captain of Zero Two is getting detailed instructions on his final approach to the pad:

> The patrol would get themselves ready and if it was a land straight ahead, you might just come straight over the top of the jungle and there the pad would be. Albatross Zero Two is down forward so Zero One can see him and then he would say, 'Okay, pad is left ten o'clock. Okay, do a 180, now' and I would do

An Iroquois
'Bushranger'
gunship with
flanking rocket
pods and
mini-guns. *Photo
courtesy of Jack Lynch*

a 180 and there would be the pad in front of me and I would just come down to a hover. There's always a little bit of apprehension there, 'Could they possibly have mined this?' Surprisingly, that was just very, very rare if it ever was.[17]

The approach to the LZ is not taken in a direct line—the aircraft will have been changing direction to try to mask its true destination. Pilot Jack Lynch continues:

You wouldn't go straight to the pad. The idea was for Zero Two to get in, drop the patrol off and then quickly take off and then continue on in that same direction. Five hundred metres out from the pad the patrol would get a call from the crewman and the patrol members would position themselves in the chopper cabin to scan the jungle as they approached the LZ. Any enemy sightings from this time would cause the insertion to be aborted.[18]

THE GUNNIES

While the Albatross Lead is directing Zero Two into pad from the 'gate' where they have dropped down to treetop level and been scaring the daylights out of the SAS patrol as the canopy flicks past only feet below their skids, the light fire team (LFT) is flying in direct support of the infil operation. Jack Lynch also qualified to fly the gunships, which required special skill levels owing to the need to engage ground targets with a high degree of accuracy. He recalled the way the gunships operated and how they flew:

> They're far enough away that they are not as a formation with
> the insertion slick. When the insertion was going on, they had

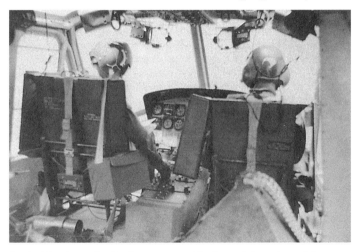

An inside view of a Bushranger gunship from 9 Squadron. Note the ammunition bins which fed the 2000 rounds per minute mini-guns and the armour-plating on the rear of the pilots' seats.
Photo courtesy of Terry Pinkerton

to be within striking distance. If Zero Two took fire for instance, as he came round to do a flare to land, the gunships would be fairly close in at that stage. And then the gunships would probably do an orbit around while Zero Two was on the ground. Then the slick would lift off and the gunships would fit in behind him again as he departed the insertion pad.[19]

BUTTERFLIES

Sergeant Nev Farley was a veteran of Borneo when he went to Viet Nam but admitted he still felt apprehensive the first time he inserted by helicopter into the badlands with his five-man patrol:

> It was pretty bloody scary, because you got choppered right into the AO. In Borneo we used to get flown fixed-wing down to a bunch of Gurkhas and then we would get a chopper up onto the border, and from then on we would walk on into Indonesia. But here, you got choppers straight into where the bad guys were. And when you go in brand new—first time— you think, 'Shit, what's here?'[20]

Nev Farley's mate from Borneo was Andy Nucifora, who was in the same patrol again with him in Viet Nam as the patrol scout. Andy reflected on the fact that he always felt a little apprehensive on the fly-in:

> Fear of the unknown is a terrible thing. I never liked it but it had to be done and up until you got inside cover, got into the treeline, I remember thinking once I would give a hundred bucks for a beer. Your mouth is really dry and then initially you're craving for a beer and then after a few hours you will settle for a lemonade and then as you get thirstier you start to ration your water, particularly in dry areas, and you're just looking for some nice cool water with lemon juice squeezed in it. I remember even in Borneo, the first couple of infils there it was the same.[21]

Bill Hindson had some good descriptions of what it's like sitting in the back of the chopper getting ready to leap out and seek the sanctuary of the jungle:

You could feel the tension increase as we approached the landing zone. Everybody would be off their seats and some would sit in the doorway ready to leap out and go for it. We would come hurtling in, skimming across the treetops, occasionally hitting the bloody things and then the pilots would do a hard turn to wash off speed, do a full 360 degree turn, bang it down—if they could—onto hard ground, and you would all start leaping out.

On occasions we would be in high grass and on leaping out would find ourselves falling bloody ten feet and have people disappearing into grass which would all be flattened out by the rotor downwash. So the experiences were different. Sometimes you could get out and go flat out straight into the nearest piece of decent treeline, and other times people would be all arse up, tangled up in bloody long grass, and shrubs and things, and we would be looking around trying to find people and they would be on their backs with this bloody great pack. We would be trying to pull them up and while all the helicopter noise is going on there's bloody twigs and crap falling out of the sky.

We would be there, instantly out of the cool of the helicopters into the bloody heat of the jungle. Our hearts would be beating, the blood would be rushing in our ears, and we could hear this bloody noise from the helicopters and we're thinking, 'How are we going to get in there and try and hide?' And we felt like the whole bloody world at this stage is bearing down on us. So, we get straight into the treeline, grab our hats or whatever and stick them on our heads, and check that we have got everything and haven't dropped anything on the landing zone. Then we get shaken out into our formation quickly and get away from there as rapidly as we could.[22]

These feelings of apprehension and a bad case of the butterflies would have been hard to detect, as Jack Lynch recalls, when he turned around in his pilot's seat to look at the patrol and give them the word to get ready to get out:

The SAS blokes are totally camouflaged, all over their face and hands, the whole works. They've got all of their gear on and they look very bulky because they've got water bottles, plastic water bladders and all that sort of stuff. They've got their weapons, ammunition, bandoliers of ammunition around them, bandannas around their heads—especially the Maoris, they were just a fucking fearsome sight. Absolutely fearsome sight, and I guess you would never know whether they were afraid or not. But it was all pretty quiet, there was never much chat going on on the way out. They weren't talking about who won the football or anything like that. It was always pretty focused. Totally focused on the job that was to be done. They were obviously totally at ease with what they were about to do—they didn't seem to have a need to know what was going on over the headsets.[23]

TOUCH DOWN

As the pad fills the windshield of the Huey helicopter the pilot and co-pilot are checking the clearance available to put the skids on the ground, as the nature of what is under the grass or vegetation is not always exactly known. Because of the fact that the pad hasn't been directly overflown in the recce by the Albatross Lead or the patrol commander, there was always an element of the unknown:

> The LZs were usually chosen fairly well from the map and aerial photographs, showing clear areas where you could obviously get a chopper in. Whether you could land or not, you wouldn't necessarily know that until you actually got there.[24]

Just before the slick lands, the pilot flares the aircraft to wash off forward speed and allow the machine to drop almost vertically onto the pad. The time to get off is measured in seconds and would sometimes catch the aircrew by surprise. The pads always contained an element of the unknown:

> You were always prepared *not* to land and the troops were always prepared to jump off from a low hover anyway. Quite often they would be gone before you touched down. Eager beavers![25]

Not all of the apprehension is confined to the men about to deplane and head off into the scrub. The aircrew bringing this flying machine down where there was a chance of the enemy also being present had mixed feelings about the possibility of contact on the pad and 'going hot'. Terry Pinkerton did dozens and dozens of insertions but always felt vulnerable, especially

> when you're on the slow-down process, you're going back from 90 knots back to virtually about 40 knots and that's the time of the decelerating period, and it's that point where you are committed and you have got a full five-man patrol on board, you are maximum weight, you're going into a pad, a hot day and you're virtually committed—there's not much else you can do. You might have a little bit of spare power to get out in a hurry but it's not going to be nice, it's going to be touch and go.[26]

Pilot Jack Lynch always felt the same vulnerability when doing SAS insertions:

> When you are slowing down and coming down on late final to the hover, and just at the hover point where you are stuck there and the troops are getting out or getting in and there's nothing you can do. You are not moving—if there is someone there in the J you're a sitting duck. Then, and when you are taking off, that last bit on finals and the last bit before you disappear over the top of the trees—that's when you are the most vulnerable.[27]

Despite the detailed briefings, the days of rehearsals, the security and secrecy surrounding the detail of where and when the patrol would insert, it was still a tough time mentally for the SAS patrol. They knew that they were on their own once they hit the deck and would only have support for about twenty minutes after they were dropped on the pad. Trevor Roderick always thought that the time he disliked the most was

> the moment of being inserted out of a helicopter. Because you get out of the helicopter, you just move away, go to ground, the helicopters take off. At that point, you're half deaf, there's still dust bloody settling, the helicopters are gone but SOP was

that they would hang around somewhere else just in case, but at that moment—if the baddies were onto you—you were bloody gone, you were dead meat. So, until you got off the LZ and into the trees, which was our home, until then, it was frightening.[28]

BACK IN THE WEEDS

The patrols were often inserted at last light, which might sound as if that would be asking for trouble as the patrol might have difficulty getting extracted in the dark. Such was the confidence in their preparations and the deception of inserting that it hardly ever crossed anyone's mind that they should do otherwise. Patrol commander Joe Van Droffelaar explains the rationale of a late afternoon insertion into an AO by chopper:

> Being last light, of course it gave you a greater cover and because you can move right up until last light, any follow-up that occurs, even the best tracker there would need light to find an LUP. Of course if you are inserted during the early part of the day and you have got some follow-up, particularly in relation to a large enemy force, your chance of surviving is going to be somewhat limited. If you got inserted later, knowing that a large enemy force could be up your tail, you can use the time of darkness to be able to hide. A five-man patrol in a well concealed location is difficult to locate.[29]

What this amply demonstrates is the belief that the SAS procedures would work, that they had great confidence in their ability to conceal their arrival and foot movement and that the patrol night LUP would be undetected by the enemy.

ON THE DECK

The patrol is off the chopper, which is quickly climbing off the pad and into safer air space. The patrol has gone from the cool environs of a fast-moving chopper with the wind in their faces to the hot, humid, sticky close air in the jungle. The sun is beating down on the men as they quickly move off into the cooler shade of the surrounding bush. Patrol commander Joe Van Droffelaar will now take us through his patrol's procedure of getting off the pad and making themselves reasonably secure:

The fact is that once you're out of the chopper your senses require five seconds to work out where you are. Everything is geared up and basically you have got to have luck. As you hit the deck you need at least 60 per cent of luck and 40 per cent of tactics to pull you through the first 30 seconds of insertion. Although you've got chopper noise in the background, you know you've got your blokes moving and once you get off that actual LZ—even if it's just two paces into the actual J or whatever it may be—there is a sigh of relief. And the relief comes almost instantly, and the body goes through stages of releasing almost 100 per cent of the fluid that you have attained an hour back at base—all of a sudden it's just pumped out of you. It's an element of nerves, anxiety or whatever it may be, and then all of a sudden the brain winds down, the eyes are focusing correctly, the breathing has come to a normal progression, and this constant pumping of the heart tends to slow down—and then away you go.

But that is the most awkward time, I should say. If the enemy is there, and you know he's there—that's no big deal. What you want to know is *where* he is, that is the important part.

A lot of blokes go very quiet; a couple of blokes in my patrol would hardly speak or wouldn't even talk. After the initial pilot brief they would go quiet and that was it. And they knew, including myself, that nothing more can be said. Those blokes, in the next half an hour or hour or whatever it takes from the time you get to the insertion point, you may not see ever again. And everybody knew that. Once we were in, after that first minute or so and you knew that everything was reasonably quiet, you then knew that you had a 50–50 chance.[30]

Once his patrol was in the jungle, Joe Van Droffelaar would then put his patrol through a series of manoeuvres to ensure that if they were hit they would be able to fight their way back out with a fair chance of success:

Once I got off the chopper, and got ourselves off the LZ, we would then generally cut at about a 30-degree angle away from the LZ. Just in case I got contacted, I could move back to the LZ and have the standby slick then pick me up. I would never head straight in. That would be done for about 15 to 20 metres as quickly as possible whilst noise was still in the air and then I would cut back the opposite way about 30 degrees.

So, now I have cleared all to my front and to my right—which is to the back of the LZ—and now I am starting to go and clear further forward, away from the LZ. I then knew that both to my right was safe, to my left was safe, to the back was safe—because that's the area I have just come from, and I'm now going to push myself further in and this is in about ten to fifteen minutes and would have covered a good 50 metres. Then the choppers were gone, and the stillness would be there. Those branches that had been pushed down by the downdraft would have moved back into place and the jungle becomes as we know it in its neutral state.

I would then take a stop and we do not move—try not to blink an eyelid—for about at least two minutes. And we would basically stand back to back in a circle about 3 metres in diameter. And we would stand there. My 2IC, he would stand back about 3 metres away from the actual four blokes within that LUP to listen to see if there was any follow-up. Once he was satisfied there was no follow-up, after about two minutes or so, the 2IC would then close in to the five-man patrol.

We would then check our bearings. The scout knew the direction we would move right up till last light or up to our night LUP. We would then, very slowly and very carefully, move off and basically try to look for indicators. That was our primary aim, to look for any indicators or sign of enemy that may have been here or may have been in the area some time ago.

We would continue to do that with a zigzagging formation, constantly changing every 30 metres or so, stopping for five minutes, moving for 30 metres, stopping for five, moving for 30. And we would try to use the best route to give the patrol the greatest advantage in case contact was made.

Once darkness came upon us and I knew the choppers had now moved totally out of range, a contact now at this time was most dangerous and had to be avoided at all costs. So we would just close in and then we would establish our night LUP.[31]

Other patrol commanders took other actions to ensure that they didn't draw the crabs when they landed. Nev Farley explains his method of insertion, especially if being targeted against an enemy camp:

> If you were going in to a specific target, we would land about two or three thousand metres distance from the camp. What I would like to do if I was going in to find a camp, I'd land and walk away from the camp if it was getting towards the end of the day.
>
> So I would walk away from the camp and spend all night there and then the next day I would go in—that's if I went in at last light . . . LUP for the night, early next morning we will go and start looking at them.[32]

All patrols had their own way of getting themselves into the scrub. Bill Hindson's patrol would do it this way:

> Then we would stop, wait until it was all absolutely quiet; we wouldn't necessarily check around your area immediately, but would wait and make sure that there was nobody—no obvious noise or movement coming in towards where we have been inserted. Then we would send a couple of guys out to check around the area a reasonable distance which was probably only 25 or 50 metres at most, just to make sure we were not sitting beside a track or on the edge of a bloody bunker system or something which was unoccupied at the time but where the occupants might have been coming home late from a party or something.
>
> That night we used to lie in a circle, feet out, so if something happened, we would sit up and be facing whatever it was coming towards us. This also enabled us to have our heads together for whispering if we needed to communicate anything. The standard of training and the lightness that people slept was just unbelievable. I still have difficulty sleeping even now, if the wind picks up or it starts to rain or somebody drives by or kids walk past on the street, I wake up.[33]

The distance from the LZ to the target was never laid down, as the variables were always vegetation, the time of the year being wet or dry season and the likelihood of enemy contact. Troop leader and patrol commander Ron Dempsey always wanted some breathing space between himself and the enemy when planning his infil location and the ingress distance:

> If there was a position that we had been given—say a suspected camp in the area—I would normally make sure I picked an LZ that was at least two days walk away from the location. Two days slow walk, which could be 1500 to 2000 metres. You didn't want to have it too close. You wouldn't want to be dumped right down beside the suspected area in case that was occupied.[34]

Other methods for creating a diversion on the insertion of an SAS patrol were tried with varying degrees of success. Bill Hindson recalled one particular insertion that he was involved with which became rather exciting as the night wore on:

> I can remember at one stage being inserted beyond Thua Tich about 30 kilometres from the Task Force base and we were to land just a couple of hundred metres from a known occupied enemy village. Whilst we were being inserted, which was just before last light, we used 8 inch or 175 mm guns from an American fire base to fire on the village to mask the noise of the helicopters.
>
> That worked very effectively. We got out of the helicopters and took off, got ourselves out of the way and then laid up for the night. As it was just on dark, we only had time to get away from the landing zone, go to ground, and listen and make sure everything was still. We didn't actually do a check around our perimeter and a couple of hours later when we were asleep, we could hear voices approaching from the village. We assumed that the villagers had decided that they had had enough of the artillery and they had packed up and were moving.
>
> By the voices, they were coming straight at us, and the interesting thing was, even though it was pitch dark—it must have been about ten or eleven o'clock at night—without anyone saying anything, every member of the patrol—without being shaken, no word or contact, no touch—rolled over, packed up, put their pack on and we were all alert. I could only just sense this—it was pitch black. The voices came straight at us. There must have been a track that we were very close to and they came to within about 30 metres and then

veered away and they went on past chatting and talking and disappeared off into the night.

I guess the most nerve-racking time was when we felt that they were going to walk right over us. We were worried that we might have been sitting right beside the bloody track. Normally, we would try to get in late in the day, find a place to hide and then hope that any enemy moving into the area the morning after the insertion would not be aware of our presence.[35]

It was SAS squadron practice for patrols that radio contact was made with the insertion agency approximately ten minutes after the insertion of the patrol had taken place using a normal code word whilst the choppers were in a holding area out of patrol noise range. The choppers have climbed back up to 1500 feet and joined Albatross Lead at the pre-located point. They would orbit for about fifteen or twenty minutes until the patrol gave the all clear. They would do that on the ultra high frequency (UHF) ground-to-air radio known as a URC–10, or URC–68 in the later stages of the war. Once the code word was sent, the choppers would return to base. If a patrol was contacted on insertion after the choppers had left the immediate area and were out of UHF range, it was not an easy task to get help, as Ian Stiles explained:

If you got bumped, you had to lay out a wire aerial and then start sending Morse Code—which is a bit hard to do if you're running! So, that holding pattern SOP was quite good. In fact, I did do an insertion once where we got bumped as soon as we landed and had to get pulled back out.[36]

HOT INSERTIONS

This initial apprehension on insertion by helicopter was brought about by the fact that the enemy rarely send you their plans and where they are going to pop up next and so there is always an element of the unknown and a sense of danger. Ian Conaghan experienced insertions in Borneo and in Viet Nam and compared the two:

The probability of striking the enemy in Viet Nam was far higher than it ever was in Borneo and striking the enemy in Borneo was normally on ground of your own choosing. From the time you got off an aircraft in Viet Nam, and quite often *before* you got off an aircraft in Viet Nam, you were hit. But in Borneo, you could march like all get-out for days on end until you got into a particular area where you knew there was a possibility of bumping someone. Viet Nam was totally different: as soon as you got off that plane—or whatever your insertion means was, it might be a boat, APC or whatever—you knew there was a possibility or indeed a probability of having a contact.[37]

Occasionally a patrol would be inserted only to find that the enemy were in the near vicinity of the LZ or actually on the LZ as they deplaned. Ian Stiles was leading one such patrol when it all hit the fan:

We landed and actually could see where the Charlie had been sitting down on the side of the LZ. I could hear voices and I said, 'Come on, let's get away from the LZ', because once you're in the jungle you can at least run a bit, but you can't on an LZ and they can box you in by coming around behind you. So we go on in.

A guy named Trevor McKenzie, he was my forward scout; and Ticka Gray, he was the radio operator with the 25 Set. We could hear the nogs talking and we listened and then we started moving, patrolling off, and I turned around to Ticka and I said, 'Have you got those choppers, make sure you've got the choppers on voice.' And he was whispering into the set, 'Albatross, Albatross, this is Bravo Nine Sierra Two Four' and trying to get them.

We moved along and we were getting a bit further into the jungle. As Trevor McKenzie was going under a bit of bamboo, I turned around to say to Ticka Gray have you got those helicopters, and then the next thing, 'Brrrp, bang, bang' and old Trevor McKenzie comes running back past me! Old Ticka starts screaming at the top of his voice, 'ALBATROSS!' into the radio.

So I pulled out a white phos grenade and I threw it to sort of give us a bit of a smoke screen, but it landed on a bush about bloody 10 feet in front of me and I turned around and started running back. We were throwing a few grenades and old Charlie is firing back through the bamboo. And he had only gone in a short way from the LZ.

I said to Chick Dimmack, my patrol 2IC, to get the 148 [M203] grenade launcher going. It landed about 400 yards [360 metres] away and I yelled bring them in closer and anyway it landed in the tree above me and I said, 'Not that fucking close!'

So the choppers saw the smoke from the white phos and then they came over and the next thing they got the door gunners firing and the gunships laying down shit everywhere. We jumped back in the chopper, we got back and there were no casualties on our side, so it was okay. We all went up the Hill and had a drink or two.[38]

Nev Farley had a great deal of praise for the 9 Squadron crewmen who would risk all if the patrol suddenly found itself in trouble immediately after infil:

The old 9 Squadron, they were pretty cool, they would come back and get us under all sorts of conditions, even to the point that if the slicks were too far away, Albatross Lead up top would come straight down and get you without any support or anything.[39]

THE SHOTGUN PATROLS

To overcome the problem of having a patrol unable to extricate itself when caught on an LZ, one of the squadrons employed a technique known as a 'shotgun patrol' similar to the armed men who accompanied stagecoaches in the days of the Wild West. Ian Conaghan deployed on several of these shotgun patrols:

We'd had a number of guys, particularly my tent mate Jack Gebhardt, poor old Jacky. Every time he got on an aircraft, someone would shoot at him—he had a real bad run. So we started a deception plan where we inserted two patrols, with the second patrol coming up the arse of the initial patrol in a second aircraft. But the second patrol was just loaded for bear. You had that much ammo on you, you could fight World War III. Then after the first patrol had its legs on the ground and they had moved off and got into patrolling mode—maybe half an hour later, depending on how far away you were from

Loaded for bear. A 'shotgun' patrol led by Ian Conaghan which was to escort a patrol into an area and be prepared to assist in their extraction if the landing zone went 'hot'. Back packs were not carried but replaced by large amounts of ammunition as evidenced in the photograph. *Pictured left to right at rear:* Trooper Lawrence (Burma) Mealin, Sergeant John (Slag) O'Keefe, Trooper Don Miller and Trooper Jim Raitt. *In front left to right:* Sergeant Alan Smith and Sergeant Ian Conaghan. *Photo courtesy of Ian Conaghan*

Nui Dat, because of aircraft endurance—the aircraft would then come back and do a full extraction of the shotgun patrol. So hopefully that deception plan had covered the guys who had just gone in and if you did hit the shit straight off the LZ, at least you had some firepower with you then and you could actually do something about it.[40]

For now, the patrol is in the jungle and heading off to its LUP for the night. The deep blackness of a jungle night where there is very little ambient light to speak of covers the patrol as they sleep with their ears open.

10

THE DAILY ROUTINE

To get a feel for the patrol's existence and what the men experienced as they searched for the enemy, we need to look at a day in the life of a patrol. While this was the daily routine, there was hardly anything routine about five men, out of artillery and mortar range, sneaking through the enemy's backyard. The 'routine' the patrols generally went through really started at the first night LUP, which was after they had been inserted by 9 Squadron in the late afternoon. The men are fully loaded with all of their ammunition, their food, water and any special equipment and radios required for their task. If it is the dry season it will be very hot, averaging around 36° Celsius during the day, and the men will be carrying anything up to the equivalent of eighteen water bottles or 18 litres of water. The vegetation will not be as luxuriant as during the wet season, when the humidity soars and the temperatures stay almost as high, averaging around 30°C during the day. In the wet season, once the monsoon has arrived, it will rain almost every day and depending on proximity to the coastline it will rain very heavily for an hour or so almost at the same time of the day.

THE FIRST NIGHT LUP

The patrol had only an hour or so after insertion on most patrol infils to get off the pad, get into the jungle and clear the area around where they intended to stay for the first night. The patrol commander would have given his scout the direction he wanted to go and the scout will be carefully moving forward looking for any indicators that the enemy have been in or, even worse, are in the immediate vicinity. The patrol would not start moving forward until the noise of the choppers had totally died away and the fauna and flora had settled down after the whirlwind created by the downwash of the rotors of the Huey. Most patrols secured the area for the LUP the way Joe Van Droffelaar's patrol got itself into its night location:

> I always maintained that our insertion LUP and our extraction LUP would always be a fish hook, or a direction by which we could move back onto our track so we could observe any follow-up and be in a position to make contact if we had to. This was what I called our 'patrol' SOPs. I used to have my own patrol SOPs and our own code of conduct. And certainly our night LUP, we used to move into a fish hook, we would then come back and the 2IC would hang back. The remainder of the patrol would be standing, almost back to back—about half a metre between each man. The 2IC would stand back to a point where I could almost barely see him. That was when I would then call him in. I would never send out any other blokes as in a clearing patrol because I had already done a reasonably good loop and there was no reason now to start moving again. Because there are two principles of why contact is made. One is movement, the second is camouflage and concealment.
>
> Generally we tried to just keep in close. As darkness fell, we would just move down, remove our packs and remain sitting there for another half an hour at least. Then we would individually knock up a bit of sleeping gear. Most blokes didn't bother to drag any sleeping gear out because they knew that things weren't too good outside the LUP.
>
> Then the guys would just relax, get some water down them, have a quick feed, which was generally small because they had a major feed when they left base and we would stay there that night. The formation in the LUP was generally a

star or a circle. We used whichever one gave the maximum cover and the best escape routes for the patrol. Both were quite tight. Everything was at half arm reach and the men were always pointing outwards. All the weapons that were carried on my patrol—none of them were on the safety catch, they were always on 'fire'. So, everyone on fire including the M203. The 40 mm HE round was removed and the shotgun or bird pellet round was then put in. The WPs were also ready to set up and at times, depending on the likelihood of the enemy moving off tracks and moving through the scrub, we would set up a Claymore mine with clacker and two WPs and time delay strapped to the Claymore. The distance where the Claymore mine was from the LUP—generally no more than ten paces, sometimes less, depending on the situation.[1]

SLEEPING WITH YOUR EARS OPEN

In a normal rifle platoon in the bush in Viet Nam, or any other conflict for that matter, the platoon runs a roster system during the night with its three machine-guns manned each by two men on a staggered picket arrangement. Everyone will spend some time during the night behind the gun looking and listening for sound of the enemy.

Not so in a five-man patrol in the SAS. The men would spend all night on picket and the LUP was designed to hide the five-man patrol where it would be unlikely to be contacted. It would be off tracks, in dense undergrowth and with some kind of cover from view if not from fire. So when darkness fell and everything in the jungle had settled down for the night, the men would simply lie on a piece of groundsheet and, with their web belts still on their waists, put their heads on their packs and sleep with their ears open.[2] One patrol commander, Peter Schuman, described the way his patrol slept the night in their LUP:

> You get to know areas and know whether anyone has been in the area for a long time or not. And if you can get yourself in the right area like a big thicket patch, a bamboo patch where you know if anyone is coming towards you they are going to make a hell of a lot of noise anyway and it's almost as good as an alarm clock.[3]

Sometimes the patrols would be forced to have a sentry owing to the presence of the enemy or if they thought they might be being followed up by an inquisitive or aggressive foe. In cases where a sentry was posted, it could only be a single man and the patrol used their own fail-safe system to ensure he didn't fall asleep completely. Peter Schuman explains his patrol's sentry system:

> If we were in a fairly active area we would sleep head to bum, that is whoever is on sentry we would put their bum between the three heads, so there was one head near your arsehole and one head near your right hip and one head near your left hip. So, if you did fall over, you would fall on someone's head and wake them up. We knew that we were just human, but if all of us were asleep we would be courting danger, so that's the way we used to do it.[4]

Sleeping in an LUP requires discipline for what most people take as a fairly simple act. The patrol cannot afford to make even the slightest sound while they are in the night LUP. Ian Stiles explains:

> It got to the stage that even if you rolled over, you would actually lie on your back and lift your body up with the heels of your feet and sort of roll over, and even that was a real exercise in itself.[5]

The patrol members never slept like logs as they were so keenly aware of their own perilous situation that they would wake at the slightest sound. Bill Hindson recalls one incident when his patrol was in a night LUP:

> I remember on one occasion, Sergeant John 'Slag' O'Keefe and myself were lying there in the middle of the night and I could hear this rustling in the dry leaves. So I carefully sat up and this rustling noise kept coming towards me. It sounded really weird, not like something walking. There was this 'rustle, rustle'. I'm thinking, 'Jesus, it's a snake.' I'm trying to think what is it, and it didn't occur to me that snakes would or wouldn't move at night or whatever. This thing is coming closer and closer and I am thinking it's an animal, it's a small

thing, it's like a snake. I reached over and got the insect spray and this thing is going 'rustle, rustle' and it's coming up just between Slag and myself.

Just when I reckon it's less than a metre away, I let fly with the spray and Slag did the same thing. I hadn't heard him move but we both sprayed this thing and it took off! It was just like that—we were so quiet, we couldn't hear another patrol member at arm's length beside you. The standard of training and alertness was such that even when patrol members had their packs off, and they had bits and pieces out of their pack, they were able to wake up, put everything back in, and pack it up in total darkness. We usually kept our basic fighting gear on our belt but we could get our packs on and weapons ready with no command. Nobody needed to wake anybody up.[6]

FIRST LIGHT

The dawn in Viet Nam and the sunset were fairly predictable all year round, with twelve hours of daylight being the norm. First light was around 5.30 a.m. and dawn at six o'clock. While the patrol was sitting on their packs waiting for first light they would go through the practice of preparing themselves for the day's patrol. Ian Stiles remembered the daily practice in his patrol:

You had a signal mirror or heliograph to signal choppers and it was part of every guy's escape kit that you wore on your belt. But we would sit down—when we were sitting on our packs waiting for it to be light—and we would do up our make-up. Different guys had different patterns—like I used to have a base of American Revlon green, then have that horrible brown Australian stuff in stripes. After a while when you had about five or six days' beard growth, you would get all these dags of cam cream hanging off you.[7]

During the day the patrol will sweat heavily carrying their packs and moving and standing for long periods in the hot, humid jungle. Their shirts would be soaking wet by the time the day had drawn to an end and many SAS men would carry a second shirt to sleep in and before they moved for the day,

Ian 'Bagza' Stiles cammed up on patrol with 3 Squadron in 1969. The dry season made camouflage and movement extremely difficult for the patrols trying to gain information on enemy camps. *Photo courtesy of Ian Stiles*

You would have a dry shirt that you had slept in. You take that dry shirt off, put it in a waterproof bag, and put your wet shirt back on—in the dark.[8]

The men slept with their clothes and boots on even if they were soaking wet so that if they had to move in a hurry, or if necessary, engage the enemy, they would not be caught (literally) with their pants down:

I used mainly a piece of camouflaged parachute silk to put over myself at night. You always slept with your boots on. We were issued with the American canvas-sided combat boots that had drain holes in the instep. These allowed our feet to breathe and were far better than the Australian GP boots. When checking your feet, you would remove one boot at a time and shake or wring the sock out, but you would always put that boot back on and do it up before removing the other boot.[9]

As the patrol departs its LUP, the 2IC is the last man out. Andy Nucifora was very particular about the sign they made as they slept on the ground in the night LUP:

> I always slept on the deck in Viet Nam. You just didn't have the cover to do otherwise. When I got up in the morning I went through the LUP and tried to cover up the marks with dead leaves. I picked it up and tried to keep it as natural-looking as possible. Any small saplings that were in the way, we tied them back, just very gently so we wouldn't split the bark. In the morning we let them go carefully and straightened them up and I would have a look as patrol 2IC and made sure it was always clear.[10]

MOVING

The light is now good enough to be able to fire through the iron sights of their rifles and engage a target and the patrol wants to move from its night LUP and get away from where they have been stationary for the last twelve hours. Leaving the night LUP was not simply a case of everyone standing up and leaving. The movement of an SAS patrol is very deliberate, very slow and always 100 per cent secure. Patrol commander Joe Van Droffelaar had a very well tried and true procedure for getting started in the morning:

> About half an hour before first light we used to wake the blokes half asleep, and I used to say to the blokes, once you have been woken you are not to move. There's a reason for that, because the senses need to start get going again. There's nothing worse than as soon as you are awake that five blokes start to move all over the frigging place. I used to say just hang loose. The only bloke that would move would be me—first, and then individually other patrol members would move whatever they had to do in the LUP to prepare themselves for the morning routine.
>
> Generally what I used to do then, because I used to be in the guts of the patrol, and about fifteen minutes before first light I used to stand up. I would have my gear on and my barrel pointing towards the ground. Most soldiers have the

weapon pointing horizontally of course and when he makes a move, the jungle moves at the same time, so we always had that barrel pointing downwards. And if there's any enemy happen to be lying there on his guts, nobody would be able to put a round through him.

So I used to stand up, have my gear on and weapon down. The next bloke would be my scout, the third bloke would be my 2IC, fourth would be the medic and last but not least would be the sig, because he was the closest to me and he generally was the last bloke to stand up. Once we all stood up we would be standing there for at least ten minutes after first light. Once we had done that, each individual man would take about two paces forward so that we could enlarge the LUP now and we would then individually sit down. We would sit down, knowing that everything was reasonably safe. We would sit for another ten to fifteen minutes and make no movement whatsoever until the actual air that surrounds the LUP gets moving. What I mean by 'get moving' is that the air tends to be not as thick in the early part of the morning, and as time goes by it tends to thin out a bit. And of course you start to hear things. Particularly the two things we were most concerned about was any noise and any smell. Once we were satisfied with that, we would then move out. The first morning LUP, the one after the night insertion, I would never have breakfast there. I would always move off. Whether I moved 20 metres or whether I moved 100 metres, I would never use that spot for breakfast just in case the enemy had or may have closed in during the night.[11]

Peter Schuman did what Joe Van Droffelaar did because he wanted to move from where someone might have inadvertently made a noise during the night, or the enemy might have been able to pinpoint where the patrol was likely to be headed. Peter Schuman wanted to leave the night LUP as soon as possible after first light and

> get into a safe area where we had good vision all around us, sit on our packs for another twenty minutes to half an hour, just becoming part of the J. By this time it would be broad daylight and then two at a time we would brew up. Breakfast was usually just a cup of coffee and a pack of peanuts for energy. And then we would continue on our patrol or, if we

were doing a close surveillance, I would issue orders then for that particular phase.[12]

LOOKING, LOOKING

The distance a patrol moved during the day would depend entirely on what their task was, what the enemy were doing and the area the patrol had to move through. Foot movement was very slow compared to a normal infantry platoon in Viet Nam. A rifle platoon could expect to patrol for up to 9 kilometres in a single day. They have the firepower to meet most challenges and have the radio and other support in case things get too much to handle. The SAS recce patrol on the other hand is living on its wits and cunning and using stealth as its primary means of survival. It can only talk to its base at Nui Dat on CW Morse Code because it is so far from base and is normally out of gun and mortar range. The recce patrol is looking for indicators that the enemy has moved through the area. All Australian infantry soldiers refer to this as 'sign' and they train to look for it.

> What we were looking for was those tracks, those tell-tale signs and, as soon as we found it, we then started to loop along the track. Just forget the area, it didn't matter, make a rough bearing towards the target. As soon as we hit the track and saw a footprint going this way or that way, or a scuff mark, or anything—a piece of mould underneath a leaf that might have been flicked up the day before when it was raining—we then started to loop. We would go about 200 metres back into the jungle, and then come back, hit it again and then start to plot the track on the map. Then we would start to get the tell-tale signs: the flies, the smell of the shit pit of the camp, the sounds of someone chopping and you knew you were on pay dirt.[13]

A patrol might move only 1 kilometre in a day but there was no set benchmark. Every patrol was different. The movement routine was to move a short distance and then halt to listen, much like a caterpillar creeping through the jungle. The distance between men who usually moved in single file was probably only 15 metres from the first to the last man—at most.

Patrolling was very slow and 500 metres would not be an unusual day. Very tiring, you're on your feet for a hell of a time. We would sustain that for about 35 or 40 minutes and then we would just rest for ten minutes. It was all about being part of the jungle.[14]

RADIO SCHEDS

One thing the patrol had to do every day was make contact with the squadron headquarters. Every patrol of the eight that were deployed at any one time would have a different time schedule in which to come up on their HF radio using CW and Morse Code and send a coded word or message with a coding system called the one-time letter pad. This was a very secure, short-time, code system that kept the messages brief and meant the patrol wasn't transmitting over a long period of time. Signal troop sergeant Barry Standen worked in the squadron radio shack attached to the squadron headquarters and operations room and explained the system:

> You would have two HF frequencies and half would come up on one and the other half on the other. There was a common emergency HF frequency for everyone and it was common for the whole of the bloody Viet Nam War and you would have different frequencies maybe for different scheds. For example, if you use an ionospheric prediction chart, it would tell you what frequencies were best at what time of the day for this month and you would work out and say okay for your morning sched you will use channel one, for your afternoon sched use channel three and channel two might be your emergency common.
>
> And if ever you had something come up on your emergency channel you knew that there was a problem because the emergency channel was something out of the ordinary. Each patrol had an hour in the morning and an hour in the afternoon, or they might only have 30 minutes morning and 30 minutes afternoon, depends on how many [patrols] were out at the time.[15]

One of the essential elements required to be sent was the patrol location state, called a locstat. Most of the other information the patrol was sent out to find would not be sent back at that time unless it was something absolutely extraordinary. The patrol debrief was the place to unload all that information—after the five-day patrol. Barry Standen detailed the basic information or situation report (sitrep) they wanted back at base:

> We had it down pretty bloody well that they could send a locstat in three cipher groups. That is all it was and that included the authentication and a grid reference. They could send a sitrep in about ten groups and after that it just depended on what they had to report. In essence they wouldn't send a lot of detail over the radio at any time unless they were asked and they would wait to come back after the exfil and then they would do their patrol debrief. They may have sent a sitrep in to say, 'an OP at such and such' and when they come back for the debrief they would say exactly what happened in there but they wouldn't try and say that information back. The idea was that they sent the minimum amount of stuff over the airwaves.[16]

A patrol could come up at any time and send a message, as the operations room and radio shack were manned 24 hours a day. Barry Standen continues:

> If they were in the shit they would just use the three-letter code word and then from that they would back that up with a communication saying that they required exfil and there would be a code word for 'require exfil'—three letter. So he might send 'Cat'. Twenty minutes later when they had pulled out of the contact area he might send 'Dog', require exfil and the squadron commander would have to work out whether he supported that—depending on the tactical situation because that patrol may be in there for a particular reason: to stir up, to find out, see what they've got; so what they may do is whip in, pull them out and put them back in 2 kilometres down the road. Drop the same people in.[17]

Barry 'Muka' Standen outside his tent. As a member of 152 Signal Squadron he participated in four operational tours of duty with the SAS. *Photo courtesy of Barry Standen*

THE COMMS LUP

The time spent in a comms LUP was kept to the minimum because the signaller has an aerial strung out and he is tapping away, albeit very quietly, on a Morse key. Two of the patrol are unable to keep their eyes peeled for the enemy because one is setting up his radio and the other is encoding the message he wants to send.

> From the time they pulled up for a comm stop to the time they closed the radio up, a good operator, you're probably looking at ten to twelve minutes and that includes encoding your five groups to say what's going on. About ten to twelve minutes because once the signaller had the patrol commander trained on the comms requirement, the patrol commander would work out how to pull into his LUP and he would work out that he has got to march on a bearing of 300 for the next 50 metres. He would give the sig the nod and the sig would

A patrol signaller, Pte 'Ticka' Gray, making a radio sched during a patrol with 3 Squadron in 1969. *Photo courtesy of Ian Stiles*

tie the wire up with a slip knot on it as they were walking into their LUP. So you wouldn't actually have to walk out and put the wire up, so the last 20 metres you were actually running your wire out.[18]

One of the times a patrol felt vulnerable was when they were conducting a comms LUP. Ian Conaghan was a signaller in Borneo and did it on his first tour of Viet Nam for a while. He also had to look after the LUP as a patrol commander on his second tour. He talks about why he felt vulnerable when getting ready to send a sched:

The patrol radio in Viet Nam was the PRC 64, an HF set, quite a tiny radio. Its major drawback was it had four fixed channels which were crystal controlled. It was all CW—even though the set was capable of voice, we never used it. As with all HF sets, the performance is very much antenna-critical, so the lengths of the antenna and so on have to match your frequencies.

The communications LUP was always a very vulnerable time. First off, you've got the sig on the set, who is no longer a set of eyes and ears and looking after any part of the perimeter of the LUP. The patrol commander is also tied up looking after either encoding or decoding.

My sig did all the encoding and decoding. Some patrol commanders preferred to do it themselves, but I figured this guy is a sig, he's a specialist in the patrol. He carries the code books—why the hell shouldn't he do all the encoding and decoding. But you certainly checked it. Just one letter transposition can turn the whole message into just total garbage. I, as a patrol commander, would always check his encoding. You would be crazy if you don't do that because anybody can make a mistake—but that time was fairly critical.

And the wire for the antenna that you had to run out also meant that there was a great possibility of someone walking into your antenna—who was then walking into your LUP—so that was always a danger.[19]

MISSING A SCHED

If the patrol missed a radio sched it was no cause for great alarm because the enemy might have prevented the patrol from establishing a radio sched LUP position and they were not secure enough on the ground to send a sched.

The duty signaller would notify the OPSO [operations offficer] that a patrol has missed a sched. Nothing would happen at that stage. You could miss a sched because tactically it might be inappropriate to try and communicate. If they missed the second sched of the day, the OPSO had the option of over-flying. He would put up a FAC [forward air controller] or he would put up a slick ship or something which would over-fly the last known area. They wouldn't try and communicate, they would just over-fly the area to see if the patrol on the ground tried to communicate through their URC–10 or whatever just to say, 'Hey, my HF's broken down' or whatever. And if they missed the first sched of the next day, well then the squadron commander would start to be thinking about putting in another patrol into the last location.[20]

PARK TIME

The SAS patrols found that patrolling in the middle of the day was not a good idea. Apart from being the hottest and most debilitating time of day, it had the potential to be dangerous, as Peter Schuman recalls:

> We had had a couple of nasty scares by patrolling through that midday period and at one stage we did walk into an enemy rest area, but most of them—if not all of them—were asleep. We were able to extract ourselves in fairly neat order, but we decided from that time on from about 11.30 a.m. until 2.30 p.m. that we would do the same as the baddies and just knock off for a midday siesta.[21]

As an infantryman who spent most of his time trying to search and clear designated areas within set timelines it was a revelation to the author to hear of 'park time'. However, the idea is one of good commonsense, provided you have a boss who is prepared to let you sit on your butt for a couple of hours. However, to be compromised was almost akin to failure if a patrol had not finished their task and too many resources had been expended just getting the SAS patrol into the area of operations. Park time's origins were explained by a forward scout, and later patrol commander, 'Bagza' Stiles:

> The idea was that because you were moving through the jungle and making a little noise and the Vietnamese or Viet Cong who had actually stopped for a sleep in their hammocks or having a midday siesta and they of course would be very quiet. I suppose there was a good chance that we would bump into them. So the risk was high in the middle of the day and we would actually stop in an LUP for 'park time' and just rest and listen.[22]

The daily routine of the patrol continued after park time. Peter Schuman continues his description of a day in the life of a patrol:

> From then until last light it was patrolling again. When we started to get to toward the end of the day, that was the danger period. It was a natural instinct, it was when animal instincts took over and it was a case of 'Where's somewhere that's safe for the night because darkness is coming around?' We were never sort of away from civilisation in the Viet Nam context, but it was that preservation thing of, 'Gee, I must surround myself with some protection against the darkness for the night.' We would eat about 4.30 p.m. or five o'clock before it got dark, then stand to and then go into a night routine. I did not do any patrolling at night. It was too dangerous, it was the fear of putting your foot into it, you just never knew what was around. You can only do the surveillance type work if you knew what was around the next corner, what was around the next tree, what was on the other side of that ridgeline. We could do that by reading sign on the way up to it. And if we couldn't see it, one of your senses was taken out. It just wasn't worth having a go.[23]

DAY'S END

As the day drew to a close the patrol would start looking for a place to hide for the night. They now had a better feel for the jungle in which they were operating than for the first night LUP but it still meant paying close attention to their security as they went through the LUP drill. Ian Stiles is thankful they always did a loop before pulling up:

> When you were moving, just before a halt, you would always do a loop, to come back on your patrol track, so the patrol commander would signal, 'Okay, stop here', and the scout would move around to the right or left and then you would loop back on yourself so you're actually back close to your own track so you could ambush any follow-up or someone tracking us—which actually happened to us once.[24]

Joe Van Droffelaar goes into some detail to explain exactly how his patrol would set themselves up for an LUP:

I had this habit of getting the 2IC to hang back. We would stand still for at least fifteen minutes, no movement, then I would send out my two blokes, that is to the area which I had not cleared. If need be, that process would take a further ten minutes or so, then the guys would be called back and individually then they would sit down. And it was the sig would go down first, followed by the scout, followed by the medic and then the 2IC and then me the patrol commander. So everything was now in the reverse to how we started the day.[25]

This insistence by Joe Van Droffelaar on set procedures and formations had a great deal of commonsense and practicality about it as he explains:

At no time did I ever point out to the blokes where he had to sit, because my LUP was exactly the same as the formation of my contact drill on the ground. When I did a creek crossing that formation is exactly the same as a contact drill on the ground, or when I did a track crossing—it's exactly the same.

So it was a total learning process that as the guys moved into the LUP, they were in a contact drill formation. The enemy could hit us from anywhere in 360 degrees, and I knew that I could have five weapons firing in any given direction.

I was the last bloke to sit down in the LUP and we would sit there for another ten minutes or so, and in those days you used to have a smoke. Depending on where you were in relation to the enemy, of course, but generally I would light up a smoke, and the cigarette would be flicked from one to another for whoever wanted to have a suck on this darn thing, and of course all movement was slowed down like a slow motion picture—so to speak. All smoke was blown in towards the ground and that was it.

Nobody used to talk. Field signals were very limited, because of our build-up training both in Australia and New Guinea and what we were doing was what we had been doing for a long time. Nothing really had to be done out of the ordinary. SOPs don't change and they would get a nudge or something telling them that makan [the Malay word for food, or in this sense to eat food] had to take place and they knew exactly what to do.[26]

The drills that the patrols went through had been rehearsed until they could do them blindfolded. There was very little need for voice communication and if it was required it would be done quietly directly into the ear and at very close range or at worst a very soft stage whisper. Silence was the key. The patrol was now at that stage of getting close to the enemy and needed stealth to ensure they would not be compromised. It is day two and tomorrow the patrol will be deep into the enemy's backyard.

11

GETTING CLOSE

MOVING IN

The SAS patrol is now in its area of operations and is closing in on the quarry. Quite often a patrol would be sent in to confirm the presence of an enemy group in a camp or if the enemy were using a particular track system or transiting from one area to another. On a recce patrol they would observe the camp or track, record what they had seen and extract from the area without being compromised. The intelligence value from that type of operation is regarded by most SAS men as being as valuable if not more valuable than a hit on two enemy walking down a track and then being chased out of the area. Ian Stiles participated in both recce and recce/ambush patrols but thought:

> The intelligence information is far better than kills. It even went so far as you would go through a dead Charlie's pockets, and grab as much papers and stuff off him before you even grab hold of his rifle. You had to get away from this mentality of 'I've got to have that as a trophy'. An AK–47 is a good trophy, it looks a lot better when you march in and say 'Look what I've got' instead of a sheaf of papers with all the members of *D445* on it or something. But that is a thousand times more

important than the AK, and that was sort of instilled in you. Even though you wanted to do some brassing up sometimes— when you had a perfect opportunity—you had it drilled into you that you had to be quiet and not compromise the patrol if you were on a recce patrol.[1]

Searching an area was hard work because the patrol is unable to move freely if it is to stay totally undetected. The patrol is allocated about six grid squares in total which is surrounded by a kilometre all round of 'no go area' for other troops. This allows for errors in navigation and to ensure that other friendly forces do not go lobbing artillery or calling for air strikes in an area where the SAS are operating. While the patrol is closing in on the target, patrolling or foot movement becomes very slow and arduous, as Ian Conaghan recalls:

> We would work four grid squares in about five, six or seven days. And those four grid squares would take us all of that time, because the term 'patrolling' is often misconstrued by people who think that patrolling is moving from point A to point B, but a fair proportion of that time we may very well just be standing and listening, or we may divert off our path for maybe 70 or even 100 metres in a direction because we had heard something or because of the lie of the land we suspected that there may be something over there. And then we would come back onto our original track. I would venture to suggest there is much more time spent listening, than there is actually moving.[2]

The seasons in Viet Nam often had a huge impact on how fast a patrol could move without being seen or heard. In the dry season the vegetation thins and is left to dry and rot on the ground. In the wet season the tropical downpours prevent the patrol from being able to hear and often see what is ahead of them. Many patrol members hated patrolling in the dry season, as Bill Hindson says:

> The problem with the dry, and in places it was exacerbated by the Americans defoliating some areas, was that we could see far greater distances which meant that we could also be seen from far greater distances. In addition to that, because of

the very dryness of the leaves and twigs on the ground, in some areas where we might have had reasonable cover from view, we could be heard moving over a long distance. It was like walking on corn flakes. To get a feel for it, you need to spread a packet of Kellogg's Corn Flakes onto a pavement and then try sneaking over them without making any noise. That essentially was the problem—we could be heard over a long distance and lacked foliage to hide us. So we had to adapt to that and that sort of made a change in the pace that we could move, and just how we moved, and how far the patrol could be spread out.[3]

In the wet season the heavy rains made some men distinctly uneasy. Peter Schuman, who had moved over moss forests in Borneo and tippy-toed through the dry leaves of Phuoc Tuy, did not dislike the rain just because he was going to get a wet bum. He saw the rain as a double-edged weapon and felt:

Absolute terror, because you can't hear anything, you can't see. We used to just stop and go into all-round defence and hope that the enemy would not come just blundering through the rain and hoped we didn't have to fight a contact because it was really bad.[4]

The other problem when it rains is that it softens the ground and when a man or animal moves over that wet ground sign is left behind which can be more easily detected than in the dry season when the ground is very much harder. Patrol scout Andy Nucifora was not too fussed by the wet and tried to use it to hide his tracks, but like Bill Hindson drew an analogy with dry breakfast cereals:

The problem you've got is leaving tracks. But then you can be careful with the tracks as well; you can walk slightly closer to the roots of the trees and leave less track and deep mud. Sometimes if you have left really bad footprints you can tidy it up and let the rain wash the rest away, so I preferred the rain because it gave you cover over noise and you can move a little quicker. In the dry it's pretty bad because of the noise factor. It's like walking on Weet-Bix.[5]

The pace that a patrol moves at is determined by several factors, not least the actual presence of the enemy. The amount of vegetation which can cover the movement of the patrol, the amount of dead vegetation littering the jungle floor which was so aptly described by Bill Hindson as walking over corn flakes, and the density of the scrub all impact on how fast the patrol can move without disturbing the branches, leaves or hanging vines. Most things are seen because of shape, size, shine, silhouette or movement and the SAS patrol would be attempting to avoid all of these as it moved towards its objective. Corporal Ian Stiles found himself in the uncomfortable position of having a more senior man dictating a pace which he knew would get them into strife:

> We would only—it depends a lot on the vegetation—make about 1500 metres a day. I remember going with Reg Beesley as his patrol 2IC at one stage and we went very, very fast. As his 2IC, I said, 'Eh look, we're going too fast here, someone's going to fuck up. We're moving too fast, we've got to slow down and just take it easy.' He was a major and I was corporal, but we keep going and the next thing the forward scout has a bloody accidental discharge of his rifle. If you go too fast you make mistakes. I didn't say to Beesley, 'I told you so!' But my dirty look did.[6]

The SAS in Viet Nam had an enviable record for its lack of mine and booby trap incidents. This is most likely because the rate of advance of a patrol was so slow that the members of the patrol had the time to take in their surroundings and actually 'see' what they were looking at. It was only rarely that an SAS patrol was chronically fatigued while patrolling and so their mental alertness kept them away from the hidden menace of mines and booby traps. Patrols did not move at night because it was just too dangerous. Apart from poking someone's eye out, the jungle canopy was often so thick that very little ambient light was able penetrate to the jungle floor. Patrols would be moving blind and as Ron Dempsey says:

> You could lose contact with the men. Some nights it was absolutely pitch black and you couldn't see two feet [600 mm] in front of you; moving along in the dark it would have been

noisy; the enemy would have been laid up anyway and they would have heard you coming. And if anything happened and you had somebody wounded or something like that, or if you got into contact—it would have been almost impossible to get out of it.[7]

SLEEPING AND THE SENSES

While the patrol is moving closer to the enemy, the element of danger reaches very high levels and the men are moving like jungle cats. Their eyes are constantly searching the ground and the trees for signs that the enemy have passed that way and during the constant listening halts their ears are straining for sounds foreign to the bush. The olfactory senses come into play and a keen nose was a bonus. Even at night the men slept fitfully and more likely dozed than truly slept, as Trevor Roderick relates:

> Your senses are heightened. We didn't have sentries at night—we slept with our ears open. Because we kept waking up. A bloody twig would fall and you would wake up. Even as a smoker, a curry eater, you could smell them, you'd really smell them.[8]

The sleeping men would be in an LUP and as previously described be within touching distance of each other. During the cooler wet season when the men were constantly wet, other factors came into play and made closing with the enemy even more tricky, as Bill Hindson explains:

> When we got to the wet season there were a lot of coughs and colds, and there was great concern because of the involuntary coughing at night. We had real problems with that. It certainly became a problem with people who snored. We would usually find as soon as someone started making a noise, the person either side went 'whack'—hand over the face. I was out on one patrol, when in the middle of the night a patrol member yelled out, 'The nigger did it!' In the middle of the night! And there was this 'wham', all of these hands

over the face and whoever it was was instantly awake. Everybody was instantly on the alert, it was just unbelievable.[9]

For those who led the patrols, the responsibility is heightened and becomes a heavy burden especially when the patrol is moving in and getting close and personal with the enemy. Patrol leader Peter Schuman found that sleep eluded him whenever he went out on patrol:

> When you're leading a small patrol, every leaf dropping wakes you up. You just can't live on your nerves. You just don't get any rest at all. It's like a nightmare, just a continual feeling of responsibility. It must be the jungle, I suppose.[10]

IT'S A ZOO OUT THERE

Many different animals inhabit the jungle besides the enemy, as the patrols were to find out when they were a long way from civilisation and using the bush to hide in. Ron Dempsey remembered one particular night:

> We were up towards the northern part of the province and we felt like something was following us and we went into an LUP and propped for the night. We could smell this 'cat' smell. It was a big cat, like an ocelot or lynx or something like that. We thought it might have been a tiger, so no-one slept that night. No-one went to sleep. Everyone just sat there with a knife and a pistol in his hand and it went around the outside of the LUP, and you could hear it and smell it moving around. And of course the guys are saying in a stage whisper, 'Did you hear the story about the guy that got dragged away by a tiger?'.[11]

WATERING

The patrol would try to carry all the water it needed for the duration of a patrol because resupplying from local streams meant going into areas where the ground does not suit a tactical fire-fight because the enemy are higher than you and can better observe you and the clear stream area offers both an obstacle to movement and a clear path for observation. The enemy used the watercourses for resupply constantly, except where their camps and bunker systems were located away from streams, where they dug wells often up to 20 metres in depth to ensure a safe water supply. For a five-man patrol with a limited set of eyes to keep a lookout, a water resupply could be a long process. Ian Conaghan recounts the problems and one type of water resupply from aircraft:

> Getting water from streams that you would cross became a tactical operation in itself. That was the other good thing about Pommy water bottles. Their big wide necks were just great for scooping up a full bottle of water just straight out of the stream. The American bottles, you can't do that with the glug, glug, glug, glug. In Viet Nam we had to work out our own patrol drills on how we would take a water resupply.
>
> I think my patrol only ever took a water drop once and we trialled a lot of methods for taking water from the air. One of the most successful ones, there was a long plastic sausage bag and it wasn't a single bag, in fact it was something like nine or ten bags all inside each other and just tied off in a big knot and that was just thrown out of a fixed-wing aircraft. Brilliant. The theory behind it was that half a dozen of these bags would burst on impact on the outer skin, but some of the bags would still retain their integrity. It was a great idea actually, very, very successful.[12]

Trevor Roderick remembered the problem for those men who were not big around the waist and trying to carry several water bottles on their web belt:

> We used to carry so many bloody water bottles around our waist the skinny guys used to have all sorts of problems. But we were probably carrying six water bottles and perhaps a wing—those little bladder things. But getting water, going down to a creek, you're vulnerable.[13]

In the dry season the extremely high temperatures of Viet Nam would quickly take their toll on the water supply the SAS patrol could carry. Some patrols ran into deadly serious dehydration problems, as Joe Van Droffelaar experienced on one patrol:

> There was one time when I physically had run out of water— we had one water bottle left amongst five blokes. On the fifth day there was contact made and I could not get to my extraction point. A rope extraction or winch extraction was impossible because the enemy was firing up at the choppers as they came anywhere near my AO.
>
> So by that time we had half a bottle and we were swigging this bottle in between the blokes and this water was getting thicker and didn't taste too well. And it got to a point that our movement of no more than about six paces was very difficult to do. No sleeping, you could not sleep, there was hunger there but you could not eat because all we had was dehydrated rations.
>
> So I took the risk of getting the chopper to come in to drop off a jerry can. Although the chopper was fired at and a round went through its tail, we did get our water. But the enemy that was in the close proximity may have only been one or maybe two and never really moved in towards the LUP.
>
> So we quickly filled up and took the jerry can which was only a third full then, and we moved into another LUP which was all pre-planned and sucked on this jerry can within that next 24 hours and then started to plan an extraction point. But at least now we had the ability to move, because we had fluid down our guts and we knew we could make our extraction point. But it was a bit of touch and go there for a while.[14]

RECCE/AMBUSH

As the war progressed in Viet Nam and the area under Australian control spread outwards from the Task Force base, the SAS patrols were pushed deeper and deeper into the outlying areas of Phuoc Tuy Province. As they were sent farther afield, the opportunity arose to conduct harassing operations to keep the enemy off balance and ensure that they felt they could never move from one location to another in safety. Once a patrol had completed its initial task, it was given free rein to ambush targets of opportunity. The art of the Claymore ambush now came into play and became a very successful technique for the SAS recce/ambush patrols. The layout of an SAS Claymore ambush patrol was usually similar to that used by Nev Farley's patrol, as illustrated.

> Normally with a five-man patrol, I used to always put two Claymores in the centre, two on the outside of the killing ground, two for flank protection, and one to the rear and that was seven. We would have at least one each and a couple of spares. My ambush set-up was normally four up front and one out the back. Sometimes I might put them out to a flank, but normally that was the set-up.[15]

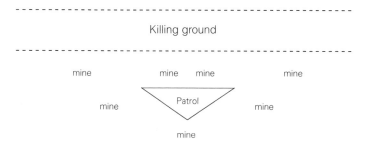

An example of a Claymore ambush as used by Neville Farley's five-man patrol

Bill Hindson's patrol soon became one of the patrols that was tasked more often with recce/ambush patrols than recce tasks and the ambush became a part of their rehearsal routine before deploying. Ambushing at night was not an option for Hindson, as he explains:

> The standard procedure was that when we put in ambushes, we occupied them by day and walked out of them by night. We didn't occupy an ambush by night. Because if we were close to a track and someone was coming down it, we would be unwilling to trigger it because we wouldn't necessarily know how many, as we couldn't see what the hell was happening. So we would pick up an ambush at night and

move back 100 metres or so and move back in again at first light and occupy it.[16]

Hindson details the manner in which his patrol set about occupying and springing their ambush:

We would know roughly the area that we wanted to go to. I always looked for the perfect area, of course, which had a huge thicket of bamboo on either side, that nobody could rush through. It would be really nice to have an area where we had maybe 10 to 20 metres or so to the track, with fairly clean, clear sight to the track and, if possible, to either side. And then we wanted reasonable cover. So we looked for buttress trees, logs or ant-hills to hide behind and still give ourselves a reasonably clear view of the track. We didn't want too much in the way of dead ground on the other side. So we wanted a pretty flat area in order to give ourselves the best possible opportunity to see VC approaching without exposing ourselves. We often set the ambush so that the killing area had a log they had to step over, and a branch they had to duck under. So, while they're doubled over and then bunched up the people behind them, we would set it off.

With a five-man patrol, we had two people in the killing zone, the medic and the forward scout usually on the flanks to guard against an approach from the sides and the signaller at the back. The signaller would have a Claymore facing rearwards, the guys on either flank would have a Claymore facing to either side and the guys in the killing ground would have a couple facing along the track. We always used to rehearse these beaut drills to meet most anticipated situations. We got real cocky at one stage and we were joking back in camp over a couple of beers about whether we would kill just one person if they came along down the track or would we let them go and look for something bigger? If there was something bigger, would we let them go and then look for something smaller? What if it was a bunch of women? Would we kill just anybody? We got real picky and choosy.

In May we were in the process of setting our Claymores in the killing zone and a woman came through the killing zone. Everybody was so astounded that we just froze and let her go! I was trying to figure out what to do because we were up and standing in a fairly clear area, we couldn't figure out whether she had seen us and said nothing, whether she didn't see us at all, or whether she just beetled on through and was about to go and tell someone.

She was obviously unarmed and we went 'Oh, hell, what will we do now?' Chase her quick! So I organised two guys to go up the track and try and find her. Of course they went along the track just 100 metres or so—they didn't want to get too far away—and they couldn't find her. She had just disappeared.

So they came back and there was an argument between John O'Keefe and myself about whether we had been compromised or not and it got quite heated. He wanted to go and I wanted to stay. On that occasion we did have a good thick clump of bamboo on the flank where she had gone, so we stayed. Four baddies came along soon after and we knocked them over and I was highly relieved.

We always just initiated with the Claymores as the problem with the small arms was as soon as there was any noise the enemy were off, so we always wanted to use the Claymore first.[17]

Springing a Claymore ambush is best done by simply firing the Claymores and if they are sited properly there should be little left to do but search the remains of the victims who have been blasted by these terrible weapons. It was not uncommon in Claymore ambushes to find the enemy missing the lower parts of their bodies as the blast and pellets acted like a scythe at a height just below waist level. In Viet Nam there were always things going bang in the night—and day—and a Claymore ambush would sound like a bomb or a mine going off, which was a common occurrence. If the patrol could avoid firing their personal weapons they would, unless there were more enemy in the killing ground of the ambush than the Claymore mine lethal arcs could cover, as Bill Hindson continues:

So we initiated with the Claymores. That was usually myself as I had the responsibility of initiating—unless we were seen or there was some other action, in which case any others in the killing area could initiate it. Usually it went Claymores first, then we each fired a magazine through the killing area and then we would get up, assault forward and carry out whatever action was needed if there was anybody still moving.[18]

175

Lying in ambush not moving for hours on end requires an enormous amount of self-discipline and self-control. Murphy's Law works overtime in ambushes and according to an army adage if you are ambushing the intersection of two tracks the enemy will take the third. The patrols have to be able to engage the enemy without giving away their position and the position they adopt on the ground in the ambush site varies. Bill Hindson found that it

> depended on the foliage. Lying was a problem in that it was too damned easy to nod off to sleep. If you were able to get a nice buttress tree or an ant-hill where you could easily sit cross-legged or something. It was better sitting up, if you've got the cover, because you can move better, but certainly you're more exposed. The majority of our ambushes and other contacts were initiated by us and not by the enemy, and because we were sitting up, we had a better view, and could also move our weapons far more easily and could actually put it into the shoulder and aim it. But if you are lying down, we could only get limited range of sight on our weapons because of lower foliage and stuff in the way. I always had a problem with firing in an ambush if lying down, because by shooting up we often shot too high.[19]

The Claymore ambushes were a lot more successful than firing into the enemy group using small arms weapons, even on automatic, as the fire tends to be frontal fire with a limited arc of fire and has a limited chance to collect moving targets. Bill Hindson's patrol had a set procedure for searching the people caught in the ambush:

> On my very first ambush patrol which didn't have Claymores, we had a six-man patrol, with Sergeant 'Slag' O'Keefe and myself in the killing ground. When we triggered the ambush by firing into a group of four VC, a strange thing happened. We wounded two and they were still struggling around and had a bit of fight in them. The other two escaped and soon we heard them calling out further up the track. It then came time—as we had done in rehearsals—for myself and Slag to move forward and we had a situation of having to shoot the VC as they were struggling to aim their weapons at us. As the VC that I shot was beyond the track, I crossed over to search

him. Slag therefore 'covered' me while I went across the track to search the bodies. From that time on, that became the standard practice in our ambushes—Slag O'Keefe covered me whilst I searched for maps, papers and weapons. Whilst we were thus engaged, two of the members of the patrol would observe to the flanks of the ambush site in case any of the enemy tried to come at us from the sides, and the signaller would be behind us covering the rear end.[20]

IN THE SHIT

It becomes evident after talking to men from the Viet Nam SAS patrols that a five-man patrol would often take on a larger group of enemy if they knew they had the drop on them and had a good chance of making their escape after the confusion of an ambush being sprung. The noise and blast from a bank of Claymores is unbelievably loud and shatters the silence of the jungle with an enormous force. It often renders those who have not been caught in the ambush into a state of shock and gives the patrol time to effect their withdrawal.

But sometimes a patrol doesn't fire on the enemy, as Joe Van Droffelaar experienced when he was on a recce of a very large enemy camp with his scout. The remainder of the five-man patrol—the 2IC, medic and sig—were all back in an LUP some 30 metres distant while Joe and the scout were tippy-toeing around the camp. I had asked him if he ever had occasion when he didn't fire upon the enemy even though the opportunity was there. His reply was amazing:

> I had moved into an enemy camp, no that's not right. I stumbled onto an enemy camp knowing that there was a likelihood of being an enemy camp and when I did get into this enemy camp, it was huge. It had been bombed, B–52 bombed on either side but leaving a strip of jungle, 150 metres wide by about 400 metres long. And when I got through the actual obstacle, which is all the B–52 craters, I got into this camp and all these bunkers and all this medical equipment.
>
> But I straight away realised that it was a staging camp and as I was slowly moving through knowing that it's not really

Sergeant Joe Van Droffelaar outside the Officers' and Sergeants' Mess on SAS Hill, Nui Dat in October 1969. He is wearing the US camouflage uniform and carrying an early version of the M203 being an M16 rifle with a 40 mm grenade-launcher underneath. Van Droffelaar was awarded the Military Medal for bravery whilst in Viet Nam. *Photo courtesy of Joe Van Droffelaar*

the right thing to do, being a bit inquisitive, and trying to work out who these bloody gangsters were, as I was looking, noises came moving through this camp and a larger force was starting to move through. So we quickly moved into this bloody pen, a buffalo pen. It was well done—it had all the bamboo and vines and the shit was about 30 to 40 cm deep, so we squatted in that, threw the shit over us and sat there as we saw this very large enemy force moving through.

But I was not game enough to open up fire on that particular occasion. We were in enough shit already and I don't think I would have ever got out of the shit.[21]

The large enemy force Joe Van Droffelaar talked about numbered over 150.

PATROL CASUALTIES

One aspect of an SAS patrol which people do not really want to mention, as it brings out a dichotomy in policy and actuality, is what action the patrol will take to extract from the situation if a patrol member is wounded. With a five-man patrol, there are four men left to carry the casualty, being two to carry and one forward to lead the way and one to cover the rear as they withdraw. The British 22 SAS standard operating procedure for this sort of action in Borneo was that the patrol would try to hide the casualty somewhere, take off in the other direction, escape and evade and then come back and try to get him.

Of all the SAS people I've spoken to about casualties, that never happened. They talked about it—but they never did it! The bond between the patrol members is too strong. The only time it was ever done was in Borneo when Paul Denehy was gored by a rogue bull elephant, but that was with a four-man patrol and he was the signaller and the patrol had no other option but to leave him with one of the patrol while the other two members sought help.

Ron Dempsey was asked what he thought about the idea of leaving a mate and if the patrol would hide the wounded man and escape and evade to effect a later extraction.

> I think the guys would probably stay with him and stick it out. It was certainly our thing that if anyone was wounded, the closest guy next to him would pick him up, we would reform, break contact, treat the wounded and get out.[22]

Even the thought of losing a patrol member by being separated was enough cause for concern, as several patrol commanders admitted it was the one thing they never wanted to face when deep in the enemy's backyard. Trevor Roderick was leading a straight recce patrol when he was faced with just such a situation:

> We found a camp, probably a platoon-sized camp, I suppose. We did a close recce of it. My 2IC, Billy Harris, did an outstanding recce on it really, and I had all sorts of trouble getting him out, getting him back. On the way out, we ran

into a sentry. I killed the sentry, we legged it and the next morning, because we had been compromised, the policy was to come out.

The next morning we were moving to an LZ and that's when we had Billy Harris and myself across the track. It was only a narrow track, the other two on the other side of the track and I saw a section of enemy (about ten men) coming down the track. So again, I opened up on them, and that was probably the worst moment of my life because we did our normal RV thing and we were missing Billy Harris and I didn't want to be the first patrol commander to lose a guy and that was probably the worst moment. It might sound silly but it really was.

We met up with Billy at the second RV and the conversation went something like this: Billy Harris said words to the effect, 'Where have you lot been?' I said, 'Where the fuck have you been? I'm gonna kill ya!' or words to that effect. The other two patrol members said, 'Can we have this discussion somewhere else please?' I was going to kill him because I was so frightened. And then we were winched out. Not under fire but the Viet Cong were following up when they fire their signal system using single shots and so forth— they were after us.[23]

Ian Stiles felt very similar after a contact with the enemy and he thought that he had lost one of his patrol members wounded when he was leading a patrol up in the far north of Phuoc Tuy Province. He admitted he often thought about what he would do if a bloke went down and his reaction was akin to Roderick's outburst:

It was always in the back of your mind. And then you really, really worried about what you would actually do, if things happened, how you would cover him. Up in the May Taos, it was pretty short and sharp contact. We pepper-potted out of this contact and I threw a grenade at the enemy and it seemed to shut them up. I was looking at the patrol and one guy was missing. I couldn't find him, I thought he was back at the RV, and I thought, 'Shit, I've lost him', and I was pretty worried but shortly he turned up. I was sort of chastising this bloke like he was a little kid. You kind of blow your stack at them because you were more worried about losing anyone than anything else. I think it's part of human nature.[24]

If a casualty was taken, the patrol had a drill to get him out. Ron Dempsey ran through the drill for his patrol:

> The first thing was that you would move in and protect the casualty, the medic would do his work on it and see what it was; at the same time the sig would be bashing up a message to squadron headquarters saying 'We're in contact and we've got a casualty'—that's provided you had broken contact. The first thing would be to break contact, carting the casualty with you, and one of the guys would just pick him up and move.[25]

BACK AT NUI DAT

Meanwhile back at Nui Dat, while the SAS patrols are tippy-toeing around Phuoc Tuy Province, the operations room and the signallers in the radio shack are maintaining a 24-hour listening watch in case a patrol gets into real strife and cannot wait for a sched to contact the HQ. The signallers from 152 Sig Troop lived with, drank with and were an integral part of the SAS squadron, being also beret-qualified. They knew the characters and natures of the men out on patrol very, very well. Barry Standen explained how this close relationship came about and how it would impact on what happened when a patrol sent a frantic call for help:

> It's very, very helpful if you're in the radio shack and you get the three-letter word for contact/sighting. It might be 'Cat' which might mean, 'Gazza has just contacted baddies'. And that's all they would send. That was the SOP. They would send, 'Cat, cat, cat, cat' and they would send that twenty times, pull up the aerial and skedaddle.
>
> It was very helpful to know the personalities that may be on the other end of the Morse key at the time and a lot of people say it's a load of claptrap that you can pick who's on the Morse key or the personality of the guy or how stressed they are. I would have to say that after you get to know the guys, if you got a three-letter word sent to you ten times,

Ron Dempsey in his tent preparing to go out on another patrol.
Photo courtesy of Ron Dempsey

once you got to know them, you could definitely say, it's not a real bad contact, because it's coming through nice and precise. It may be a bad one or it might not be because this particular guy is excitable. And you could say with a reasonable degree of accuracy, 'Hey, get the bloody gunships up, this guy's in the shit.' Or you could just trot in there and say, 'We've just had a contact from Three One.'

I believe the troops in the field appreciated the fact that there was this intimate knowledge of what was going on and sometimes a private soldier, a signalman, would read it the way it was sent rather than the content and say to Tony Haley, 'Get the Bushrangers up, there's something going on here.' And it was the fact not only that the operator had the ability, had this knowledge, he knew he could go to Tony Haley, Reg Beesley, or Dale Percival Burnett in 1 Squadron; to walk in and he could say, 'Hey, I'm not sure but I feel . . .' And someone would say, 'That's good enough for me, sig. Go back and do your job, I'll take it from here.' And things would start to happen.[26]

What happens when the patrols got into contact is covered in the next chapter—when the enemy reacted to the SAS patrols getting up close and intensely personal.

12

GETTING PERSONAL

SAS patrols are not out in the jungle to advance to contact as Australian rifle platoons and companies did in Viet Nam. If they had a contact with the enemy, most of the time it was either a deliberate ambush as part of a recce/ambush patrol which was carrying out harassing activities as a secondary role in that patrol, or the enemy walked into the patrol and they had no other choice but to engage the enemy and then exfiltrate. To get away from the enemy takes quite some skill, especially the more aggressive North Vietnamese Army and the Viet Cong Main Force soldiers, who were as well trained and drilled as their Australian infantry counterparts. To survive a contact a patrol must have well defined, well practised drills, good to excellent shooting and weapon-handling skills and a bit of luck does not go astray. Often survival from a contact depends on the harsh reality of 'the quick and the dead'. To show just how this occurs, Bill Hindson relates on how one needed to be alert at all times.

We had four VC walk into our ambush and we didn't have Claymores. So we initiated with small arms and got two out of four. The problem was that as we moved into the killing zone to search the dead, both of them still had fight in them. They were both wounded. One was on his knees and his weapon had been knocked away from him and he was reaching around for it—Slag O'Keefe took care of him; and the other one that was on my side that I was heading for was on his hands and knees and had his weapon and was swinging it around—he had just picked it up and was swinging it around towards me as I approached. So we then had a bit of quick-draw exercise to see who could outdraw the other.[1]

SHOOT AND SCOOT

When engagements are taking place at 15 metres or often less, there is no prize for second place. The man who wins will be the one who is faster to bring his weapon to bear, a more accurate shot and have the better battle-craft skills such as firing position, camouflage and movement in battle. The SAS were trained to carry out a drill called the shoot and scoot. Peter Schuman went to Borneo and his patrol in Viet Nam used the drills passed on to him by 22 SAS:

My refinement of the shoot and scoot was—well it probably wasn't a refinement—it was the confidence you have in one another. If we did have a contact and there were usually more bad guys than there were of us, my scout would go into the kneeling position and just fire from left to right and because he was in the kneeling position he was then firing at the centre of the seen mass of the people that were standing. He would fire a magazine from left to right on automatic, so there's a 'brrrrp'! As soon as he started firing his first shot, I stood my ground in the standing position and fired over his head, single shots into the contact area. Not aiming at a target—this is just kicking up a bit of mayhem with two weapons going 'brrrrp' and 'bang, bang, bang'. As soon as he had finished his magazine he was beside me and reloaded.

I then finished my magazine, I started to reload and we started crawling back and the sig started firing automatic with his Armalite and the medic would then run up to the sig with his SLR and he used to throw either a CS gas canister or an HE grenade strapped to a gas canister or white phosphorus. It didn't matter—it was his call, whatever the scene was. If there was a lot of milling around and he had to blind them, he would use a gas canister or a white phosphorus. If there was only a couple of people that were putting their heads up, he just hurled an HE grenade in amongst them.

Fire his magazine and he had the second compass that was set on the bearing that we had chosen for our escape route. And he would take the scout position. So by now we are all reloaded, we are up to him, the order of march was reversed, except me—I had moved to the number two position. And it was just three of us there, crump, bang, bang, bang, bang. Compass, away we went. Worked every time. It was quick.[2]

To draw a comparison and illustrate how closely the different squadrons operated, Joe Van Droffelaar's squadron used this type of shoot and scoot drill:

> In most cases I used a normal, standard IA [immediate action], squadron SOP contact drill. That is the staggered formation where the forward scout remains and fires down range. Not all contacts are to the front, sometimes slightly at two o'clock, sometimes slightly at ten o'clock, but the primary aim was to get the blokes off the direction of advance by taking one or two steps to either left or right and then pump as much firepower to the front as possible.
>
> Your primary aim was to check your right or to your left and then your front, because in case the enemy decided to do a left hook or a right hook, which happened nine out of ten times in my cases. During this process there is total confusion, particularly for the last two blokes, not for the first three blokes because they knew what the hell was going on. But most contacts were over and done with in about ten seconds flat.[3]

To pull off a shoot and scoot and come out the other end unscathed usually means the patrol will expend a fair amount of ammunition in that initial burst of fire. Bill Hindson's patrol loaded their rifle magazines to assist with this shoot and scoot drill:

> I think when we thought we were getting into something hairy, we wanted to put a lot of tracer into the magazines so that—from the bad guys' point of view—they could see a lot of tracer coming at them, as well as the noise of having a lot coming at them. They could physically see the tracer which gave the impression that we had more firepower.[4]

The expression that 'bullshit baffles brains' is very true in the SAS notion of throwing as much lead at the enemy to get him to keep his head down while the patrol took off. The other thing that also helped was the reports from the weapons. The 7.62 mm SLR, or a .308 calibre rifle, was a noisy beast which didn't go bang, it went boom! It was often referred to as 'the elephant gun' by the Diggers and it was by far the noisiest rifle and probably the hardest-hitting weapon in the war that was not a machine-gun. But when you get these beasts firing on automatic and in unison, the noise level was dramatic:

> The sound of an SAS contact is just awesome. There is no, 'Bang'—I wonder what that was?—'Bang'—a few more shots. Whatever is happening? If we got away the first rounds, it would be automatic and it would be a full magazine, maybe if there were unders and overs—we would have grenades going off, and rapidly joined in by the other patrol members. So it would rapidly escalate into a huge amount of fire by five people putting down automatic fire and grenades and so on. So we could recognise when one of our own patrols had a contact, and *knew* it was an SAS patrol. It could not be anybody else.[5]

The patrol members all used 30-round magazines wherever they could as it gave a longer burst of fire, lengthened the time between magazine changes and allowed more ammunition to be carried loaded. Nev Farley ran through his patrol's SOP on the initial burst of fire:

> We used 30-round magazines, and most of the blokes carried a 30-round magazine on their weapon. Because the idea was that when you had a contact, you deliberately fired as much ammunition as you could, and if you had those bloody SLRs on fully automatic, firing a 30-round magazine, and if the flash eliminator was taken off it, you would think, 'Fuck! What have I hit here?' Because it sounded heavy, and fast, and automatic, and it would just make old Charlie think, 'Shit, I've hit something big here' and it would stop them, rather than race in and try to take you out. Because they think they have hit so much firepower, it's at least a bloody company, and by that time we've got ourselves on a back bearing and fucked off out of there. But, once that first magazine was gone,

from then on that was our rules, you fired well aimed, single shots. But it was quite okay to fire a full mag for the first part of it in the initial contact. It's pretty bloody scary when five blokes all open up at once. There's a lot of noise and if you've got three SLRs on fully automatic with a 30-round magazine, shit flies everywhere.[6]

The SAS patrol SLRs were converted to automatic by the squadron armourer, who also removed the flash eliminator to shorten the weapon's length thereby making it easier to move through the vines and branches of the thick rainforest:

The back sight was set so that it couldn't be lowered, so it was up at all times. The armourer fixed it up and put it on fully automatic for us, and with the flash eliminator taken off, took off the bayonet boss and all that shit. They were pretty nasty weapons. It creates a long flame. You could shoot and cauterise the wound at fifteen paces![7]

THE CONTACT RV

Once contact was broken after the initial burst of fire and the enemy were keeping their heads down as bullets, grenades, CS gas and whatever else the patrol had was thrown at them, it was time to get the hell out of there and put time and space between themselves and the enemy. It was important that the squadrons had a fairly standard drill, as men moved between patrols if someone was sick or away on another task or on rest leave. Joe Van Droffelaar explained what was the standard drill on breaking contact and getting to a rendezvous point (RV) for his squadron:

As the contact would start I always maintained that the first RV would be behind the 2IC at a visual distance. Some blokes used to call it a rally point, I used to call it an RV . . . If you're not there because you can't get there, then the patrol RV would be the last stop we made and generally—in most cases I suppose—it would be somewhere to the rear about 100 metres or less from the contact area. And that RV point would remain open for one hour. Then we used to have what we called the second patrol RV and that would be the RV or LUP, that previous night.

We used to change my RVs because sometimes you had to work out the time and space it would take the bloke to get there, particularly if he's got the enemy between the RV and himself, so sometimes you would have to make some radical changes. Sometimes I would say, forget all the RVs, our primary RV will now be our extraction point and our alternate RV will be the insertion point—provided we had not made contact on that insertion point.[8]

CONTACT!

When the silence of the jungle is shattered by the deafening roar of a contact, the men of the SAS patrol experienced immediate adrenalin release and it was a time when all the hours spent practising drills and conducting rehearsals came into play. The mind is very focused at this life-threatening time and the men who experienced a fire-fight are able to recollect years after the event exactly how and where a contact occurred. It is indelibly engraved into their memory banks. Some contacts were 'good' even though they might not have occurred as originally intended. Trevor Roderick recalled one incident:

We were looking for a radio operator nicknamed 'Fred' and Westmoreland was the boss and the American general promised an extra R&R in the country of your choice, for the organisation, the troop or the American squad or whoever got this Fred. And lots of patrols went after Fred.

We were looking for Fred and it turned into an immediate ambush, which is not an SAS job. We went out to fight, six guys, we had a Bren gun or two Bren guns, some extra ammunition and so we were ready to ambush and what happened was we thought we were onto Fred. We found spots where we felt he had set up his aerial, set up his radio set.

They reckoned he was on a bullock cart or the movement of the wheels on the bullock cart were recharging batteries and also giving him cover for this radio operator.

Anyway, we found this spot. It had jungle on one side, there was a narrow but deep creek and then a hut. A couple of us went across just to check this hut out and to check this area where we thought the radio operator might have been operating and then we went back over the creek and rejoined the group.

Again in an SAS patrol there's a bit of debate, it's not just the platoon commander or the troop commander, or the officer or the sergeant says this is what we're going to do, you know. Everyone knows who the boss is, but 'This is what I think we should do fellows', 'Oh yeah, but'. That sort of routine, and we were debating whether to go across the creek as a patrol or stay where we were because the creek was running. It was narrow, wide enough that you couldn't jump it but it was very, very deep and running and I was hesitant about getting sprung halfway across.

And whilst we were sorting this process out, the baddies walked in! And we just upped them from the other side of the creek and then there was some fire returned and we took off. Mainly because of the obstacle between us and the killing ground and I wasn't game to take it any further, so we took off. The squadron flew in, did a mini-op the next day and they gave us five kills out of that. It might sound gory, but they gave us five kills because of the matter splattered on the bloody walls of the hoochie, heads and stuff like that. They gave us five kills and I thought that was all right.[9]

When the patrol goes on a *close* recce of the enemy it normally goes into an LUP and the patrol commander and his scout drop their packs and venture forward while the remainder of the patrol form a firm base to support the two who are now getting really close and must be very careful not to get sprung as they are now two against too many. Ian Stiles was out on patrol with Sergeant Fred Roberts, who was awarded a Distinguished Conduct Medal for his efforts as a patrol commander. Medals were far from Ian Stiles' mind when it all hit the fan one memorable afternoon when he was the sig on this particular patrol:

A lot of patrols would patrol for days and see nothing. We had everything on this patrol. We had two really good ambushes; we had air strikes coming in; and here I am only 21 years old, got hold of this radio handpiece and I am directing bloody air strikes. Two of our blokes got wounded with bloody shrapnel. I told the FAC, 'We're running out of smoke here' and the next minute this chopper came flying down the road and there were people shooting at it, and they dropped this sandbag. How they knew that we would need this extra smoke when they were flying around up there—it must have been part of their SOPs. He dropped this sandbag full of smoke grenades and it went down about 150 metres along the overgrown road. There were too many bad guys down there for me to go and pick up the smoke and then I said, 'No, that's too far away'. And he came in and dropped another bag. It was still probably about 50 metres away. I said to Dennis McCarthy, 'Come on, come with me, and we'll go and pick the smoke up.' I thought about it later, and I thought, 'Shit! He mightn't have wanted to come with me.'[10]

The SAS patrols had to be skilled in talking to forward air controllers as they would be the only agency capable of placing accurate supporting fire between them and the enemy who were intent on destroying the five-man patrol:

Well, we were next to an LZ or rather an 'RZ' as we were roped out, and there was shrapnel coming through the trees from our allies' bombs. We had American OV–10 Broncos, Vietnamese Sky Raiders and Australian gunships, and later two American F100s supporting us. It was a pretty awesome feeling. Keith Jackson asked, 'What did you tell the FAC your name was, Westmoreland?'[11]

SLEEPING WITH THE ENEMY

Sometimes a patrol will get so close to the enemy that they can hardly move. Joe Van Droffelaar found himself in just such a predicament and his patrol nearly died from lack of water because they couldn't move without being sprung by the enemy. It was always a matter of judgement just how close a patrol could go to get the information they wanted without jeopardising their safety. Nev Farley was up close and personal one day and found he was in more strife than he could handle and had a night and morning he will never forget:

My task was to carry out a reconnaissance to see if elements of *274 VC Main Force Regiment* had moved into an area. Because the infil was a couple of hours before last light, I decided to lie up for the night south of the infil LZ, and the next morning go north, past the LZ towards the recon area. When we left the chopper, we entered the scrub and the place was like Roma Street railway yards. There were tracks everywhere.

While trying to find a way out, my scout, Andy Nucifora, came across an unknown device. It was a snare used by the VC to catch small animals. They were normally placed on a camp perimeter. Luckily, I had been told about them by Des Kennedy, an old soldier who won a Military Medal in the fifties and had already had a tour of Viet Nam with the Training Team [AATTV].

The patrol was doing a U-turn to move away when a perimeter clearing patrol bounced into us. The light was fading, but you could make out that they were wearing bush hats and webbing. Next thing I know, my 2IC, Bob Mutch—who was the tail-end charlie—opened up using one in one tracer—tracer and ball—in his first magazine and you could see the strikes as they hit the VC.

Andy Nucifora opened up from the flank to give support to Bob, who was caught up in a bush. I was calling out to Mutchy to see if he was okay, but getting no reply. When I started moving back to his location I noticed that there were fireflies in the air, the only thing was that these fireflies were tearing the shit out of the foliage around me!

About the time that I had given up hope of seeing Mutchy alive again, this object [Mutch] exploded out of the bush like a Polaris missile and shot past me doubling at the high port. Next thing I know, I'm leading the patrol from the rear. When I caught up with the others, we were tripping over bunkers and getting caught up in black pyjamas hanging on clotheslines. That night we had a 'sleepover' with what later turned out to be the whole of the *274 VC Regiment!*[12]

The scout in this patrol was Andy Nucifora, who remembered a bit more about the sleepover with *274 VC Main Force Regiment*:

I saw these muzzle flashes and there was three of them and I fired back a couple of bursts. They stopped—whether I hit anyone I don't know because they were in the dark and I was in the open. Very uncomfortable. Bob Mutch opened up and I could see where his muzzle flashes were so I was quite happy that he was still okay. Then Nev said, 'Come on, let's get out of here', so off we went and then we got into some pretty heavy stuff and we were running into bunkers and God knows what.

'Break right!' 'Break left!' We bumped into a bunker and by this stage it had got dark and it was right on last light when it happened and it was pretty dark in the jungle anyway . . . I saw someone going into a bunker and I thought I'm not going down there and boom, boom, gave them a couple of shots in there but I don't know if I hit anyone or not.

Bob Mutch got caught up between a couple of trees and Nev raced back and said 'Come on' and got him going and then we just sort of zigzagged all night. Tripping over graves, bloody clotheslines, I got hooked up in a clothesline with rows of pyjamas and other stuff.

We were told later there was probably upwards of 1500 . . . It was a regimental headquarters plus, but there was just so many of them that we were breaking contact with small parties and there was quite a bit of tracer flying around. No-one in the patrol was getting hit and that seemed quite good. We stopped for a while and we got going and we bumped into a few more and then eventually we got into a cleared area with four huts and I remember the sig was trying to set up the radio and was having problems in the dark and couldn't get his aerial wire out. So Nev asked me to help him set the aerial up . . . We set the comms up but we didn't do any good.

I think it would have been about two in the morning. The initial contact I think was around about 1700 hours and I can't remember what time it finished—it might have been about ten o'clock . . . We had a lot of minor contacts. When Nev said, 'Andy, help set up the wire for the aerial', I said to him, 'This is exciting isn't it?' I remember saying that and doing a bit of shit-stirring but he just ignored me completely. Probably thought 'Dickhead!'

I think we slept with our ears open for sure because you just dozed with your ears open around the big tree, we were just all together. We got mortared; I think there were four rounds fired and they were spaced about 50-metre intervals and they were coming closer and I reckon one or two more and they would have been right on top of us. I was praying that night. I don't know whether I was scared or not—I would have been apprehensive. I probably was scared. I know that every time I got off that chopper I was shit-scared. But I was praying and going 'God, no more, let that be the last one' and it was.

And the boys reckoned they all prayed that night for a little while—until they dozed off. I think we all accepted it and we talked about it later. We didn't say anything for a couple of weeks actually. I don't think anyone said anything and then we were talking in the boozer one night and I was convinced that we would be dead in the morning and everyone else was but we accepted it, quite frankly. It was probably part of the training that we were mentally very tough because I thought we were going to be dead in the morning, but let's see how many we can take with us—because we couldn't see us getting out.[13]

After a fitful night of wondering whether the enemy was going to open up again with mortars or sweep the area with a clearing patrol, Farley decided it was time to take leave of the enemy's hospitality and exfiltrate. It actually turned out to be easier than any of them had thought, but their hearts were in their mouths as they furtively crept away on their guts, or as Nev Farley so succinctly put it, 'Next morning we were trying to sneak out by "walking" on our basic pouches while Charlie was having breakfast.'[14] Patrol extractions are covered in the next chapter, but to finish off this contact and show just how much coordination is required in getting a patrol out, Andy Nucifora relates the extraction of this patrol:

Just before first light we started crawling—very, very close to the ground I might add. I was very conscious of my arse sticking up and I was really tucking it down but anyway it wasn't too bad because we could hear them talking and having breakfast and making quite a racket. We were zigzagging through people for an hour and a half or more but they were making a lot of noise, so we were able to get away fairly cleanly. Once we got out of a cleared area back into the thick stuff, reasonably thick, we could see that there wasn't too much around us—there was a bit of movement over to our rear over from where we had just crawled.

We got in the treeline and then we tried calling our headquarters again, which was very unusual. By that stage they were alerted anyway, they told us later, and we couldn't get through. So there was a low-winged Yank Bird Dog flying around and Nev got onto the URC–10 and was able to make contact.[15] Scared the shit out of us initially because he had a very loud voice, but I remember Nev saying to us, he said, 'Okay, we've got through'. The Bird Dog said, 'Can you show us a bit of ID?' and someone flashed a mirror, he saw our mirror and he said, 'Okay, got you' and then Nev said, 'Can you get away a bit because you're drawing the crabs . . . Just fly over away from us a little bit', and he said, 'About 50 metres due east of you there is a clearing . . . I'll get everything set up for you to get you out, and when I give you the word, run towards the clearing.' . . .

We didn't have to wait that long probably about twenty minutes to half an hour, and I reckon they would have been quicker because the slicks were all fired up and waiting but they had to wait for American gunships to RV with them. When they came in they said, 'Okay, 30 seconds and you start running . . . Righto, now make for the LZ due east.' So we ran and as we ran the gunships came around and started shooting behind us and then the slick came in and we were on that and out of there.[16]

It must have been incredibly nerve-racking for the patrol surrounded by literally hundreds of enemy, knowing that their chances in a fire-fight would have been very slim indeed. To show that these men are human after all, I asked Andy Nucifora how he felt when he knew the odds were stacked against them that night, and he replied:

Probably a little bit scared, but I was in full control of myself and I remember thinking that we were going to be zapped in the morning. I didn't see us getting out alive. There was no way anyone was going to capture me, unless I ran out of rounds, or it was out of my hands, but I don't think we saw it as gloom and doom, any of us. We were prepared for it, we were prepared to accept that it was going to happen. Nev [Farley] told me the same and Bob [Mutch], when I last spoke to him, he did say he thought he was gone that night. I remember sneaking around and there was mist everywhere and

I thought shit. He said the same thing, he said he was quite prepared to take on as many as he could. I think everyone felt the same.[17]

THE DEAD MAN'S GRIP

Just how close, scary and personal this contact business is could be no better illustrated than by what happened to Bill Hindson when his patrol had just successfully sprung an ambush using two five-man patrols—the other was Nev Farley's patrol—in early June 1967:

We were sent out to ambush a well used track. We had been in Viet Nam a few months and had successfully tried a few five-man ones and then we thought we'll try and go for something bigger. We had discussed larger ambush patrols over a beer or two—like, 'Nev, you hold my jacket while I get stuck into them, but have it ready in case I come running past.' It was our third month in Viet Nam and we were very confident.

We went in on the evening of the 30th of May and we were out on the second of June. We set up an ambush and unlike the five-man patrol, we had early warning groups on either flank. We set up the killing group which was five people and had three for flank and rear protection. And then we sent out the early warning groups—and the 'group' was a single person with an URC–10 on either side. There was a bit of debate about who would volunteer for that . . .

We set up the ambush with Claymores beside some ant-hills on the track—we had been able to carry in twice as many Claymores as normal. We had a couple of Claymores either side of an ant-hill in the middle of the killing area, and they were aimed down the track and overlapping with others aimed back towards the middle. Back from that we had the killing group which was myself in the middle with Slag O'Keefe and we had a couple of other people in pairs either side of that. We had thoroughly practised all of this and the early warning people up the track were supposed to be out 100 metres to warn us on the URC–10, 'There is x number coming', so we could leave a little group and we could hit a big group.

So that was fine and by this stage I think we had only been in a day and gone out overnight and gone back in to set up the ambush again and it was just a bit after midday when the early warning group reported on the URC–10 that we had VC approaching. The only problem was, because he was feeling a bit insecure talking on the URC–10 with the enemy so close, he waited until the group had gone past! Of course he wasn't out the 100 metres we thought he was, and as he is telling me there is four VC coming, I look up and straight ahead on the track there were four VC and one of them is looking straight at me because there is this voice coming from the radio in my hand. He is looking at my camouflaged face peering at him and this voice is saying, 'There's four VC coming'. I'm thinking, 'Shit, they're here.'

So we initiated the ambush. We actually hit that guy and one other—so we got two, and thought we wounded the third and the fourth VC took off through the scrub. We then did the usual thing: searched the area and subsequently withdrew. The interesting thing at that time was, I think out of the first series of ambushes, in mid-April, my patrol was initially the only one that was doing a thorough search of the bodies. Even if we had got a couple and there were still two enemy running around, we were able to get all the photographs, all the documents, the weapons, the whole bit. Take photos of them as well and then withdraw.

On this occasion, the guy that we had knocked over was lying there and I was searching him and he reached up and grabbed me! It sort of set me back a little bit. He wasn't going for his weapons or anything—he was lying on his back and he was full of little holes. But he grabbed me on the left wrist and I was a bit taken aback and wrenched my arm away, and Neville Farley came up and secured him while we continued to search him. He wasn't quite dead.

So we did the usual thing, got all the documents and gear and decided that because of the possibility of the others coming back we then decided to get on out of the area and make sure we didn't leave any witnesses. After we returned to camp and had been debriefed, we went up to get showered and I jumped in the shower and had this sharp stinging sensation on my left wrist. As the dying VC grabbed hold of me, his fingernails had torn my skin right through my shirt! My adrenalin was going so fast at the time, I didn't even realise it.

That patrol was successful in that we achieved what we

wanted to do. Although we didn't get all four VC, we learnt a lot of lessons from sending out the early warning group and we didn't do that again! It was just a bit too stressful for the individuals sitting out there by themselves.[18]

GUERILLAS AND GORILLAS

Getting close and personal in the jungle can be hazardous for many reasons, not the least the enemy's intention to blow you away. However, not all confrontations are as straightforward as one would expect. Trevor Roderick recounts his first 'contact':

> It was classic! And it was in Borneo, I went down on one knee and didn't bloody fire a shot. The enemy was a big orange orang-outang. We thought we were being tracked because of movement and suddenly, honest to God, this orang-outang just came out of nowhere on the track in front of us. I was forward scout at the time and there was no 'Contact front' or anything like that, we all just went into our drills and there's this big fucking gorilla standing there. And as quick as he appeared, he disappeared.[19]

After a contact, the patrol is often compromised and finds itself in a position of having to withdraw from the immediate contact area and exfiltrate their patrol AO. Like everything else an SAS patrol undertakes, this was a procedure that was constantly rehearsed, practised and trained for and required a lot of coordination between the patrol, their HQ ops room at Nui Dat and the agency tasked to lift them—in most cases the choppers from 9 Squadron RAAF.

13

GETTING OUT

'*I would hang a medal on every bloke from 9 Squadron who went down the hole for an extraction.*'—*Reg Beesley, OC 3 Squadron 1969–70*

PATROL EXTRACTION

Whether a patrol has had a contact and 'gone hot' or not, it will at some stage still require to be airlifted out of its AO. The basic procedure for a patrol not in contact was that the patrol would signal by CW transmission (Morse Code)—usually the day prior—that it wanted to be extracted at a certain pre-designated place and time. The choppers from 9 Squadron would be tasked and with helicopter gunship support would RV with the patrol at the designated LZ. Patrol commander Ron Dempsey ran through the procedure for standard extraction when not in contact:

> You would get your orders the day before from your sched and they would come up and say, 'Okay extraction is planned for 1100, or 1300 hours from your planned LZ . . . We would move to that area . . . and at 11 o'clock—making sure that

we didn't get there too early—we would move in, clear the whole LZ. Move to the designated position where we told the choppers to come in and pick us up, and just wait until we heard the helicopters . . . Pick them up on the URC–10 and have a talk to them and say, 'Right, you are to our north' or whatever and then pick them up with a signal mirror and then they would come in and say, 'Throw smoke' and we would throw smoke and 'I see red' and 'Red confirmed' and in they would come. We would clear by actually moving around the whole LZ. It could take a couple of hours by the time we cleared it all round. And then they would just drop the slick down, we would leap on board and away we would go.[1]

The patrols could never be too careful when exfiltrating, as the enemy might actually be following them up in the hope that they could bag a bigger prize and bring down a chopper and its crew.

There was one extraction where we suspected that we were being followed up and we could actually hear the movement after we had done the clearing of the LZ and we could hear them on the other side. The gunships just came in and brassed the area up and we didn't hear any movement after that, so while they were brassing it up the slick just came in and picked us up and away we went.[2]

Terry Pinkerton was grateful that the briefings given to the crews by the SAS were so thorough because he had a situation which showed just how cunning the enemy could be:

One of the SAS patrol leaders got hit not long after he had got in. And this is where briefings are very important. He had a five-man patrol and it was a hoist job and we went up there, did all our air work, got the okay to come in with the usual popping of smoke grenade identification procedure. We came in with the hoist. It was a small cleared area just near a crop of trees but we couldn't get to the ground, so although it was a hoist, it wasn't a high hoist but it was probably about 35 feet [10 metres].

I'm counting them coming out of the trees—I counted one, two, three, four, five, six. Six? Bang! He's not one of the patrol and that's one of the decisions I had got to make right there and then. And of course it was probably one of those times when I don't know whether I got a hit or not, but he never appeared again.[3]

The 'normal' extraction—if ever there was such a thing—was simply the reverse of the air–land insertion technique described in Chapter 9. Pilot Jack Lynch described it:

> The crews were all there, Albatross Zero One, the mission commander, would give his briefing and then it would run about the same. He would know where the pad was that the patrol was going to be pulled out from, and he would direct in the Zero Two aircraft as if it was an insertion. Except this time the gunships would probably take a more active part. If there was any likelihood of contact they would probably actually put down some fire while the extraction was going on—particularly if they knew where the enemy were or on which side of the pad they were. It was more or less straight in because there's no point in much deception at this stage.[4]

COMING OUT OR STAYING IN?

Some squadron commanders were reluctant to extract patrols if they had only just been inserted, as the resources needed to get them in were not inconsiderable compared to what most infantry organisations were allocated for an operational helicopter deployment. Reg Beesley tried to instil an ethos of patrols staying in the bush even though they might have had a contact and therefore possibly be compromised:

> My squadron was the fourth to deploy. Previous squadrons usually deployed patrols for five days. In addition, patrols were extracted following a contact. These factors together with the flight pattern had, over time, forged a definite operational SAS signature. To offset this, the duration of patrols was changed, and patrols stayed in unless they were totally compromised. Rope extraction was introduced along with patrol resupply. A distinct advantage in increasing the duration of a patrol was that it allowed a longer period between patrols, thus alleviating the stress factor and allowing greater time to recover from injuries or health problems.[5]

Major Reg Beesley commanded 3 Squadron in Viet Nam during most of 1969 and January 1970. He led his squadron on an operational parachute jump during its tour of duty. *Photo courtesy of Reg Beesley*

Beesley would always listen to the patrol commander who was out in the bush because he knew too well that here he was back in Nui Dat controlling the show from the safety of SAS Hill. He maintained that,

> while the extraction policy was accepted, there was a need to be flexible—noting that it was essential to believe and accept the view of the man on the ground.[6]

Ian Conaghan did two tours of duty in Viet Nam and his thoughts reflected the overall belief by the squadron that the patrol commander getting shot at knew what was best:

> On a number of occasions patrols would lay an ambush, kill some folks, get back out of the immediate contact area, take a resupply, and just go straight back in and lay another ambush

202

again but not necessarily in the same place and then get some more kills. And that was fairly successful. It was generally the patrol commander's call and often some guidance from the squadron commander of course, but the bloke on the ground has to call the shots and he is the only one who is in a position to be able to do that.[7]

This policy of Reg Beesley's had its moments and one particular patrol commander was not impressed when his call for extraction was not totally supported by his boss. Nev Farley recalled an incident when one patrol commander arrived back at Nui Dat after a harrowing hot extraction and was a bit excited:

The patrol commander came back, he opened up his shirt and spilled all the empty magazines on the OC's table and got up him and said, 'When I ask to get out of this place, I mean I fucking well want to get out!' He had used up all of his ammo and was just shoving the mags back in his shirt. And he just walked in and spread them all over the OC's desk and they went everywhere.[8]

HOT EXTRACTION

If the patrol required what was called a 'hot extraction'—that is, they were under fire or in contact and needed help—they would send a very short three-letter code word over their HF radio and when the Albatross Lead, his slick and gunships were overhead they would play it from there. If they were unable to raise the ops room at Nui Dat, the patrol would activate their URC–10 emergency beacon and any aircraft transiting overhead could pick that signal up and through a series of convoluted links would eventually get help from any aircraft in the area to help get the patrol out.

If the patrol is in contact it means that the enemy will sooner or later figure out that the people shooting at them do not number as many as them and will then become more aggressive and possibly pursue the patrol in the hope of winning a fire-fight and inflicting casualties. For the patrol it is a tough time. They will be trying to get to their nominated exfil LZ without the enemy in hot pursuit. Patrol commander Peter Schuman described the situation of a hot extraction as 'pretty scary', which I can only assume is a gross understatement. His notion was that the patrol had to take out—kill—the enemy scout or commander in order to establish a clean break and get away from the contact site, but it was not easy:

> Kill the eyes, kill the eyes all the time. It's fire and movement and then you've just got to wait—it's almost like waiting around the side of a building and as the baddie comes towards you—bang!—kill him and that gives you about a fifteen-minute break while they're trying to sort themselves out.
>
> We were chased for a few hours. We had had a contact, we got hit, it was after we had had a contact, withdrew what I thought was a fairly reasonable distance, got the aerial up and started putting in a contact report. And then your heart drops into the bottom of your stomach when you hear this 'Jibber, jibber, jibber' and it's, 'Oh no, not again!'
>
> We don't know if it was the mob from the camp that we had hit or just another group—a fluke—I don't know. Two guys just walked on us and anyway we knocked them off. We hadn't seen a lot of sign going into this area but that's not surprising, because sometimes the track systems might run one way and you're coming in at an oblique angle where there were no tracks, and all of a sudden you're in a hornets' nest.
>
> We certainly stirred up a bit of a hornets' nest and people didn't like us. The two guys we knocked off might have been a reconnaissance group and the larger group were fanning out just trying to find us. And they did and from that point onwards it was just a running battle and we didn't have time to get our message out and every time we tried to get an aerial up—the aerials in those days meant you had to get about 30 metres of aerial out for these little radio sets—and it was just impossible. We were dragging this bloody aerial through the jungle trying to get this radio set up and get away.
>
> We extracted ourselves and we had a couple of contacts on the way back and I was heading for this large LZ and I knew that if we could get there, there may be a chance we could get the ground-to-air radio because there were no aircraft—we had tried that—and there was no aircraft in our area.
>
> Finally we got to this LZ, we had had about three contacts, two contacts during the day, plus this running fight. And we got back to this LZ. I got my guys right in the centre of it

and it was about 500 metres all around, so here was the four of us like Custer's last stand, back to back in the middle of this LZ and we got a message through to a FAC and over the treeline came a slick and two gunships and blew the sides of this paddy field up and rescued us.

That was hard, real hard. That brings out all the skills of leadership, and you can see the guys' eyes looking at you and saying, 'Shit, what are we going to do now boss?' They know what you are going to do, because you can't get the radio message out, but they're just waiting for you to say it.

'What we're going to do guys is get back to this LZ,' and you haven't got a clue whether there's another bloody group waiting at the LZ to knock you off. It's just trying to instil a bit of hope into it and that's real hard.[9]

While the patrol is moving through the bush looking for a place to LUP and set up their aerial, the men from 9 Squadron are back at Nui Dat in the Alert Hut, probably playing cards (but they would never admit that) and waiting for tasking for a variety of jobs. Terry Pinkerton, a helicopter crewman on two tours and survivor of many SAS insertions and extractions, talks about the waiting game:

Well, you were always sitting around waiting for the balloon to go up. I think even though you had other things on your mind, we used to just do things and in the background it was always that thought that you're going to get that call, especially if you're on Albatross Zero Two. Zero Two was always a switch-on call for everybody—really on a day-to-day basis because you could get a call at any time.[10]

When the call to go to the aid of an SAS patrol did come through from the command post (CP), it had an immediate galvanising effect on the aircrews, as Terry Pinkerton describes:

It's like switching an electric charge through everybody. The instant that word comes through from the CP, everybody is in a new gear. It's unbelievable to see the difference in a bunch of guys just slacking around—waiting for the next task—sitting in a pool of sweat on an old army PVC mattress. Everybody's out. Getting their gear together.[11]

The 'gear' the pilots are getting together is mainly the equipment they will wear while flying. In Viet Nam the pilots and crewmen wore a two-piece Nomex flying suit with a nylon webbed overjacket which carried basic survival gear in case they were shot down or crashed. They also wore a pistol belt with a side-arm, usually a 9 mm Browning pistol, a water bottle or two, first aid dressings, spare magazines, survival knife and the like. The crew scramble to prepare their aircraft and the mission commander, Albatross Lead, will depart for a briefing with the captains of each aircraft.

The Zero Two crewmen who will do the pick-up are

> straight out to the aircraft. The pilot would go straight away to the CP to get the final instructions as to where—all the locations, the points, all the pertinent requirements that he's going to need—plus Zero One captain. So both captains go up there. In the meantime his co-pilot would do all his pre-flights, get ready, and have it all cocked and ready to go. Then we would regroup and we would have a brief at the Alert Hut, which is just on the side of the pad. The captain gives any special briefing required and we climb aboard. If it was *really* urgent, the captain of the mission would brief airborne.[12]

The helicopter pilot's view of all of this organised chaos was described by Jack Lynch:

> In a real emergency situation it could be any slick that's in the area or any slick that's available to get out there and get these blokes out. It was usually with gunship cover and sometimes artillery cover. Usually we would have to try and secure a pad for the extraction. But a lot of the ones that I can remember, as a slick pilot, there was always a great sense of urgency to get out there and get these troops out of this situation.
>
> Quite often we would just have to navigate to the grid reference that we were given, make contact with the patrol and then just get into the pad and get them out. They would give us a quick brief on what the situation was on the ground and then if we had time, try to get the gunships in, coordinate them with the patrol leader as to where the enemy were. They would start putting down fire and once they had established

their fire pattern, in would go the slick at the direction of the patrol leader. We would just go down, land, or hover.

Pretty soon you would see them coming in from the edge of the trees or wherever they were and then just lob on board. Quite often they would be shooting as they came in and they would quite often shoot when they were in the aircraft as well. In fact, on rope extractions they would occasionally be shooting as well.[13]

The crewman of the slick designated to bring the patrol out has a particular role to play, as he will be the man to either winch the patrol up or deploy the ropes if they are carried. He also tells the pilots how far they are from trees and what clearance exists and what else is going on down on the ground. He gets pretty busy, as Terry Pinkerton relates his role in the extraction procedure and talking to the patrol on their URC–10 radio:

> On your way out, as soon as you get in radio distance, 'Beeper, beeper, come up voice.' So that you can tell them you're in the area and then they switch over to voice and eventually you start talking to them and usually you can hear a lot of puffing and panting and saying how urgent it is. Lots of radio traffic. You've got air-to-air, air-to-ground, all going on flat-chat. And you're listening to all conversations, because the pilots are talking to each other on UHF air-to-air and talking to the ground on FM. Plus your intercom. So you had flicking of channels, and all sorts of stuff going on at a million miles an hour and of course you're checking your gear and you're on hype mode. It's an adrenalin rush. It's different. It's something else. You're really trying to find out what state they're in and where the bad guys are.[14]

The pilots are unable to look down or to the rear of the aircraft and so the chopper crewman who has a door gun and the door gunner on the other side of the aircraft act as eyes for the pilot. Pinkerton explains that they were painting a picture for the pilot:

> A total picture and it's constant, it never stops, it never stops. It's a continual patter that never stops from the time you slow down or even start to slow down; from 300 metres back, it's then basically your scenario and the pilot panders to your

instructions that you are giving from the back. At this point in time the pilots are sitting there, they're using their expertise but you're playing the scene as the crewman. You're doing all the calling, move here, move there, do this, do that and it's his expertise that finally comes through of course, because if he hasn't got it—you haven't got it.[15]

While the pilot is at the mercy of the crewman and trusting him to give the right information, the dense jungle obscuring the patrol means the crewman talking to the patrol is relying on the patrol commander to guide the chopper in on the radio:

You're listening to the radios and so you're listening to him too, you're listening to everything and you use every means that you can to locate him on the ground. Because you are relating what he's talking about to what you are seeing on the ground. And the pilot's hoping to God that you have got it right.[16]

WINCHING OUT

If the Zero Two aircraft was unable to land because of the lack of landing space or if the patrol did not have the time to get to an LZ, then one method of extraction was the winch. The Huey helicopter was equipped with a winch with 120 feet [37 metres] of steel cable which could hoist two men out at a time. The two men would link arms through a harness arrangement to stop from swinging into each other and to assist the crewman when they reached the skids of the chopper. It was a slow process and one which was reasonably vulnerable if the enemy were anywhere around, as the chopper would be hovering for quite some time. During a hoist operation, Albatross Zero Three, the back-up slick, would sit to the right and to the rear of the hoisting aircraft to give cover in case it came under fire. Ian Stiles recalls one memorable winch extraction and describes how it was done:

It was the first patrol on the second tour, and Freddy Roberts was a sergeant and I was his 2IC. It was the first patrol in country, so I did the forward scouting first. We actually moved in and we set the comms up. We were in the middle of this area where the enemy were building this camp. And there were a lot of trees cut down for overhead protection of trenches and their bunkers.

We had arrived there pretty early in the morning and we set the comms up—we had our aerial out—and the next thing Viet Cong are moving around and chopping trees down and dragging them past us and we're trying to get the aerial back. Anyway we get it all away and we sneak out of there, but I think we must have been seen and they came down a track.

By this stage, I had reverted back to tail-end charlie, and I was last to move off. We had just done an LUP and our guys were going off at an angle and the Charlie were coming down this track at another angle, and then they heard something and they stopped. Their forward scout stopped only about 20 feet [6 metres] away from me and he was down behind this bush and I was just waiting. I was trying to get our guys' attention, and they didn't look at me and walked off oblivious to what had happened. And shooting started, so I shot this poor bloke who was about 20 feet away and then I just ran like shit to catch up to the rest of the patrol.

9 Squadron had stopped getting us out by ropes and they came up with the idea of winching us out. After sending a coded message to base camp, the choppers came to pick us up after quite a while. Our pick-up chopper was hovering and the drill was that there was going to be two guys going first and then one and then the last two guys. So I went up first with one guy, then the single guy and then Freddy Roberts came up last with the sig.

When I got up in the chopper, there was the crewman operating the winch bringing up the other guys. So I sat behind the M60 door gun and I could see the bloody green tracer coming towards us and so I was acting like a B–17 door gunner, you know, and blazing away with this bloody M60. Couldn't see Charlie—just muzzle flashes, green tracer coming in and the M60's red tracer going out.[17]

ROPING OUT

Another method, and definitely more spectacular—at least to see—of extracting was to drop five ropes which were attached to the centre of the cabin through a system called a RAD or rope attachment device. This device held the ropes in place and if need be could be released by the co-pilot pulling on a lever which released all five ropes and allowed the men to get away from the aircraft once they landed. The rope extraction, or as it became more commonly known, a Karex or karabiner extraction, worked basically with the aircraft hovering over a winch point, the ropes dropped down to the anxiously waiting patrol. They hooked onto the ropes by using a karabiner they carried on either their web belt or a Swiss seat which they wore or put on just prior to extraction. Once they all hooked up, they linked arms to keep the mass of bodies together and flew to the nearest safe pad to be dropped off and re-board the aircraft for the flight back to Nui Dat. It was not simply accepted by the air force hierarchy that rope extractions were a good thing as Squadron Commander Reg Beesley recalled:

> The air force weren't very keen on the rope extraction, because there was a possibility of the aircraft having to auto-rotate with five bodies hanging underneath the aircraft. But it enabled chaps to go into a patrol AO and not have to be continuously looking for a landing zone. It gave us greater flexibility in an area. They could move and hopefully in a cleared tree area they could put the ropes down and up they would come and out they would go . . . It was also designed as a quick way of getting a man out if he was wounded or injured without trying to take the whole patrol and go to an LZ and hope that it was secure.[18]

The pilots themselves didn't mind too much doing a rope extraction because it meant that they spent less time in the hover and being a potential target for the Viet Cong. Jack Lynch indicated he preferred to rope the patrols out if he couldn't land his machine:

> Winching was slow. The rope extraction method was a pretty quick technique, because . . . it would be all over in twenty seconds. The ropes were just coiled, just lying there and then, in the hover, they would be thrown out and they would just tumble down. The patrol would be out on a perimeter, the helicopter would come to a halt, hover, stabilise, down go the

ropes, they would then hook on and the crew chief would get a thumbs up signal from the patrol commander, the crew chief would then tell the pilot to take the weight, he would monitor it once they had taken the weight and make sure they were stabilised, lift them up clear of the jungle and then roll forward very slowly until you got translational lift, and climb up to about 1500 feet above small arms. To see this group of guys hanging there—that also reinforced our opinion of these guys that they were absolutely crazy.[19]

Quite a degree of skill is required from the entire crew on this type of extraction. It is not just a case of 'They're on, let's go'. Pilot Jack Lynch explained:

The most difficult situation occurred when one or more ropes would stretch much more than the others. We could end up with a couple of clusters under the chopper . . . but generally they used to try and link together in one cluster. There's just one mass as far as the helicopter is concerned, so they are not trying to pull the helicopter one way or the other. It's just this one mass that ends up directly underneath the helicopter, and then it's a matter of lifting up, get above the trees, lift them up in the hover so we're just out of ground effect hover now, maybe 100 feet plus, and then we've got to lift them up so that they're clear of the jungle and the treetops. Then it's a matter of very slowly moving forward and when we're actually flying, they're sort of back on an angle of about 15 degrees. Just the drag on them has them back on an angle—it's a spectacular sight to see![20]

Joe Van Droffelaar had a reputation for hot extractions and survived nine of them all told. Here he recalls the patrol's view of one:

The contact was quite a simple one. We were moving through some defoliated jungle and in actual fact we had moved into a forward enemy command post. The enemy opened up with an MG, missed the forward scout and myself, probably because of his inability to shoot straight. We engaged the enemy and pulled back. The following day we decided to attack the enemy camp—which we did and successfully killed the enemy, there was only about two or three blokes—and then pulled back thinking that everything was okay. It was during the actual pulling back that a subsequent contact was made again and a large enemy force was then moving up our tail.

We continued to move back for quite a fair way, about 200 metres. We got into an area which we had already moved through which was buffered by reasonably good thick jungle. The enemy basically started to delay his movement and I found that to be an ideal situation to get on the URC–10 to call in the choppers.

I called on the sig to throw out his wire [aerial] which was a common practice. He would throw out a bit of wire which he already had attached to his sig set and the 2IC would switch it on and he would then tap away and at the same time observe his front or whatever he had to do. The sig would then tap away and he would generally say, 'Joe, she's a go' or give me the thumbs up and we would wait for Albatross Lead which was the first chopper, generally hovering up around four grand [4000 feet].

On this particular incident, there were no choppers available and the enemy were starting to close in. The Bushrangers—we could hear them, but they were in support of another patrol—and I happened to pick them up on the URC–10, and they informed they would be there as soon as possible. The enemy continued to close up and close up and then we started to fire a couple of shots. The scout gave me the drum that he would hold them back while I still tried to communicate with Albatross Lead.

It all felt very long, but I don't think it was—it was probably only about five to ten minutes, but by that time the enemy had a feeling of where we were and they had us surrounded somewhere between 180 and 320 degrees. A good 30-plus enemy but they tried to make pinpoint at this stage; and they knew what procedure would occur once choppers moved into an area—there would be some smoke or some identification on the ground with smoke.

Anyway, Albatross Lead tells me to hang off and I was very dubious at this time about throwing smoke because most of the time they would tell you to throw smoke which is much, much too early, and if you had another contact there would be confusion between the enemy, you and the smoke and trying to call in Bushrangers. So I was always hanging back about throwing this bloody smoke. So once I got the word from Albatross Lead, four minutes at the roping zone—

that was generally the time given to the patrol. But whatever that lead time was, that is when I used to say to the blokes to get their Swiss seat.

All it is is about 25 feet [7 metres] of rope with one single karabiner and wrapped around the guts about three or four times, through the legs a couple of times, making sure you had a couple of good reef knots, throw the old karabiner on—don't worry too much about the weight on your back. Most blokes would have a small karabiner on the back of their pack which they could clip onto the rope and just hang tight. Most blokes were very quick in getting that Swiss seat on!

There wasn't too much time delay, because it was a simple thing to do and should take you no more than a minute. Most of the blokes already had a Swiss seat on their belt which was in a pouch and it was attached to their gear.

As soon as they got the seat on, I requested to throw smoke. The bloke that used to throw the smoke was the bloke closest to the enemy. As soon as smoke was thrown, and when I say 'throw', the Number 83 smoke was laid down, the pin was removed and was held down by his hand until he got the word from me. When he let the smoke go it was pointing in the right direction—downwind of course.

As soon as that was done I used to close the blokes in and that was done by the normal fire and movement but without the firing. On this particular incident as soon as the movement of the patrol started, the enemy started to open up. So what we did was we returned the fire as much as we could.

I was talking to Albatross Lead who informed Bushranger that they could see up to 30 enemy moving near the smoke and they asked for clearance from Albatross Lead to fire in. Albatross Lead asked me how far away I was from the smoke and I said about 5 to 10 metres to the south and as the patrol was closing in, the bloody Bushrangers were doing as many sweeps.

It always surprised me the pick-up slick with the ropes— you would never hear them or see them, but by that time the Bushrangers are pumping the stuff in. You are keeping your eyes open to the other flanks, especially to the rear and to the areas the Bushrangers have not put any fire into.

By this time we are back to back, the 2IC is now on the URC–10, Albatross Lead would guide in the slick and the slick would generally be about 30 seconds or 15 seconds and knew what the score was and would come over the jungle, basically pull up like a car; the arse end she would drop down; ropes would then be thrown out; the blokes would grab a rope as quickly as possible and lock on.

So we used to quickly put the link rope through and lock on and give a final burst of fire and basically empty our mags and hang there with one arm around the rope, hand on the weapon. Those blokes that could fire, generally about four blokes, we would pump out as much fire as we could, change mags on the uplift, get clear of the jungle. As soon as we were clear of the J we would cease fire. Generally the lift to the top of the jungle was quite quick and in most cases Bushranger would go underneath you and provide covering fire. And that was generally a hot extraction.

They always tried to get the blokes off the ropes as quickly as possible. I never used to hang on to the ropes for too long—ten minutes, could be fifteen minutes—by that time we all had got our balls up near our throat. You could hardly bloody walk, some blokes were in quite some pain. But the SOP was to get yourself to a clear LZ; the LZ would then be cleared by Bushrangers once again; get yourself off that bloody rope; get into the chopper as quickly as possible in any order using the fire and movement again and away we go.[21]

The throwing of smoke to indicate a patrol position becomes almost a double-edged weapon in that the enemy may also be able to see the smoke and then bring fire to bear on the patrol. Trevor Roderick had some ideas on throwing it:

They would just come up and 'Callsign 11 this is Albatross 20. Throw smoke.' 'Nooo!' Sometimes you threw smoke, other times no way in the bloody world. They were so used to dealing with battalions, and then there would be this pregnant pause, 'I say again throw smoke.' 'No!' The main form of marking your location for extractions was to use smoke, but on a few occasions smoke would compromise your location if the enemy were close. But we had marker panels and signal mirrors.[22]

What the air force feared most actually happened on one occasion and Terry Pinkerton was the crewman on board when, at a critical time in the rope extraction of a patrol, the aircraft lost power:

We went out and picked up this patrol, and it was a hot extraction up near the May Taos. We pulled them out and everything went fine, everything went as by the book. Not a problem. The five guys were all firing on the way up. We had all our predetermined pads that we were going to fly over to, to the nearest 'cold' pad in that area.

I suppose it would have been a distance of maybe five clicks to the north-west or directly west from where we picked them up and we were just coming in on finals and they were just over the trees and there was a big lurch and I heard this noise right in the transmission area. We had this momentary loss of power and of course as soon as that happened—'Nugget' Hibben who was our CO was flying at the time—he lost momentary control of the balance. This pendulum effect started to happen and of course all of a sudden it got to now you see them [the SAS patrol swinging forward and aft of the slick], now you don't! And we are only about 180 feet in the air and just coming over the edge of the trees. It must have been terrifying for the patrol underneath, absolutely terrifying . . .

Of course 'Foxy', who was the co-pilot at the time, he was sitting there with his hand on the RAD, waiting to release it and as soon as they were on the end of a swing and they were just over a bit of a lump in the ground I yelled, 'Release!' And as soon as they released they were on the ground in a crumple, but at least they were sort of only one or two feet above the ground when they got released—at most. They were swinging at probably 20 miles per hour [30 km/h]. As you can imagine, 120 feet below swinging at a fairly decent rate, their speed was more than comparable to a very good para landing . . .

Then all of a sudden, of course with the loss of weight, up we went and the next thing, John Hazelwood—who is in the gunship Seven One, he said, 'There's a rotor just went past me going through 3000 feet!' and he said, 'I think it's yours.' The next thing I knew we were upside down, and I'm not a Catholic, never proposed to be a Catholic, and I went through the rosary. I started repeating things that I didn't even know about for a few seconds and then of course in the meantime I was trying to tell them what was going on in the back. And the next thing it righted itself.

We crashed in this paddock, a few hundred yards from where the guys were, and the next thing I know I'm out, grabbed my M60 and went straight over to the SAS guys and

Amazingly the crew walked away from this destroyed chopper after it lost power whilst extracting an SAS patrol who were dangling some 100 feet underneath on a rope extraction. The helicopter was later destroyed in situ. *Photo courtesy of Terry Pinkerton*

set up a position. They were still gathering themselves and we had done all this and I set up a position there with the M60 and I was going to take on the world.

The aircraft had landed on its nose, then tail, and then bounced around and I think Foxy, all he got out of it was a broken thumb. May, who was the gunner, he got a badly ricked back out of it. Foxy got a broken thumb where he pulled on the RAD trying to release the guys. 'Nugget' got out of it unscathed virtually; and all I got was a broken helmet where the transmission came through the side wall and bashed my helmet to pieces on the way through. And there it was, the transmission was just sitting out about 50 feet [15 metres] in front of the aircraft. Lord knows where the rotor ended up.

Zero Three came in and picked us and the SAS patrol up. Zero One, Zero Three, they were all there. We had the gunships overhead anyway. They stayed there on station until we went back, dropped off the SAS patrol, picked up a demolitions group. We went to hospital—they took us straight down to Vampire [pad] and put us in hospital for a check-over and all the rest of it. They came back out again with the demolition group for the aircraft and destroyed it in situ.[23]

BACK AT NUI DAT

The key players in the squadron headquarters are the signallers that take the message from the patrol that they need extraction and the operations room, who then have to coordinate the whole shebang with the RAAF, possibly Task Force HQ and any other agency likely to be able to assist the patrol. Barry Standen spent two tours working in and around the sig shack attached to the ops room as well as going out on patrol and he proudly remembers what it was like when it all hit the fan:

In the ops room, the minute you received a code word that said someone was in the poop, the squadron headquarters became an ops room. The orderly room were on standby because you might need drivers to take someone to brief the RAAF on what was going on because if someone was in the poo, you may not want to use the switchboard to send the information down. You may want to send someone down to brief. Security was paramount. People sometimes think we were a little bit bloody neurotic about it—but it's a lot easier to be conscious of it rather than pay the price . . .

The machine went into motion and it's a very pretty sight, probably an inappropriate word to use—but when the machine starts it is very, very efficient. And the sig says to the OPSO, 'Hey, Three One is in contact.' The first thing the OPSO will do is listen to what the sig has got to say—I think it's bad, I think it's this. I don't know, all I got was very very faintly in the background I got 'Cat'. Three One is in contact. He will notify slick and Bushrangers, he will notify the squadron commander. The squadron 2IC takes over administering command while the OC is tied up with the extraction. So everything goes into motion, it's not just the ops room, it's everything and it works very well. Seldom did I see hiccups in the machine.[24]

Once the word goes out that there is a hot extraction under way, the SAS also had a standby group ready to go to the aid of a patrol or a downed aircraft crew if need be. Reg Beesley ran through the squadron SOP on what they would be doing:

> There was two teams of five on standby at Nui Dat all the time. I don't mean sitting around with their equipment on waiting to be called out—they were within the troop area and so forth with all their gear ready to go. With the time to jack up the helicopters, time for the helicopters to arrive, get down to Nadzab—our pad at Nui Dat—it was a necessary thing to have and I think I used it a couple of times. One I used when Dave Fisher went in, and I took it out. It was the first time we actually rappelled into the jungle.[25]

MAN DOWN

If a patrol takes a casualty and is still in contact, it is in deep trouble. For a start there is one less set of eyes and one less weapon to engage the pursuing enemy. Then there is the problem of getting the man out and getting him to a point where a chopper can either land or winch the casualty and the patrol out. The standard operating procedure if somebody was shot or wounded to the extent that they couldn't keep up with the patrol or move with the patrol was that they were to be moved as far as necessary to hide them and the patrol would move away and come back later to recover them. That SOP had come out of British 22 SAS experience and passed to our SAS in Borneo—but had not been put into practice in Viet Nam. In August 1966 when Russel Copeman was seriously wounded, the remaining three members of the patrol carried him to a point where they were winched out. The standard procedure in 1 Squadron required a wounded patrol member to be moved to a safe place and camouflaged. That doctrine persisted and SAS did not have anybody that got into that sort of predicament until the patrol of Bill Hindson's in August 1967, where he had five guys in an area heavily populated with enemy and one of his patrol members, Noel De Grussa, got shot:

> There was no doubt in my mind at the time, and it wasn't something that I sat down and considered, what we should do

or how we should do it or anything. Alan Roser sighted the enemy on a track as he went to cross it and he fired off his burst and we then started to peel off and withdraw with Alan heading past me. I started to move and we started getting all this fire, so I basically went to ground.

I was sitting firing back and Alan had gone, and I got away about three magazines and Alan comes back and asks, 'Are you hit?' I said, 'No!' 'Good, because Noel is!' And shit! I thought. 'Right, let's go!' I leap up and go and have a look at Noel and there's blood all down his leg. So I arranged for Alan to lead the way, and for Gerry Israel, our medic, and Pieter Van As to help Noel to walk and to carry his weapon and equipment while I brought up the rear. So we headed off and I was expecting to be pursued by the baddies. We probably went no more than 50 metres and instead of Noel hobbling along, he actually collapsed.

So at this stage we said right, put him down, and we need to fix him up quick. Gerry Israel gave him some morphine, and then applied a field dressing to his leg. At this stage we could see that he had been hit through the thigh; it didn't hit the bone and the bottom part of his trousers is like somebody has poured in a bucket of blood. He had just collapsed on us through loss of blood.

While Gerry and Pieter attended to Noel, Alan and myself were observing towards where the enemy were and there was no movement back there at all. So we agreed we've got to get communications and at that stage I pulled the top on the URC–10, so we were sending out a distress beacon. Noel was the signaller and we had a patrol where the only one who can send Morse is Noel and this is not good. Real problem.

Again it did not even enter our minds to leave Noel behind. So we patched him up as best we could and Gerry and Pieter pick him up and we're off again. We go about another 150 metres and he is just dead weight and almost passing out. We didn't jettison anything—intentionally that is. I lost my hat and three magazines initially back in the contact site.

So as we are getting towards where we finally stopped I said to Alan, 'Look around for a place to hide.' And there was an area where there were a couple of ant-hills and a small depression and a reasonable amount of foliage—not totally thick, but where we could be hidden from view from about 20 or 30 metres away. We laid up in the middle of this stuff and Noel's pretty ratshit by this stage, so we've still got the URC–10 beacon going. I said, 'Right, this is it' and I was thinking it could be Hindson's last stand.

We couldn't hear anyone, we certainly weren't being closely followed as far as we could ascertain. We had put down a fair amount of fire in the contact site, I thought, and had got out of it. I don't know how long it took, but the next thing I hear this American voice and there was a twin-engined Beechcraft overhead and he asked me what was wrong.

I said, 'Look, we are a reconnaissance patrol from Nui Dat, contact them and give them this code word.' He questioned me a bit and I said, 'Look, get onto Nui Dat and give them this code word.' I wasn't terrified or anything, I was dead calm, I wanted to make sure he had it nice and clear. I wasn't about to say we had people shot, who we were or what we were doing, just give them the code word—which was the code for 'we've got a casualty'. So, right he says and the next thing he's joined by an FAC. Beechcraft, a forward air controller. Then another one comes, Beechcraft, two FACs. Shit!

Then Noel suddenly comes good, says, 'Run out the antenna quick!' So we ran out the antenna, Noel sends the code and by this stage he is a little perky and we were real conscious of all of this attention over the top of us. There's no clearing, nothing, and it's maybe 30 metres of foliage above us. Thick. I thought this is going to be interesting.

Anyway they sent out the usual rescue mission. I'm not sure whether they actually had a patrol or not on board one of them, but they had the usual couple of gunships, Lead Albatross is up high trying to direct the slick onto us because by that stage apart from the code word we had also given our location so they could home in on us and no doubt the FACs had done the same. So the helicopters are on the way, this is wonderful, but I was thinking, 'How the bloody hell are we going to work this out?'

So we've got a marker panel which is about the size of three A3 sheets of paper and a pencil flare, a tiny little thing. I thought we are going to have to guide these guys in to us. Meanwhile, the sky is getting real busy. We've got the Beechcraft, two FACs, a trio of Sky Raiders—propeller jobs— and somewhere way off I can hear some jets as well.

The helicopters arrive and they're asking, 'Give us directions, give us directions.' So I am on the URC–10 talking direct to them and I could hear them approaching, so I am saying, 'You're on line, you're on line. Go left, go right.' And they're coming closer and we could hear this one on the treetops coming right at us. He was right on target for us and as he got just above us the rotor downwash parts the trees.

'This is real good,' I thought. So I put up the pencil flare so he could see right where we are. As the pencil flare shot past his canopy, he went wobble, whoosh! Probably thought that was tracer. Not good. Anyway he's gone and the next one comes in and this one was right on target and we guided him over. So we've got him sitting on top of us, the trees are bent back, there's twigs and shit going everywhere.

At this stage the gunships decide to join the party. I don't know how they quite did it. One did a run and as they laid down a line of fire I had given them directions to where the contact was and where we thought the enemy were. So while the gunships are doing a run on us the slick lowered the winch and on the first lift we put Gerry and Noel in the double harness and they started going up. The door gunners are firing off to the sides while they are winching them up.

There's all this clattering and shit going on—the gunships are coming in, running down the sides of our position and laying down great streams of bloody machine-gun fire and the next thing they are back and doing it in the opposite direction, coming in, facing one another with us between the two. It seemed like all hell is going on. I figured by this stage everybody in South Viet Nam knows where we are.

I think by now they're going to know we are here, so we may as well put some fire out there as well. So the first two went up and it seemed to take a bloody age to get Noel and Gerry up and on board. They were 9 Squadron choppers and bloody magnificent, just unbelievable. They put down the winch again and you think right, what's this going to be, is it going to be one now and two last or two now and one last? Two now. So we put Alan Roser and Pieter Van As in the harness and up they went.

Now, there is just me on the ground. I was starting to think to myself, that this is a real lonely place to be. The gunships are still doing their thing and blazing away and at this stage there are two F-100s, doing this huge bloody loop and off to one side the Sky Raiders are also circling around and all these FACs stacking up. Bloody brilliant!

Eventually, down the harness comes again—thank Christ—

and I get into it and I think to myself, I'm going to lay down a few rounds here myself. The door gunners were firing and there is bloody brass falling out of the sky all around me. Our guys are in the doorway of the chopper shooting as well. I'm up on the winch and I thought, 'Oh, I'll give them some from the waist.' Never fire from the waist when you're getting winched. I started firing from the waist and by the time I get to the top, I'm spinning like a top!

The crewman grabbed me and hauled me in. Noel's sitting there looking fairly pale, but pretty happy with life at this stage when the door gunner says, 'I think I've got one and maybe a second!' And I'm thinking I couldn't see them, shit! Anyway we are on the helicopter and we were out of there.

At this stage the gunships lay down everything they have and we're off. As we're going away in come the fighter aircraft and start laying some bombs and rockets and while they're doing that, this huge trail of smoke comes up out of the canopy at them. So there was something in there. I don't know what, but whatever it was on the ground was getting a bit angry that they were getting so much attention, so they shot back and that was the last I saw. So we are thinking this is pretty good, we're all safe. Thank Christ.[26]

Just when everybody thought that they were home and hosed a small incident now took place inside the aircraft that nearly brought the whole show undone. Bill Hindson recalls what happened as the chopper was heading back towards Nui Dat and the Field Ambulance:

It was August, we had been in the wet season a few months, and as some of the patrols had had coughs and colds, a few months before this, the OC had allowed our patrols to take a water bottle of Bundaberg Rum, so that we can use it to ease our coughs and this plastic bottle of rum appears. The pilots of course had been sitting at the hover for bloody ages while all this shit was going on, so they're pretty stressed and they're damned hot sitting in their bubble. So whoever had the bottle of rum held it up and indicated to the pilot, and the pilot goes nod, the bottle goes over with the cap off, and pilot takes one clean sweep, thanks, swig—not knowing it's straight rum! The bloody helicopter nearly fell out of the sky. It was unbelievable—you should have seen his eyes, it was just absolutely incredible.

He gave it back to us and we all got stuck into it and finished it off. We were all happy that we were out of it and flying back to the base and we flew straight down to the medevac pad. The helicopter comes in to land and as we were landing, I'm sitting in the doorway, Noel's in the seat beside me and as we touch down and I look out and everyone from the squadron is there. The OC, the intelligence sergeant, there's the medics, the rest of the troop and as I start to get out of the helicopter, Dale Burnett comes running over asking, 'How's Noel?' I replied, 'Oh, he's fine,' and I look around and Noel has just collapsed and falls out of his seat! 'Aah, let me change that.' So anyway, that was it, they took him away and patched him up properly and off he went down to Vung Tau.

We were pretty fortunate. As a result of that action and because that was about the time I was coming up for R&C down in Vungers, the whole patrol got to go down there and we spent a bit of time going to the hospital talking to Noel. Noel's view was very interesting. Noel didn't think he was going to get out of that—at all. When he got back to Australia he was in Hollywood Hospital and my fiancee was a nurse working in Perth at the time, and I had written to her and told her to go and see him. He told her he thought he was going to get left and didn't think any of us were going to make it. So, he was very lucky.[27]

But sometimes luck runs out and for one of the patrols in 3 Squadron during the 1969–70 tour just such a time arrived. The New Zealanders had a troop attached under command of the Australian squadron and Terry Pinkerton was the crewman on board a 9 Squadron chopper sent in to do the extraction:

Unfortunately during the first movement in the morning, the Kiwi guy, his name was Campbell, he popped up when he shouldn't have and the enemy must have been watching them. They may have been seen from the previous night on insert, and they had made camp pretty close to where they came in because it was a late insert. He got shot through the head straight through the eye.

We got called out, and it was up in the May Taos, so it

was a long ride out with the gunships. There's lots of mayhem going on on the ground and they had been moving for some time, ever since they had first contact that morning, and they were running low on ammunition. So we get there virtually just in time and it was a hoist extraction. It was so dense I had to use a jungle penetrator, because you just couldn't take the chance on slings because they could get caught up on a tree going down.

The patrol strapped him on with another guy—there was two of them on there. I had to deal with that on the way up and that wasn't easy because you're trying to pull off a few shots with your M60 with your spare right hand and pulling in two guys and one is basically—at that stage not known to be dead, but badly injured—and get him on board.

It was not easy and to maintain a surveillance of the aircraft and whatever else is going on; and gunships coming past and blooming streams of rockets and mini-guns and all this sort of thing. It's a scene which is unbelievable really. It felt like forever to get them in, a million years I would say. Because you can't make the hoist go any faster and it will only go so fast. It's got a maximum speed going down and half of that coming back up again because you've got two men still fully equipped, except for their ammunition. They still had all their food on board and everything like that. So it was very heavy.

We got out of there and went straight back to Vampire pad and of course all the time I am trying to tell them that he is still alive—and that was my job. I had a dual role, I suppose. I'm still taking pulses and they're looking at me and nodding and then when I felt for the last time they knew.

Well, as soon as they saw that I was doing it for the last time, they all fell to pieces and started crying. It was awful. It was a scene I hadn't experienced before and will probably never experience again. When you have got people with weaponry that would make an armoury look puny and they're in pieces.[28]

This episode didn't end in the chopper. The patrol had to be debriefed and relive the moments when these men who had trained together for years—lived, ate, slept and drank together— had lost one of their mates, one of their 'family'. The squadron commander at that time was Reg Beesley and he said it was one of the hardest times of his career when he was standing in front of four Maoris, built like brick shithouses, at a memorial ceremony for the Kiwi patrol sergeant. Sergeant Campbell—one of the best patrol commanders I had, made a mistake, instead of walking back from the track and coming back onto the track again and leaving some distance while you're doing it, he walked up the side of the track and the VC did exactly what we were doing. He died and it took 45 minutes to get a helicopter to him. But he died en route.

Those blokes hold their feelings pretty tight, there was no running away from the problem. I wasn't going to have a memorial service, but Ross Bishop talked me into it. The reason I wasn't going to have it was because five guys could go down the next week or two and I would spend most of my time having services. But the piper broke me up, as the tears rolling down the cheeks of these savage warriors was too much for me.[29]

The SAS men are not superhuman and have emotions just like the rest of those mortals who go into battle. They bleed, they die and they cry when they lose one of their own. They might be tough as teak and hard as nails but they still have emotions like fear, apprehension, loneliness and sadness when they suffer a loss. Trevor Roderick said the casevac procedure for his patrol was quite simple: if you took a casualty, they would put him

over the shoulder, go like shit, break contact and yell for help. Our medics were very well trained, so, over the shoulder and call for help. The biggest worry was losing someone and not getting the body out. Not taking them home, that was the biggest worry.[30]

THE FISHER INCIDENT

Roping out was hazardous even without the enemy shooting at you and it was highlighted when, on one particular extraction in September 1969 with Joe Van Droffelaar's patrol, Private Dave Fisher came off his rope. His body was never recovered and he is today listed as one of the six Australians still missing in action from the Viet Nam War. Ian Stiles was a member of the same patrol and recalled the extraction and the events surrounding it. It was Ian Stiles' belief that Fisher had hooked up through the wrong loop on his rope and had pulled the loop out and was unable to hold on:

> What had happened, Dave Fisher had actually hung on to the two bits of rope, which was enough tension to support his rope and as soon as he let go or moved his position or something, then bang, he fell away. It was sort of a bit of disbelief. Wondering what had happened, whether he was still alive.[31]

Private Fisher had fallen back down into the jungle and the patrol was unable to land and search for him. Joe Van Droffelaar describes being unable to return to the actual extraction point while still airborne:

> I think that was the toughest time. Toughest time because at the time I did not think that there was any fault on anyone's behalf. We got ourselves onto the other LZ which was a bastard of a place, a bloody swamp waist deep in water. Contact was made at the other end of the LZ. Heaps of firing going on, rain was thundering down and knowing that I had just lost a man; knowing now that I was prepared now to rappel down by using those ropes—and they refused. The simple fact was that there was an enemy force on the ground that was too large. It was a tough time.
>
> When we finally got back on the Hill, Major Beesley was there with a standby patrol and gave them a quick brief. The squadron didn't say too much, nor did anyone else. Blokes knew that these sort of things . . . can happen. After the number of hot extractions that we had done, our luck maybe was finally running out.[32]

Once the HQ back at Nui Dat had been alerted to the accident, Reg Beesley went out to the area with the standby patrols to search. They actually rappelled into the area from the choppers. After an unsuccessful search by the SAS, a company from one of the rifle battalions scoured the area for several days to no avail. Joe Van Droffelaar now had a patrol to look after through a difficult time.

When the blokes finally got back into their lines, they went through their own personal grief, I suppose, saying well you know we've lost a bloke. I don't know what the standby patrol was going to do under the command of Beesley at that particular time and there was nothing that I could do. I basically sort of hung back and had a couple of beers because the debrief would not take place until the next day now, and so I had quite a number of hours that afternoon to reconcile in my mind really what may have gone wrong, or what the likely cause of his coming off the rope was. The ropes were basically in the process of being investigated. We were on the slick that had the ropes, so the ropes were taken back by the Q store and taken up to the int section. I just decided to have a dhobi [shower].

And slowly the reports started to come back from the pilots and door gunner and they told what had occurred there. The ops officer—he was starting to take notes and I finished my shower and was changing clothes and was told that a debrief would be conducted the next day. So I picked myself up a feed and I told the blokes to have a feed and just hang tight. I started feeling quite relaxed by then. It must have been the two cans per man per day. By now the sigs were saying that contact was made on the insertion point as the standby patrol tried to get in. So I thought, well he's gone and just get on with it.[33]

THOSE MAGNIFICENT MEN IN THEIR FLYING MACHINES

Talk to any SAS soldier who did a tour of duty in Viet Nam and you will hear nothing but praise for the men of 9 Squadron. They had to find the patrol, then either come in and land or hover while they were roped or winched out. The pilots and crewmen seemed oblivious to all the mayhem that was going on around them but when pressed they admitted they did at times feel apprehensive. Jack Lynch did several hot extractions and felt that, even though he was worried about being shot at, he was otherwise occupied:

It is an interesting thing to ponder because you know that troops are in contact and when you get there, there's going to be fire directed your way. I can't actually remember really being that scared. You're so busy doing things and I think that is the main thing. You've got radios to talk on, you've got to pre-record grid references, you've got to plot the location of where you are going to, you've got to work out the artillery and you are so busy doing all these things. You're too busy to be scared, you really are! All of the times that I knew I was going to be shot at, I knew that there were troops on the ground who had been shot at far worse than I was about to be shot at, and there is a certain patriotism that comes out in such circumstances, I think.[34]

Jack Lynch also thought that the odds were with 9 Squadron, given the number of times they had been in contact and the casualty rate:

We lost very few aeroplanes, we got shot *at*, but not many people actually got *shot*. Certainly in my year—and 1969 was a pretty active year—compared to the 135th Assault Helicopter Company who got really badly mauled, our province was very quiet.[35] No big weapons. I didn't see an RPG fired in the whole time I was there. I saw one lot of .50 cal in the whole time I was there, and I'm glad that I only saw one lot! Because that is the thing that used to frighten us the most. Choppers would usually survive small arms. There was just the odd lucky round, unless you got really badly stitched up in the hover or something like that. But under normal circumstances as a gunship, or as a mobile aircraft in an operation, we might wear a few rounds, and that aircraft would be soon patched up. There might be the lucky golden BB that got a crew member or something, but it was very rare, very rare.

I think in our mind we probably played those odds a little bit. 'Hang on a minute, no-one's been shot doing this,' or 'No chopper's been lost doing this' and so those sorts of things probably all went around in our heads—all at once. But we were focused on doing our job, and doing all those things associated with it.[36]

Crewman Terry Pinkerton agreed with pilot Jack Lynch on the issue of being scared when going in for a hot extraction:

You have got too much on your mind. Too damned busy,
you have got to do your job. It doesn't even come into play,
it's as simple as that. Too busy doing your job.[37]

Watching the bush for the appearance of the patrol could
sometimes be startling, as Jack Lynch recalled when he was on
one hot extraction:

They would be firing as they came in and then they would
continue to fire, which was sometimes a little bit startling.
Because I had told our door gunner to hold fire, I knew he
wouldn't be firing . . . We were doing a rope extraction and
they were firing. I knew the door gunner wasn't firing and I
knew the gunships had stopped and we actually thought it was
the enemy firing at us. So that was always an exciting little
time when the SAS troops fired. I would have been doing the
same thing too! Hanging under this fucking chopper! I would
have been firing also, but that was always a startling little thing
to hear all this automatic fire going off and from your position
in the captain's seat, you don't know whether it's from out
there, or out there, or what, or as it turned out—from the
patrol.[38]

Sooner or later the pick-up slick, Albatross Zero Two, is
going to get shot at as the SAS patrol scramble to climb on
board or are hooking up their ropes. Jack Lynch recalled the
first time he got shot at and he had only been in Viet Nam a
matter of days:

I can remember an extraction that was on one of the fire trails
up north of the Hat Dich and I was with Jock Alexander and
we were Zero Two and we had to pull this patrol out—they
had become hot. They had moved to this fire trail and things
had cooled off. But as soon as we came down to the hover,
we thought it was the patrol shooting, it was actually Viet
Cong shooting and they were shooting in front of the aeroplane. They were shooting about a helicopter length in front
of the aeroplane. And we discussed this later on and the word
was that they had always been told that to shoot down a
helicopter you fired about an aircraft length in front of the
aircraft. So there we were hovering and they were shooting
in front of the helicopter! But then when the patrol came on,

they gave themselves covering fire whilst backing into the helicopter. That was the first time I had experienced the SAS just bloody shooting in that covering withdrawal technique. They had it down to a fine art. Then they kept firing when we started to pull out as well, along with our door gunners. My heart was thumping pretty well. That was one of the first patrols I had been involved with pretty early in my career.[39]

The choppers did not go in blindly with a cavalier attitude. After all there are at least four RAAF lives at stake on a slick and commonsense must prevail. Jack Lynch said that even though the patrol might be in strife:

There was no point in getting shot down if you were going in to try and pull someone out and get everyone shot down. If you could hold off for a few minutes and maybe get some more fire in on the situation, you might then be able to do the job without being shot up. It was always a judgement thing.[40]

Sometimes the bullets being aimed at the patrol and the hovering slick found their mark. Ian Conaghan was on one such extraction when the chopper got hit:

I was the first guy up in the winch and I was in the aircraft and it's hovering and the door gunners are blazing away with machine-guns and so on. I went straight over to the port side of the aircraft and the door gunner was fairly hosing away like you wouldn't believe, and the co-pilot was hanging out the window with his 9 mm pistol! In the meantime, there's a couple of Sky Raiders rolling past laying down strafing runs, followed up by Huey gunships doing the same thing. There's a lot of shit going on around here, and I was pretty impressed—it was like Luna Park!

And the door gunner grabbed me and pointed down and I saw all these fucking Charlies and I near shit myself. I thought, 'Oh my God!' and the next guy up on the winch and into the chopper was a guy by the name of Johnny Ward, and he had an M79. But I was in the doorway, so John passed me the M79 and he just kept feeding me ammo over my shoulder, and all I was doing was slamming rounds into the breech of the M79 and pumping them out.

And the next thing that same door gunner—I looked over
my shoulder at him and I can distinctly remember him because
they wore white, chamois gloves—he grabbed his shoulder and
blood just pissed out in between his fingers on his shoulder
and with that hand grabbed me as if to say, 'I've been hit,
what do I do?'[41]

BUSHRANGERS—THE GUNNIES

To help take the heat off the Zero Two slick which is trying
to extract the patrol, the Huey gunships would accompany most
extractions to ensure that the patrol had a better than even chance
of getting out. If the enemy began firing at the patrol or the
aircraft or even if the patrol believed the enemy were close to
the extraction point, then the two gunships would go into action.
The gunship callsign was Bushranger Seven One (for the lead
gunship) and Seven Two (for the following gunship). The
procedures they went through were designed to ensure maximum firepower was placed between the patrol and the enemy
and with the greatest opportunity for the enemy to give their
lives for their cause. The men who flew the gunships were
selected for their task because it was a difficult one requiring
very good flying skills, good coordination and an ability to keep
a cool head when all hell was breaking loose and the enemy
might also be trying to bring your aircraft down. Jack Lynch
ran through some of the tasks the gunship lead has to contend
with while putting fire down to help a patrol:

As a gunship operator in a contact for instance, as the lead
gunship, you are talking to the troops on the ground, you're
talking to your other two aircraft. If it's a really heavy situation,
you might even be doing the forward air control for fighters
that have come through. And you're talking to artillery maybe,
talking to your co-pilot, selecting mini-guns, rockets, whatever.
You're talking to your crew chief and gunner, and directing
them to fire or hold their fire, or whatever, and by the time
you get all of those things going, you've got plenty to keep
your mind off the actual worry of being shot at.[42]

Jack Lynch did a fair portion of his tour of duty as a gunship pilot and describes what the procedure was for the gunnies when they arrived at the scene:

> Sometimes if it turned out that Zero One was not available, the gunships would coordinate it all. If Zero One was available to coordinate it all, he would have the details of where the pad was and direct the rescue aircraft in. Then he would orbit high so he could control things from up there. When Zero One was not available, the gunship lead would do all of the coordination of the rescue aircraft plus the fire support. He would have to get the patrol to throw smoke for identification. Then he would direct the pick-up slick in as well as put down firepower with his other gunship.[43]

There was always caution when the gunships rolled in to lay down fire with their 7.62 mm mini-guns and 2.75 inch Zuni rockets because

> the smoke could come up in a totally different point to where it was popped from. So there always was a bit of caution to begin with and that is why we would normally only fire a few rounds, or punch off a single rocket which we knew was well clear, and then we would get some feedback from the patrol on the ground such as, 'Okay, that's too far away, bring it in closer.' Then we would start looking for dead branches on a tree or some tree that would give us some visual cue as to exactly where to fire, as well as referring to the smoke.
>
> Quite often we would fire a mini-gun as well—to give ourselves cover on the break or just before we broke off the run. As we broke the pass, the door gunner would fire into the same area that we had fired. He would be closely watching where the rocket and mini-gun fire went anyway, plus watching the smoke for smoke drift and so on. We always had to be careful with that.[44]

The fire from the gunships is nothing short of awesome. The mini-guns are capable of laying down thousands of rounds per minute but always only fired in two- or three-second bursts as they flew onto the target. That was enough to put hundreds of rounds into the bush and about one every square metre of ground. The rockets had a high explosive warhead which was almost the equivalent of a 105 mm artillery round in blast. The weaponry was deadly accurate, as demonstrated by the safety distances that the pilots used to coordinate their fire. Jack Lynch remembered them as

> 50 metres for the mini-gun and 100 metres for rockets. There were occasions where those limits went out the window, especially if the enemy was inside those distances. We have had patrols that have said, 'We'll take cover—just keep marching it in.' There was one patrol four or five kilometres south of Xuyen Moc in a little swampy area with bamboo around the edges. I was on gunships and this insertion went hot. The insertion chopper actually got off and got airborne and then the patrol got fired upon. The enemy were right there and the patrol called for an immediate extraction and that's when we had to bring in really close fire. We were actually chopping off the bamboo over the top of the SAS patrol members' heads. That was pretty close! It was successful because the bad guys stopped shooting and the patrol pulled out safely.[45]

OOPS

Even the most thorough of pre-flight checks and safety procedures will not stop an accident or a situation when Murphy's Law comes into play. Jack Lynch was flying gunships one day when he was tasked to go to the aid of Joe Van Droffelaar, who was having trouble getting a clean break from the enemy and was in dire straits. It should be mentioned that Joe Van Droffelaar has a stutter which is noticeable but rarely an impairment. Jack Lynch takes up the story when he arrived overhead and had made contact with Joe and his patrol, who were running for their lives:

> This was out south-west of the May Taos, and Joe had been out for a number of days and had been pursued by these enemy, had gone hot and had called up requesting an extraction. I was in a gunship and we had a light fire team and we were the closest to the area at the time. We were then diverted straight out there because he's gone hot and needed some cover.

So we went out there, established contact and he was breathing heavy and stuttering a little bit, and eventually we established where he was and he knew from his knowledge of the area that there was a pad down to the south and he was working his way down south. We also found an area that had been bombed out with craters like B–52 craters or something like that. We said yes, that's the area to go and he was heading down towards that. In the meantime, he is being hotly pursued by a number of enemy who were intent on brassing him up.

So we went through this standard practice of getting his location, got him to throw smoke, and then we set up an attack pattern. He is in fairly thick, fairly high jungle and heading south down there and we were actually in a pattern going north–south. The enemy were over on the western side of him. He threw smoke and once we had seen where he was and the smoke started to come up, I rolled in and punched off what I thought was one rocket that was going to land to the west of the patrol. Then we would be able to work out where the enemy was from that.

But . . . there was a fault in the system and all fourteen rockets went off together and there are seven on each side— just in those open tubes. We discovered later there was a stray voltage in the rocket control system . . . It must have been a loose wire that did not show up until disturbed by the forces involved in flight . . . We still don't know what could have caused it, but . . . all the rockets went off together spread all over the bloody place, all literally around the patrol.

As I broke around, my wing-man, Bob Treloar, is now getting ready to roll in and I heard him say, 'Fuuuck!!' over the radio. And I am coming around, my heart is thumping and I thought, we have just wiped out a patrol. Because the fourteen rockets, each had 14-pound [6 kg] HE heads on them. Even though they're not a really big weapon, it's about the equivalent of a 105 mm shell and to blanket that area with fourteen rockets was just a frightening situation. From what we could see they went all around the coloured smoke the patrol had thrown. The smoke from the rockets might have drifted to one side, but it went all around, and I'm sure there were rockets on all sides of the patrol.

I get around onto downwind for another pass and Bob Treloar was getting ready to adjust fire on what Joe says—'Too close, too far away, bring it in, take it out' or whatever. And up came this voice, 'B-B-Bushranger S-S-Seven One, that was b-b-beautiful, can you d-d-do it again?!' And of course that broke the ice for us. We knew then that we hadn't creamed the patrol. Probably one full pod went between him and the enemy and that was probably what he was really excited about when a lot of ordnance landed between him and the enemy! But, a very tense moment. I was really pleased to hear Joe's stuttering voice.

Well after that I still had mini-guns, Bob Treloar had rockets, Joe adjusted our fire. I think we came in a bit closer to the patrol and then we just kept firing on the western side. Joe just kept moving down south and finally got to the pad. We called for another gunship who had a full load of ammunition.

Joe then worked his way probably another 100 or 200 metres to a big old crater area as a slick arrived. We were still giving covering fire on the enemy side as they were still pursuing him. Interestingly, they didn't fire at the choppers. I don't recall seeing any tracer—they used to have green tracer. I just didn't see anything and the other gunships didn't see anything and the slick didn't see anything. They were able to land, pick Joe and his patrol up and get him back to Nui Dat safely.[46]

SPIT IT OUT, JOE

Joe Van Droffelaar is a bit of a legend in SAS because he is a character and he is also a bloody good soldier. His stutter is well known and became even more well known after one particular day during a hot extraction when his stutter kicked in worse than usual. Joe doesn't mind telling the story against himself:

I have always had this stuttering problem and talking over the radio has been a problem and on one extraction I had a problem getting certain words out and when the Albatross Lead asked me what the enemy situation at that particular time was in this heavy contact, I tried to get out, 'There's two zero [twenty] Victor Charlie to my e-e-e- [east]' and as much as I tried I couldn't say 'east'. The pilot kept saying, 'Say again all after Victor Charlie, Bravo Nine Sierra.' And I'm going, 'Bravo Nine Sierra One One, the situation is so and so—' and still couldn't say it. Finally I had to think how can I get the bloody word out, and my 2IC is saying, 'Give me the bloody radio Joe and I'll bloody say it!' So I said, 'Albatross Lead this is Bravo Nine Sierra One One. Two zero Victor Charlie are opposite of west', and he said, 'Do you mean east?' and I said, 'That's it, roger'. And that is when the gunships came in and gave it heaps. I suppose that is one of the funny times and I suppose Albatross Lead still laughs about it.[47]

ON BOARD

After all the drama and chaos of an extraction, the patrol is finally on board and the patrol, who have just spent the best part of a week in their jungle greens or camouflaged clothing—sweating, sleeping on the fetid rotting floor of the jungle and not washing during that period—clamber into the cabin of the chopper. Terry Pinkerton, who sits in an open area at the rear of the cabin, replied to the question of what the patrol smelt like and if he noticed it:

Not really. I guess what's happening at the time overlays all of that. You're just pleased to see them. I used to carry a bag in my aircraft and I used to carry cigarettes and whatever, and some blokes used to carry a little pot of tea and they would give them a cigarette and a pot of tea on the way back to SAS Hill. So we were more interested in their welfare rather than how they smelt. Remember, the doors are open, there's lots of wind around, you're sitting in the back of the aircraft and you've got full air-conditioning.[48]

Not so for pilot Jack Lynch. He obviously had no air-conditioning up the front end of the Huey, as he can vividly recall the odoriferous gale that accompanied the boarding of these SAS men:

Oh, they certainly did smell. A smell difficult to describe. The nearest thing that I can come to, harking back to when I was a kid, we had an old haystack and in one corner it developed a leak in a big storm once. And that corner got wet and it all rotted and it got this really musty smell. It wasn't too offensive, it was just a different sort of smell—pungent. There was a certain pungency about it.[49]

If the eyes are truly the windows to the soul, then Jack Lynch must have seen some interesting things when he turned around in his pilot's seat and looked at the patrol that has just climbed into his chopper after five days deep in the enemy's backyard. He thought they looked

> usually pretty relieved. Their eyes told a lot—the eyes are the first thing that come to my mind. In the helicopter there is a lot of noise, and they all seemed pretty pleased to be on board. Never saw them scared, but probably just pleased to be on board and another patrol over, I guess.[50]

The patrol is aboard the chopper and he has to get the chopper out of a pad and airborne without pranging into any solid objects. Jack Lynch always thought this was the time when the aircraft was most vulnerable—when they were trying to get forward speed to get the lift to get out of enemy small arms range:

> The most difficult time from a pure operational, flying the aeroplane, point of view is if there is any limitation with the pad; if we're surrounded by high trees and we've got these really heavy men on board and it's a hot humid day. We might have to really fly that aircraft to its limits. And that's probably the most difficult—it's just the physical flying of the aeroplane and making sure we don't over-torque it, and that we have got enough power to actually get the thing off.
>
> There were some occasions on which the Zero Two pilot had to back right up to the end of a clearing to get the longest run possible, the problem being that in a helicopter you need about 15 knots to get into what is called 'translational lift'. At that point the air inflow through the top of the rotor gives extra lift and the aircraft gives a lurch into the air. If there was no wind—not unusual in a hole in the jungle—then it could take a few runs to get the lift to exit the pad. Seeing 100-foot [30 m] trees fill the windscreen can be a frightening sight. The lurch into translational lift under such circumstances was always good for the heart rate.[51]

But for now, the patrol is thinking of other things as they head back to the relative safety of Nui Dat and a few days off before the next patrol. The flight back home will take up to 40 minutes and mates, real food and a cold beer await the incoming patrol.

14

TARGETS DOWN, PATCH
OUT

BACK TO THE HILL

When the helicopter landed back at the SAS pad called Nadzab, a routine swung into place which meant that the hard-earned information could be quickly transformed into military intelligence. A patrol debrief was done to extract the most important information and the SAS int staff took possession of any documents, weapons or equipment the patrol had brought back with them. Most patrols carried a small camera of the Minolta 35 mm variety and, if able, took photographs of the faces of the enemy that they had killed to enhance the intelligence files on which enemy were operating in Phuoc Tuy Province and environs. When the SAS first arrived in Phuoc Tuy Province, and with only two infantry battalions on line, SAS patrolling was done at a frenetic pace with little time for rest between patrols. Peter Schuman recalled the first six months of his tour in 1966:

> The day you came back in, it didn't matter what time it was—five o'clock in the afternoon or ten o'clock in the morning—you were debriefed by your own int staff, that was Tom Marshall and Jock Geldhart. If there was anything important out of that brief, you then went up and got debriefed by

Lance Corporal Bob Allen of 3 Squadron in 1969 returns from a patrol. His face reflects the pressure of SAS patrols which operated deep in the enemy's backyard. *Photo courtesy of AWM Neg. No. MISC/69/0363/NV*

the Task Force intelligence and operations staff. Any equipment that needed to be changed was done straight away, and then showers and a day's rest. So that's day one and day two. Day three was rehearsals, so back down to the range and do contact drills, live firing and briefing and day four insertion. And you just kept on going.[1]

After a while the pace slowed and less demand was placed on the patrols and they were able to better rehearse and prepare for their missions. This was just as well because the patrols were going out deeper and with less support available to them if they got into trouble. The system that operated when Reg Beesley commanded a squadron in 1969 indicates how the patrols tended to operate for the greater part of the war:

When they came out there were two types of debrief. Firstly they would come out, land at the DZ, go and secure their weapons in their hoochies etcetera, have a quick sit-down debrief by the operations officer particularly on any sightings . . . and then went off and had a shower, a meal and got themselves plastered or had a few tubes together. The next day the whole patrol would be debriefed fully by the operations officer.[2]

The close working relationship between the SAS and 9 Squadron RAAF manifested itself in a mutual admiration society and one which benefited the SAS enormously when it came to getting away from the Task Force base for a spot of relaxation. This mutual respect was very sincere and was summed up by Reg Beesley when I asked him what he thought of 9 Squadron and the fact that they would help get the SAS men down to the 9 Squadron base camp in the relative safety of Vung Tau for a rest between patrols:

I reckon they were great. Achieved through socialising, they had a good understanding . . . of what the SAS were doing. The guys made good friendships with the door gunners and the pilots and so forth. They didn't stay much at Nui Dat, so I would take the opportunity to send fellows down for a couple of days and stay with 9 Squadron, get a bit of shit off their chest, come back. It's amazing what a good swim does![3]

Probably not a great deal of time was spent swimming when the men were down in Vung Tau. The young Diggers were more into tasting the American beer that was on offer and tasting other delights of this coastal town, which had something like 3000 bar girls plying their trade to the thousands of servicemen from the allied nations fighting the war. Nev Farley recalls when the patrols used to get down to Vung Tau when they were probably supposed to be somewhere else:

We got on so well with 9 Squadron, they would bring blokes back off patrol, and then they would pack up and go and get a night down in Vung Tau and nobody would know they were gone, except for the key personnel who knew of their whereabouts. In the morning, the choppers would fly them back and you would get the OC walking out to get on a chopper on one side and the chopper would deliberately land on the far side of the pad and the Diggers would be rolling off into the long grass on one side, and the OC would get on board on the other side and then take off. And all these Diggers would come out of the scrub, all still half-pissed, hung over, all this sort of thing.[4]

The RAAF men from 9 Squadron had great respect for the men from the SAS and the manner in which they went about their business. I asked them to explain what they thought it was about the SAS that made them different from other infantry they worked with:

> The SAS fellows just seemed to be one step further on—more focused. Their responsibility for everything seemed to be spread across the board. Everyone seemed to have the same level of responsibility and ability. In the briefings, they were just superbly prepared. The detail they went into about where they were going, what they were doing and so on, it was just superb. It helped you understand about how they were operating.
>
> But five blokes going into the jungle by themselves—I thought they were just absolutely crazy! It was awesome and probably became even more awesome as the time went on and I fully realised what they were doing. I used to enjoy at times—especially later on if I was on a helicopter that pulled a patrol out—to go and sit in on the debrief and to hear what went on was just amazing.[5]

Pilot Officer Jack Lynch attended one debrief in particular which followed a hot extraction and listened to a patrol member explaining the patrol's actions during the events preceding the extraction:

> I'm not sure whether it was Jim Phillips' patrol or not, but they had set up an ambush with Claymores, etcetera, and they had this killing zone and along came these Viet Cong or NVA and the patrol leader set off the Claymores. But the enemy kept coming. The numbers were such that the initial kill wasn't enough to stop them coming through. And this young private soldier, he was sort of fair-haired, he was of German extraction and baby-faced but he was just as cool as you could imagine—I remember him talking to the OPSO in the debrief and he's describing what he saw in the kill zone: the Claymores, where the other patrol members were, and how the patrol leader had set off the Claymores. And then he said, 'They kept coming

and I fired at the first man and got him between the eyes, fired at the second man and got him between the eyes.' And he got about four or five blokes like that, and then with this really impassioned plea he said, 'I'm really sorry, sir, then I went to automatic!' It was just the most amazing thing. And I thought, Christ! I would have gone to automatic a long time before that! That's when I realised that here are people who are just superbly trained and just so mentally attuned. It was just a little bit beyond me actually.[6]

The men from the SAS really appreciated what 9 Squadron did for them down in Vung Tau, but even more so when the patrol was out in the field and they were calling for help to get out of a tight spot. Like many others from the SAS, Bill Hindson expressed great admiration for the 9 Squadron aircrew. He thought they were

unbelievable. They were inserting patrols under fire, extracting them under fire, and for me, hovering—for a very, very lengthy period of time with all that shooting and stuff going on—knowing that they were a bloody sitting duck. They're the only thing that's visible, close to the canopy and clear as day. It's probably difficult to see from a long way away, but from a reasonably close range, 50 to 100 metres, you've just got to fire at the noise. They were just brilliant, they were there every time and never knocked anybody back—at all. There was one occasion where one of the co-pilots got so excited I think he had his 9 mm pistol out and he had his arm out the side window, and he was firing at the enemy that were shooting at a patrol. I thought, that was pretty bloody stupid at the time—Just drive the plane, thanks!

They were great and I know our guys really appreciated it; when they went to Vung Tau they used to go and visit them. There were some SAS members who used to go down there on leave—we thought—and we would be going out on an insertion and would check the guy in the helmet in the gunner's seat and find it was one of our own troop! The buggers were swapping jobs for a bit of excitement![7]

The admiration the SAS felt for 9 Squadron is probably best expressed by Barry Standen, who also felt that 9 Squadron had a lot to do with the success the SAS enjoyed:

Everyone should have been knighted as far as I am concerned. From the air frame fitters to the OC or CO. They were fantastic. Nothing was ever too much for us. They were fantastic and they were the difference for a lot of our patrols. I honestly think that much of 9 Squadron.[8]

Being able to get out of the base and into an environment where the men did not have to worry about a direct threat to their persons or their mates, did not have to have a weapon within a hand's reach, or sleep with their ears open, was a tonic for their minds and their bodies. There is a basic need to release the pent-up emotions from living with danger 24 hours a day for five or six days. There is a physical and mental requirement to loosen the strings that are stretched taut. Ian Conaghan reflected on the value of the 9 Squadron haven:

That was really cool because it was getting you out of the Nui Dat environment and going somewhere where there were real buildings and sort of get on the piss to your heart's content and not have to worry about security or any of that sort of bullshit. It was really great.[9]

The tension and danger does not always manifest itself in the form of a contact or a fire-fight. Sometimes the fact that the patrol has not had a contact can be just as unnerving, as Ron Dempsey explained:

We only got shot at once—I think some fellow up the road must have poked his rifle in the wrong direction and let off a round. We sat in an ambush for ten days on this track, but nothing ever came past. It bucketed down rain every day and we sat there, cold and wet and miserable, waiting for something to happen. They relieved us with another patrol who came in—two patrols, it was a double patrol ambush—and they sat there for seven days and nothing happened and they pulled it up. I think someone went in about a month later and a huge mob went down the track. I think they gave up counting when they got to 300 and something there. But whether you were in contact or not, it was the knowledge that someone was out there and it was the tension. I think a lot of the guys after six months and even later on were starting to succumb to it.[10]

RELIEF

The patrols would arrive back at the Dat with the adrenalin still pumping through their bodies. Many times they had got out of strife through their own excellent battle-craft, good shooting skills, well rehearsed and practised shoot and scoot drills, brave helicopter crews and a dash of luck. All of this adds up to a mental and physical cocktail that was quite explosive. Barry Standen described his first contact in Viet Nam and how he felt when he got back to safety:

It was pretty good, it was pretty well rehearsed shall we say, because this repetition thing comes in. But the first shot rings out, and you go right back to people like Alan Seale and the Beast and Swamp Fox and you can almost hear them saying, 'Return fire! Come down the funnel' and so on, and all your training comes out and it's not a conscious thing. I mean all you have got to do is locate the contact and then you react. And I was surprised at how it went, the first contact . . . because things happened very, very well . . . and probably when I got back to the Dat, I bloody near shit myself. But at the time, everything you rehearsed went like clockwork and the helicopters appeared when they should have and it was like a choreographed scene out of a movie. Everything went the way it should have.

But in all cases after the contacts I have had, my reaction was when I was back in the Dat and you unloaded your weapon and you put it down and you sort of take that first deep breath and you say, 'Shit, I got out of that one.' And then your hands would start to shake a bit and you would start this nervous giggle and putting your arms around guys and doing the bonding thing that you would normally accuse someone of being a poofter for doing five minutes before.[11]

The only squadron that did nine months in Viet Nam served about three months longer than almost every SAS soldier will tell you was their physical and mental limit. The British SAS, who had much more experience and history to call on in these matters, believed six months was the optimum period for sustained operations. The patrolling is extremely demanding and it came down to an army manning problem that squadron tours in Viet Nam were twelve months and not the preferred six months as in Borneo. Peter Schuman was on the first squadron tour in Viet Nam and he thought the toughest time he faced was

> about six months in when I started to get run down. I started to get pneumonia. I knew I was going down, but I became pig-headed, I didn't want to admit anything to myself and to the guys around me. I started to hide my fear and every patrol became harder and harder and then one day I realised I wasn't doing my job and was likely going to cause people problems. About eight days into a patrol I was shaking so much and I'm not sure it wasn't just straight fear because I was buggered. Couldn't think straight. I started to get the hot and cold shakes, and Jock Thorburn my patrol sergeant said, 'It's time to go out, mate.' I went down to the hospital for about a fortnight, came back in again and did a couple of reasonable patrols—not a patch on the early days and really just a shadow of my former self. It was just rest, I think. I think your courage starts to ebb away after a while after you have had a fair few hairy contacts and you just get out by the skin of your teeth. You think, 'Shit, the next time might be it' . . . and you get the combination of all these things. And that's why I used to admire the scouts. They were under more pressure than I was, a different pressure I suppose, but they were just that good, I used to just take my hat off to them.[12]

Ron Dempsey was also a troop commander and agreed with Peter Schuman:

> One of my patrol sergeants, he had just had enough. Every time he got off the aircraft somebody shot at him. He would be in, they would take him out and throw him back into another LZ, and a day later he would again be shot at as soon as they got off the aircraft. And they would just move off the side of the LZ and they would be in contact, and back onto the aircraft. I think it was around September, he had enough. You could just see it, so I went and saw the SSM and said, 'Look Jim, this guy's had enough, what do you think?' . . . And he said, 'Yes, I believe it', so he went back home. Later he said it was the best thing that happened, he just couldn't

have taken any more of it. He would have completely collapsed
I think.[13]

MAINTAINING THE EDGE

Between patrols the troops need to maintain their basic battle-
craft skills which will ensure their survival when they confront
the enemy. Nev Farley had a technique that kept his patrol's
shooting skills at the highest level:

> We used to do a lot of weapon handling—we used to fire off
> all our old ammunition after every patrol. We would go onto
> the range, just at the back of the Hill, and fire into a bank.
> We gave away firing at beer cans because they were too big,
> so we used to fire at shotgun cartridges, and place the butt on
> your chin and work with both eyes open and do that all the
> time. It was really good value.[14]

Sometimes these shooting skills were transferred from static
targets to ones that actually moved. The SAS troopers would
get a little bored or seek other forms of excitement when back
at Nui Dat and their improvised 'target practice' had the benefit
of maintaining the edge. The squadron 2IC was a captain who
unwittingly provided the targets for the Diggers' sport:

> For recreation, he used to make model aeroplanes and fly them
> up on the chopper pad. They were controlled on a wire. He
> would be flying them around, and the blokes used to get in
> the long grass with silenced Stirlings and blow them out of
> the sky! He would be going brrrr, and then boom and he
> couldn't work out why there was this sudden . . . crash.[15]

The key to patrol survival often centred on the patrol's ability
to send their radio messages clearly and with little confusion. As
the Sig Troop detachment sergeant, Barry Standen often would
collar the infantry signallers when they were back in base and
hone their radio skills:

> When they weren't in the field we would say, 'Hey, last time
> you were out you were pretty bloody hopeless. You had a

contact and you sounded like you were stuttering', you know. And this is on a Morse key and it's difficult—but some of them did. And we would say come in and if you have got a week or two weeks between now and your next Warning Order, sit in the bloody radio room, get used to the Morse key, get used to listening to people in the boonies so that when you are out in the boonies you can appreciate the other side of it. And it was very, very well received, especially after the first shot rang out. Everyone wanted to learn a few of the survival skills of communications.[16]

REHEARSALS

The soldiers still had to practise drills and occasionally they would experiment to refine or devise new techniques for special tasks. One such rehearsal revolved around a requirement to snatch a prisoner. Ron Dempsey was asked by the squadron sergeant-major (SSM) to help refine a snatch procedure:

> We were trying to test mace for the snatching of a prisoner. The SSM got some of this mace and the plan was we would test it out on one of the troopers and if it worked properly then they could use it. The plot was that one guy would hide behind a tree and as one of the enemy walked past, he would spray him in the face with it. And so, this was all set up and the SSM was hiding behind a tree and a trooper wanders past and he sprays the trooper in the face with this mace, and he turns around and whacks him and nearly knocks the SSM's head off! . . . It didn't work very well so we gave up on that idea.[17]

The physical demand on the soldiers was quite extreme and most patrol members suffered significant weight loss on patrols. Bill Hindson explained how it affected his group and the reason for the weight fluctuations:

> It was normally a week between patrols, but could be up to ten days. It was supposed to be a week on patrol then a week off. There were times when we were going out and putting in ambushes which were triggered after three days and if they

didn't adjust the week off when you had a three-day patrol, we got a bonus with a couple of extra days off back in camp.

The problem with the longer patrols was the need to carry more food and water. Sometimes this could only be achieved by reducing the daily food intake, resulting in patrol members losing weight. We started out with Australian dehydrated rations but quickly went to the American long-range patrol packs. It was intended that soldiers consume one pack per meal but owing to weight limitations we used to take one pack for the whole day. Invariably some of the patrols where we were constantly in close proximity to the enemy meant we couldn't cook, so we either didn't eat it or ate it dry; or we cooked a very small portion of it. So instead of three meals a day we were probably having half or less. So the routine could sometimes result in a cup of coffee in the morning, and some cheese and biscuits or sweets for lunch.

That was certainly the case on our patrol where Noel De Grussa got shot. We were stationary for over two hours watching a track and decided to have lunch, which was some sweets and a drink of water because of the proximity of the track just some 10 metres away. So we got to the stage where, through lack of sustenance, we were finding it harder and harder to get up and move quickly with the weight of our packs. We just couldn't stand up quickly without getting giddy.

We would start out fitting comfortably into our trousers and, as we started each morning, we would be tightening the trousers another notch. I had occasions where I was in danger of losing my trousers because I had no further capacity to tighten them. When we were out on patrol we were losing inches off our waist every time. Of course when we got back to camp and onto the regular meals again, plus beer or soft drinks and so on, our weight would go up. So we were on this big see-saw week after week after week. I don't know how we did that and managed to stay reasonably fit.[18]

Barry Standen found the same problem and his experience on four tours of duty came down to the type of life the patrols were forced to endure—

the simple logistics of living on dehydrated rations. I mean I used to make a joke about it and say that every time I went to the bloody thunderbox, I used to drop a little bloody silver bag and it said, 'Add water and mix'. Your insides, your body must have been so confused. I mean, a couple of times I went out and didn't have a bloody hard hit for five days! Because I was just bloody so concerned, you know, we might be in a little bit of trouble and I just didn't want to drop my daks. And then you would come in and you would have a skin full of bloody beer, you would go down and have all the freshies that you could get—rations, the bloody powdered eggs and all that sort of crap. And the body must be internally bloody haemorrhaging, it must be almost ready to explode. When you do that on a continual basis, something has got to give. Not only the pressure, the mental pressure, I mean the body just wears out.[19]

FUN AND GAMES

The relationship between the SAS squadrons and the aircrew from 9 Squadron continued throughout the entire time both units served in the Viet Nam War from early 1966 until late 1971. The good relationship didn't mean that one unit couldn't take a swipe at the other or go in for some serious leg-pulling:

> We put '9 Squadron takes it up the A' on one of the roofs of the buildings and 9 Squadron had just dropped a mob off and they were flying over and they saw the bloody thing and they almost stopped in midair. That night we were lining up to get a meal and everybody is standing around talking, the next minute two bloody choppers came over and they threw everything at us—flour bombs, bloody frangers full of Mercurochrome, there was shit everywhere and they bombed us in the Mess line![20]

Bill Hindson remembered the day his B Troop was bombed and how the RAAF cunningly got 'permission' to drop their ordnance after them they had spotted the uncomplimentary signage:

> Bob Ivey, the ops officer, is sitting in the operations post which is an enormous bloody bunkered structure. It was normal practice whenever there was an air strike or artillery to go anywhere near our area of operations, to check with us to see whether we had any patrols in the area. On this occasion we were asked for clearance for fire into a grid square. Off went

Bob goes check, check, check, our patrols are all up there—
nowhere near it, so he gave the clearance. Then he realised,
'Hang on, that's our place, that's Nui Dat, that's us!' But before
he could call back these bloody helicopters come zooming
over the squadron and bombed us with toilet rolls, condoms
full of mercurochrome and bags of talcum powder and they
beat us up a treat. Of course, many of us didn't even know
what the hell's going on and we were all ducking for cover
and while stuff is going everywhere. Then the helicopters lined
up to take photos of the mess and off they went. Later, they
all drove up the road to gloat and we all had a huge piss-up
that night. But they were brilliant.[21]

The pilot's perspective on this tribal warfare and payback was
remembered with no shortage of glee by Jack Lynch:

I was involved in that. What happened was that we got
cardboard boxes full of condoms full of water and they had
various mixes of flour in them as well, I think. And then we

Gunship pilots Jack Lynch (right) and Bomber Brown relaxing with
a Bud after a day in the air. *Photo courtesy of Jack Lynch*

WHO CARES WHO WINS!
WHAT TIME IS EXTRACTION?

The wall of the boozer in 2 Squadron's lines in 1971. The SAS motto has been embellished a little. *Photo courtesy of AWM Neg. No. P0966/97/45*

just hovered up and of course, curiosity would get them and they came out to look up. We waited until there was a reasonable number of blokes there and then the troops just kicked out the condoms and bombs.[22]

The relationship was a lot stronger than a few condoms full of coloured water splattering onto unwitting heads. The RAAF crews would often visit the boozer up on SAS Hill and, in the vernacular of the day, 'tell a few lies' and consume large amounts of beer:

Occasionally we would go over to their set-up on SAS Hill, just for a few beers and a few sausages or whatever, and a bit of a yack. The relationship was very close between 9 Squadron and the SAS Regiment—to the point of being the closest relationship that I can remember in operating with the army. Because there was a mutual trust, and certainly in the year that I was there, I know that if they were ever in strife, there would never ever be any doubts about choppers going in to pick them up. And likewise, if we ever had a chopper down in the jungle, they would be in—one of their jobs was to come out and protect us. There was always someone on standby and a couple of slicks would go and get SAS troops, and they would come out and set up a defensive perimeter around the downed aircraft. So there was this mutual trust and respect that was just the most powerful that you could have between two services. That's what I recall about that spirit. I had great admiration for them and there was mutual trust and admiration.[23]

The tribal ethos prevails, however, and a chance to get 'one up' on a colleague, especially one from a different service, is strong, sometimes stronger than the bonds of professional military behaviour. Pilot Officer Jack Lynch recalls one particular visit up to SAS Hill:

The SAS guys had this stencil made up and they painted on the roof of the little bus stop type shed down there at Kangaroo pad that said '9 Squadron Sucks'. It had this helmeted head with a '9' on it doing very rude things to a part of a man's anatomy. It was just their way of stirring us up. So one night we went up to their compound, again just for a few beers and a bit of a chat to sort of release a bit of pressure. We had all these blokes occupied—there was probably eight or ten of us—and we were talking away and having a great old time. What they didn't know was that two of our blokes had snuck out and were actually up on the roof painting an equally rude description of SAS characters.

But we were to learn a little bit later on that night. We had borrowed a jeep from someone over the other side of Nui Dat. While our guys were up on the roof painting this sign about SAS sucks, they also had some blokes out, cans of black spray paint, and painted the entire jeep—seats, windshield,

The SAS men socialising with their 9 Squadron mates between serious times at Nui Dat. The rapport between the two units was excellent and allowed for close cooperation between the two Services. *Photo courtesy of Terry Pinkerton, 9 Sqn RAAF*

headlights, the bloody whole works! We got in and thought, 'Oh, it's just the moisture and the humidity.' A bloke got in and was driving and said, 'I can't see a bloody thing' and there was shit all over the windscreen and as he pulled his hand back, in the dim glow of the lights from the SAS complex we could see his hand was black, and he said, 'Oh, fuck!' The whole car was painted, and that was a little bit of fun on us.[24]

Being bombed in the Mess was not always due to the RAAF. There was one terrifying time when the ammunition dump located below SAS Hill exploded—but it didn't stop the intrepid warriors from the SAS from enjoying a cold beer:

We were sitting up on top of Nui Dat and there was an ammo dump down near the airstrip and it was about five o'clock in the afternoon . . . We were just standing in the shower, scrubbing away, thongs on, and all of a sudden, these things started whistling overhead, explosions going off all over the place, and we thought, 'Oh, shit we're being shelled!' So everyone rushes out, wraps a towel around him and straight up to the tent, and my bunker which was just outside the tent was chock-a-block full of guys who weren't going to run any faster or further than that! I couldn't even find my flak jacket or my helmet—somebody else had those on.

So here I am running up and down the road in my slippery thongs in the mud and eventually got into a bunker and there were rockets and shells bouncing along the road between the tents. I think we had about four grenades came through the roof of the officers' and sergeants' mess. Luckily they didn't go off and they just sat on the bar. The ORs' canteen took a few hits too and boxes of white phos exploded about 1000 feet above us.

I think some rounds started leaking and the filler started leaking out of them and they get a bit hot and sweaty and off she went. One of the ordnance guys was injured when he pulled it all outside so it wouldn't all go off, but he got very badly burnt when the white phos went off on his arms. Anyway, after this when it all quietened down—it wasn't incoming it was just the ammunition dump blowing up—we all got dressed up and went down and had dinner . . . But there's all these grenades lying everywhere. We wanted to have a beer and the barman was a bit reluctant so we . . . just sandbagged around them, but I think most people bought their beers quickly and then left the Mess alone. They came along the next day and took them away.[25]

The types of incidents that would be recalled were not always 'war stories' but often small incidents that would never rate a mention were it not for the fact that the patrol was deep in the enemy's backyard and trying very hard to be serious and not be compromised before they completed their mission. Bill Hindson told a few stories about his patrol and one in particular which revolved around his troop sergeant John O'Keefe, who goes by the nickname of 'Slag' and is a large-framed burly character and not entirely the sensitive new age guy that would normally fit into the scenario that Bill related:

One of our very, very first patrols, I was patrol commander and John O'Keefe was the 2IC. We were moving along in an area where there were a lot of barking deer. This was in April and we had only arrived in March. As we were moving along, there was some movement, so the patrol stopped. Then the signal I got from the scout indicated an animal or something and as we started to move again and I looked down, and there was this little baby barking deer that had just been born, lying there all manky. I thought, that's interesting and because of the doe running away, at this stage we started to slow down a bit and we were in single file.

So everybody is trying to give a field signal for a baby deer, and there's a strange field signal going back and everybody is wondering what the hell it is. As each member in the patrol comes past this baby deer, it is doing what newborn deers do—try and get on its feet. So we're gradually moving and after a few minutes, Slag O'Keefe is adjacent to the deer. We look around and it's finally on its feet and it gives him the deer look for 'Daddy'. As we start moving off, it's wobbling off after Slag. Just hilarious, absolutely hilarious. We get back to base after that, and Slag's saying, 'Bloody deer, should have kicked it in the guts. Horrible manky little thing it was.'[26]

The boozer was always a place where the men could congregate and let off steam, if necessary air their differences, and enjoy each other's company. The entertainment provided in Nui Dat was pretty basic at the best of times but occasionally would climb to heights most unexpected. Barry Standen recalled just one such time:

We put on a bit of a show one day and there was a sig called Tweety Hickinbotham. Now, Tweety was built like a matchstick, and he came out and he was doing a strong-man routine and no kidding, he's in these leopard-skin jocks and a pair of GP boots, and nothing else on him. Now he looked like a rag man because there's no fat on him. He's just a skeleton held together with bloody skin-coloured Glad Wrap. And he says [in a deep voice], 'Now I will show you how I will rip apart so many sheets of toilet paper!' And he says, 'And you will notice that I am not tearing them on the perforations!' And it just about cracked everyone up and you had to be there to see this guy. You have got to picture a five foot eight guy, who weighs bugger-all. Three stone wringing wet sort of thing and he's standing there in a pair of GPs and a pair of leopard-skin jockettes tearing toilet paper apart in the middle of a war zone! I mean, shit! And it goes back to this essential requirement to be able to laugh, to let the steam out—especially at yourself.[27]

The incidents which sometimes brought forth great mirth didn't have to be about a particularly humorous happening, as Hindson continues:

> It was just strange; some of the incidents where we are actually out there—in the jungle—deadly serious and something would happen and everybody would be cracked up rolling around laughing. Early in the tour we had to cross what looked like a piece of fairly swampy ground. As we went to cross, the scout just sank in water up to his waist. I'm the next guy along and I'm laughing and trying to help haul him out. I go to move, fell in, and now he's laughing. He hauls me out. Finally, O'Keefe, who is probably the weight of about two of us and the last patrol member, also falls in. As we try to pull him out, others fall in. By this time we are all covered in mud and wet. We finally get him out and everybody is just rolling around laughing and killing themselves. And we're out in the middle of the bloody jungle, for Christ's sake.[28]

Patrol leaders trying to be deadly serious can sometimes become the butt of others' humour in the very egalitarian environment of the SAS, as Barry Standen recalled:

> I was in Pancho Tonna's patrol in Viet Nam and we had just pulled a hit on a track and knocked a few guys over and we were going out to check and search the bodies. I was Pancho's sig, so I was next to him and we were behind a huge tree that had fallen down and that was where we actually were when we initiated. It was a small arms ambush, a sort of opportunity target. Pancho screams out, 'Flanks out!' and the flanks go bloody out and he says, 'Follow me, men' and he stepped over this bloody great tree and went flat on his face and his bloody weapon went barrel down in the mud and I mean he couldn't have fired if there had been a follow-up—he was out of action, there were no two ways about it. Flat on his face and his barrel went straight in, almost vertical—doinngg! And he's trying to pull it out and I mean at the time I was probably having this little nervous giggle, but Jesus, when I got back I just couldn't bloody stop laughing over it. I mean

it could have been bad, we might have knocked off the first couple of men of a bloody company or something—who knows? But, yes, that was something out of a bloody play, 'The cavalry are coming, follow me men, whoosh.' Flat on his bloody face.[29]

If a patrol suffered a casualty the entire organisation was affected because it is a small group and everybody knows everybody else, probably better than any other military outfit in the Australian Army. How did they feel when they lost someone?

It doesn't affect things. There was a lot of black humour. No, it doesn't affect things, not in my experience. We were professionals. Shit happens.[30]

Not affecting things did not mean that the members did not feel the loss or grieve for their mate—they simply got on with their job. At times after incidents like when Dave Fisher fell off his rope and was lost, or other members were seriously wounded or killed, a sometimes macabre sense of humour can pervade an organisation. The SAS was no different from many other army units when one of their own is lost in battle. Barry Standen agrees:

Within the 'family' it is I guess 'black' humour by definition, but it's definitely a release mechanism. But it's also the fact that you're recognising that it could have been you, this could have happened to you. So, even though you're saying such like, 'The bloody dingbat, he shot himself', or he fell down and broke his neck and, 'What a bloody arsehole'. What you're really saying is, 'Shit, you know, I have got to learn from this. You know, that could have been me. There has got to be something in this for me to take away.'

The other thing about black humour is it's very, very much a family affair. If someone from outside the family tried to use that humour inside the family, they would be torn to pieces. It would be like bloody hyenas on a carcass. Yes, it is black humour by definition, but it's family humour. It's like an inside joke, I guess and it's part of the maturity and the training and the development that you go through.[31]

In between patrols and during their time in country, the SAS squadron would occasionally undertake a semi-official exchange program with the American Special Forces troops in various places around Viet Nam. The rationale was explained by Squadron Commander Reg Beesley, who was keen for the exchanges to take place:

> I believed there was a good opportunity to learn a little bit of the techniques of other special forces, particularly the American Special Forces. I went to Special Force commander, at Long Binh, and they had a secret compound there training people in cross-border operations into Cambodia. They also gave us some bits of equipment and access to parachuting. Their Recondo School was located at Nha Trang at a special forces group. I went there and established very good liaison. Each time I did it, the Australians topped the course, which was good. The only unfortunate thing about it was it was during their ten-day or twenty-day break, but it was exposure to other special forces activities and they gleaned something from it. The way of doing demolitions, the way of asking for air strikes and so forth.[32]

The visits were sometimes more hair-raising than normal SAS recon patrols. Reg Beesley debriefed his men after some exchanges with the US Navy and thought the SAS troopers did not appreciate their time with the US Navy Sea Air and Land (SEAL) teams:

> The SEALs were located down the bottom of the Rung Sat. I had two SEALs come up and two of our guys went down and went on an operation. They reckoned they would rather take field punishment than do it again! It was real cowboy time.[33]

15

THE OPPOSITION

The enemy the SAS faced in Borneo was rarely seen compared to the exposure they had to their foe in Viet Nam. In Borneo the SAS patrols would trudge for days and days to get across the border and then spend weeks or longer searching for him and then might only hear or catch a fleeting glimpse of their opposition. Not so in Viet Nam. They often ran into the enemy within hours of getting off their choppers, or as they were getting off their choppers. The enemy in Viet Nam were more plentiful and the topography lent itself to a greater opportunity to cross swords. Trevor Roderick fought both the Indonesian border terrorists and the Viet Cong guerillas, as well as both Viet Cong Main Force and North Vietnamese Army regular soldiers. He thought the enemy compared this way:

> When you had a contact with the Indonesians, there would be contact, you would put lots of fire down and you would go back out through your RV system and there would be a pregnant pause before they returned fire. With the enemy in Viet Nam, they returned fire almost immediately and they followed you up, they tried to get you, which is a bit different to Borneo.[1]

AS A FIGHTER

Many of the men interviewed for this book had numerous contacts with all types of enemy in Viet Nam and at different times during the SAS period there. Consequently opinions vary, but there is a constant theme which emerges about their foe: no-one in the SAS took their opposition lightly. Peter Schuman went almost straight from Borneo to Viet Nam and reflected on how the initial contact quickly got their attention when they saw their enemy at close quarters:

> When we came out of Borneo, my troop of 21 guys . . . 2 Squadron was deploying into Borneo, 3 Squadron was being raised for Viet Nam. I think about fifteen of my guys plus me all saddled up with 3 Squadron. We just went from B Troop to J Troop—it was a case of just changing names. And we thought we were pretty shit-hot, because we had been through the Borneo campaign, we had a campaign medal and we were SAS and for about the first month in Viet Nam we were, because we were just up against village guerillas around Hoa Long. I guess what you would call easing ourselves in, getting to know the area, and we had a little bit of success, and I think the baddies thought they better have a little bit of success too. They put a few guys who were a little bit tougher than the local boys into our area and that was pretty exciting. They were fellows who used to kneel down and look you in the eye and fire at you without blinking an eyelid.[2]

The enemy in Viet Nam came in three basic categories: the local village guerilla commonly called the Viet Cong, the VC Main Force regiments who were better trained, better equipped but still mainly South Vietnamese men with some imports from the regular North Vietnamese Army to stiffen them up and train and lead them. Finally there were the battle-hardened North Vietnamese Army soldiers. The NVA were well trained, well equipped and highly motivated. The SAS men compared them in various ways:

> There was a big variation in capability from the local people through to the regular force. I remember that on one of our patrols, I was looking at this guy coming through the woods

and thinking he was the biggest bloody VC that we had ever seen. And there was a difference in the way they moved. On a number of patrols we were pretty taken aback. Early in the tour we often saw groups that would be wandering around talking and pretty slack and treating the whole province like their backyard. Then we would come across a Main Force group that would actually be patrolling along. They would be in a formation and it might be a bit slack towards the back, but they had the weaponry and they clearly had the training and they looked bigger, better and more disciplined. That was a real concern, especially when Frank Sykes ran into this group and they tried to outflank him and he just had contact after contact after contact until he got clear. At one stage they could see enemy running around to their flank, sprinting around trying to get behind them. For a five-man patrol that makes your hair stand on end. I don't think they liked it too much.[3]

Peter Schuman had a similar incident to the one mentioned above and thought about the Viet Nam enemy in this vein:

The local village guys I think were a bit of an embarrassment to the structure. They were brave guys because they were the ones that took a lot of the brunt of the casualties. They were essential to the overall VC movement, I suppose. The NVA were pretty reasonable down to section level—their section commanders were pretty good. Their next echelon up from that were fairly cumbersome. Their battle drills were very slow to react . . . I can't recall the VC unit, but I remember hitting a mob of hard-hats one day, the old green pith helmets and red scarfs, and they were good. I recall one guy—I guess he was a corporal—after the initial contact, I can remember lining this guy up and firing about three shots at him and I missed him every time. But he just knelt there and he was giving field signals and he would have been about 30 metres away. I could see him through the jungle. This guy was as calm as a cucumber. There was bits flying around him. He was that good, he said, 'Okay, all I've got against me is a light automatic rifle that's sort of firing somewhere and I've got someone who is putting aimed shots in—but I'm 30 metres away and he's not that good.' I was firing at this guy and out of the corner of my eye I could see this machine-gun group go to the left flank with a rifle group following up and I thought, 'Schuman, you're gonna get done, get on your bike, son.' So, I rounded my boys up and said, 'The battlefield is yours today, sir.' Yes, they were good. I had a lot of respect for them.[4]

RESPECT FOR THE ENEMY

The SAS patrols do not vary very much in this feeling of respect for their former adversary. The SAS patrols were put deep into the enemy territory, or as most of them tend to say, in his backyard, so one would expect their security to be less than spot-on. Neville Farley was the patrol commander who 'slept with the enemy' on one memorable patrol and escaped by the skin of his teeth:

> I thought they were bloody good because they could virtually get around with zero equipment and patrol and be prepared to take on a large formation. Then again I didn't see them take on big units, who would have been much better equipped than SAS patrols. When I saw them they were patrolling in their own backyard. To be able to put up with what they did, living in the scrub for months and months, probably years on end—I've got nothing but respect for them.[5]

Nev Farley's scout was Andy Nucifora both in Borneo and later on their first tour of Viet Nam. He naturally had similar views to Farley and harked back to 'bed and breakfast with the VC':

> Well, I think I respected them pretty well but I never under-estimated them because I think it's silly to do that. But I think if they couldn't catch a patrol of guys in the middle of their own headquarters, and pure and simple they were making a lot of noise etcetera, and I thought well they can't be all that good.[6]

Barry Standen looks back on his time with a lot of deep feelings and tried to put the whole conflict and his part in it into some form of perspective:

> They were fighting for a cause, we were fighting for a cause. I mean, we were professional soldiers. Regardless of whether

they were VC, Main Force, NVA or political reactionaries, they were soldiers just like us and I mean it was a classical military conflict. We happened to have air, artillery and every other kind of superiority you could lay a bloody pencil to, but at the end of the day, it was a classical military conflict. Where it was professionals against professionals—some were more professional than others.

But I don't think you can take anything away from the VC. I mean they were bloody real mushrooms in some cases there, you know, kept in the dark and fed on shit. Thinking that they could shoot down gunships with bloody bows and arrows sort of thing and the invincibility of their cause and you know they went to their death in the thousands, believing in their cause. You know, in retrospect, you have got to admire their commitment.[7]

Probably the only group that didn't draw too much respect from the SAS were the guerillas who were really only part-time soldiers, often placed in the position of either assisting the Viet Cong or suffering some form of punishment from extra taxes to much worse. Peter Schuman recalls occasions when the enemy didn't want to play:

It was only towards the end of our tour, sometimes you would probably get an NVA unit who was tramping through your area and they would really get stuck into you. Going out towards Long Tan, you know the 3rd Platoon of the Long Tan Volunteers would have a go at you, and they would say, 'Shit, not today fellas we'll go back and start ploughing the fields, we don't want to play with you'.[8]

Trevor Roderick had experienced all types of enemy and made a comparison which was only to highlight the difference and not compare their capability or delve too deeply into their tactics. He found:

The minute we started going more than two or three clicks away from the Task Force base, the Nui Thi Vais in particular, the Nui Dinhs, we ran into the VC. The NVA were tough. I felt that they were better than we had been briefed. For example they would try and stay in contact. I thought their battle drills were pretty good, there was less of a time gap between when we initiated, because we always initiated contact, always, and the time gap between that initiation and their reaction time was bugger-all compared to the Indonesians, and that's the only comparison I can make.[9]

Joe Van Droffelaar got into the enemy's face quite often and had this to say about the enemy:

I found the enemy very professional . . . in the way they conducted themselves. I believe particularly the NVA soldier was a good fighter. If they had had the resources and the air cover that we had they would have been a good opposition . . . In the later part of our patrols, we were being pushed further and further into the May Tao Mountains. And a lot of the contacts that I did make were with either NVA-led or they were NVA, but they were quick, they were decisive and aggressive. They had aggressiveness and a will to follow up, even when they were being delayed by WPs, and being delayed by Claymores and they still continued to move up. But the average bloke would hang back a bit and say hey, this white stuff is not for me! But these blokes continued in some cases, to either divert or move around towards where the actual explosive charges took place.[10]

Some men didn't spend too much time thinking about the enemy because they brought the whole issue down to some fairly basic and quite true essentials—kill or be killed:

I had a lot of respect for him, but my thoughts didn't dwell a hell of a lot on him. To me the enemy was the enemy. If we were eyeball to eyeball he was going to do his damnedest to kill me and I'm going to do my damnedest to kill him. I didn't see him as a family-loving father. You should be detached to a fair degree. He was just a target.[11]

Some of the men deliberately put thoughts of the enemy out of their mind so they could concentrate more acutely and focus on the job at hand—killing the enemy and not getting yourself or your mates killed in the process. War is incredibly brutal and it takes men into a place and time which is far removed from normality and part of that process is the desensitising effect it has on men and the latent effects later in their lives when they return to normality. Andy Nucifora was brutally blunt and indicated that he was just doing his job. He thought of the enemy

just as enemy, just as anyone that got hit and that's their problem. I didn't feel sorry for them. In fact I was very aloof and I cut myself off with the enemy and I didn't want to have any feelings to do with them.

I remember once we searched one guy—and we used to go through all their pockets and if we found anything significant and throw it in our packs and try and gain items of intelligence value. But I just remember once this guy had a little sort of a handkerchief or a napkin and he had it all embroidered with typical Far East landscape and design. And it was very, very nicely done and it was really a work of art and I thought, gee, I wouldn't mind having that for a souvenir, but I really didn't want to have someone else's property. I have seen photos of guys with their wife and a couple of kids and it didn't do anything for me.

It's only looking for trouble, I think. You really just don't want to let those thoughts like that in, because you won't be thinking about your own guys. Even thoughts about your own guys getting hit. You might think about it but you must put it out of your mind—you don't want to dwell on anything like that. You just don't want any distractions, because there's a job to do and you have to concentrate on that.

In fact I remember once someone asked me, 'How did you feel about coming up against the North Vietnamese?' I don't think it really mattered, I said—I had nothing personal against the North Vietnamese, but if they had sent Yanks against us I would have shot Yanks. It wouldn't have worried me.[12]

A JOB TO DO

Not too many men felt 'sorry' for the enemy, even though they accepted the fact that they had inferior equipment and less military firepower. For the SAS patrol member on the ground, when it became 'the quick and the dead' and survival of the fittest, fastest and more cunning, the law of the jungle tended to take over and 'it's him or me' became the rule. Trevor Roderick didn't feel sorry for the enemy and

> I didn't despise him either. We used to talk about what it might be like. Not feel sorry for him, but talk about what it might be like sitting under a B–52 strike. And under napalm, and having CS gas pumped down your tunnel when you're down there, but I never felt sorry for him. I don't think I had hatred for him. Sometimes when you read about what they did to captured servicemen and Viets and tortured them and stuff like that, after a moment, but no. I guess we just looked upon them as just targets. So, knock them off.[13]

Neville Farley was adamant about feeling sorry for the enemy:

> Oh, shit no. I guess, being a regular soldier I didn't feel sorry for them at all. I was there to do what I had to do and if they were on the receiving end it was all the better for me.[14]

Some men did have some room for compassion when it came to the business end of their job and Ian Stiles said that he felt sorry for some enemy, in particular those who were probably just porters who were killed in ambushes.[15] Barry Standen did feel sorry for the enemy and put his feelings into these words and brought out one of the great truisms that soldiers are merely pawns in the greater scheme of things and simply tools for war, which is after all an extension of foreign policy:

> If you go in and have a fire-fight and you knock over one person and they didn't get one of yours, you have got to feel compassion for the fact that this is really the classical bloody Roman, man-on-man shit. This isn't about 'All the way with LBJ' or any of this, it's toe to toe, you or me. This is gladiatorial. And at the end of the day someone has got to go. Now, it comes back to you or me buster. You know I never felt sorry enough to lay down for them and I never felt sorry enough not to fire when it was appropriate to do so, but I'm now speaking as a mid–50 year old. But at the time we were fed so much crap about them, that I used to think that they were pretty bloody ordinary people and the world would be better without them. But when you look back with 35 years of reflection, they were doing what they were trained to do

and they were exactly the same as us. They were just soldiers being pushed around by politicians.[16]

Others felt otherwise and were adamant that it was nothing more than a job to do and a dirty one at that. Bill Hindson didn't feel sorry:

> Not at all. In fact quite the opposite. I made it a particular point where I wanted to protect my soldiers, our soldiers, at all costs. I didn't want any of them hurt. There was to be no trade-off—that ten enemy would be worth 'x' amount. There was to be no trade-off, nothing was worth an injury and nothing particularly was worth a death in our squadron or in my troop in particular. I had absolutely no sympathy for them at all.[17]

ON KILLING

No sane person would ever enjoy killing another human being, but there comes a time when the element of fear is overtaken by another feeling—when a warrior comes out of a confrontation as the victor. Trevor Roderick had that feeling when he survived his first contact:

> Absolute elation. Because I got him before he got me! Absolute, utter elation, and to be honest, it sounds brutal but you got pissed on the strength of it. You got one, you beauty. Well, you're professionals, so you don't bloody worry about it and you're not going to dwell on it.[18]

The savagery of war hits home when a soldier is standing over the corpse of another human being and the thought naturally goes through his mind of the frailty of life. Barry Standen said:

> I think the toughest thing I have ever done is to have to search bodies after a contact. You tend to realise that the baddies aren't much different to yourself and you look at these people at your feet and you think there but for the grace of God. And you realise that dead body doesn't have a race, a colour,

a religion, a political ideology, an identity, a nationality. This poor bastard, two minutes or two seconds before, was probably thinking of doing to me exactly the same as I did to him or as our patrol did to his group. It's very sobering and it's something that haunts me today. It's very hard to take that sort of thing out of your mind.[19]

One of the 9 Squadron pilots thought about the enemy and admitted he was glad he was detached from the ground fighting. He thought about what he had been told about the Viet Cong before he arrived in Viet Nam and what went through his mind shortly after he met them on the battlefield:

I certainly reappraised in a very short time. There was no respect for them in the way that you develop a respect for a conventional enemy. We didn't have any sense of that before we went up there. We heard blokes talk about them, but there was no respect for their talents. They were just the enemy, bad guys, gooks, whatever people called them, and we didn't have that respect initially, but we soon learnt it. We started hearing debriefs of missions, debriefs of SAS patrols, as to how many there were and what they were doing. It was a lot of fun initially, and then you realised that this was pretty serious business and the enemy was very serious. And they had been at war for a long time—like centuries—and they were pretty committed to what they were doing. And they deserved respect and that's pretty much what they got.[20]

EPILOGUE

Success can be measured in may ways when looking back on achievements. From the reconnaissance point of view of gathering information and intelligence and keeping tabs on the enemy—without the enemy knowing they were under surveillance—then the SAS patrols which operated in Borneo and crossed into Kalimantan on their 'Claret' operations were a huge success. In Viet Nam the measure of success at that time was more focused on the body count from harassing operations culminating from the recce/ambush patrols and in that regard the SAS patrols were enormously successful.

There were very few SAS casualties from both conflicts and a perusal of the SAS Roll of Honour since the SAS Company was first formed shows only one Australian SAS soldier killed as a direct result of enemy action. The other casualties were accidental deaths. There were approximately 298 contacts with the enemy in Viet Nam; the SAS inflicted 492 kills, 106 possible kills, wounded another 47, possibly wounded 10, and captured 11 prisoners. A total of 5366 enemy were sighted in 801 sightings.

In Borneo there were three casualties, all non-battle. Lance Corporal Paul Denehy died as a result of being gored by an elephant and Lieutenant Keith Hudson and Private Robert Moncrieff were presumed drowned while crossing a river. The

Australian and New Zealand casualties in Viet Nam were: one killed in action (Sergeant Graham Campbell), one died of wounds (Private Russel Copeman), two accidentally shot while on patrol (Second Lieutenant Brian Jones and Corporal Ronald Harris), one died from illness (Private Geoffrey O'Shea), one killed in a grenade accident (Sergeant George 'Chicka' Baines), and one missing in action (Private Dave Fisher).[1]

In that regard therefore, the SAS has enjoyed a great deal of success. The soldiers who operate on the patrols measure the success of their patrol a little differently. Ian Conaghan thought:

> People get the wrong idea, don't they? For instance I just saw in that book that's just been published [*A Pictorial History*][2] there's a picture of Frank Cashmore and the caption states that he 'led the most successful patrol ever'. I disagree, because I believe that many patrols, through recon or surveillance, achieved missions that had far-reaching effects on the overall Australian results—even though they may not have fired a single shot. In these terms, the most successful is almost impossible to gauge. I think body count does not necessarily indicate the success of a patrol. The success of a patrol is achieving the mission. If you have achieved the mission, whether it be to go out and kill someone, or whether it be to go out and gain information, then it's a successful patrol. Quite often if you went out and killed someone and your aim was to get information and you were compromised by killing someone and had to be pulled out—you haven't achieved your mission. So really the patrol is unsuccessful in that instance.[3]

THE BORNEO EXPERIENCE

The reasons behind the success of the SAS in Viet Nam? One trooper who went to Borneo as a young man and returned a much wiser trooper thought;

> Borneo was the greatest thing that ever happened to us, because it was the best training. We got trained by 22 SAS, we actually did the time over there, and it was all long-range patrolling. We didn't know what we were going to do in Viet Nam, but it still came down to long-range patrolling. Where

271

you had small teams, you had to be secure at all times and that was the best bloody training ground and I think it saved so many lives. The fact that we learnt our lessons in Borneo rather than in Viet Nam—I think that's why our casualty rates were so low . . . It was just a fair dinkum training ground.[4]

Barry Standen, who did back-to-back tours of Borneo and then two tours with the SAS in Viet Nam, agreed that Borneo was to be the proving ground for the SAS doctrine and procedures which would be proved in Viet Nam:

> Borneo was a great training ground as it turned out. I would have to say, as an opinion only, that had SAS not been committed to Borneo prior to Viet Nam, my belief is that they would have taken substantial casualties. I don't think our training for jungle warfare was adequate if you take Borneo out of the equation . . . You would like to think that the military mind had intended it, but it might be a coincidental thing. SAS had a fantastic record in Viet Nam and I think that largely could be hung off the experience in Borneo.[5]

NEW GUINEA

The SAS trained in New Guinea and did much of their initial team-building on the exercises against the Pacific Islands Regiment (PIR) and on the 'long walks' that they undertook in the country. It moulded the patrols and troops together and created that invisible cement that was required to hold a small group together in difficult situations. The SAS went to PNG instead of the normal training grounds of Canungra and Shoalwater Bay because they found that deploying overseas and exercising in a tropical environment produced better results. Trevor Roderick did both types of training in Australia, as he also deployed to Viet Nam as rifle company 2IC in 1971. He believed going to PNG and exercising against the elusive and cunning men from the PIR was the best thing that happened to the SAS after Borneo because:

> We thought our shit didn't stink and the PIR really brought it home. I don't think we were over-confident, but the

Indonesian experience really gave us confidence. Forget the officers, because the officers get posted every couple of years, but the NCOs in Borneo formed the nucleus for the squadrons of SAS that went to Viet Nam . . . and I thought that was very important . . . They were early days [1966] for SAS and I think the resources were well managed.[6]

THE VALUE OF A GOOD RECCE PATROL

The success of a patrol is not always measured in a body count after a bank of Claymore mines and 300 rounds of small arms has been directed at the enemy. The original purpose of SAS patrols was to provide reconnaissance and as it later developed in Viet Nam after 1966, the value of a well-directed harassing patrol far outweighed the expense of getting them in there. They were a very cost-effective weapon against the Viet Cong and North Vietnamese Army units in Phuoc Tuy Province, but the value of their intelligence reports and information brought back also needs to be considered. Ian Stiles explains:

> We would patrol until we found a well-used track, and sit on that track and watch people move up and down, and get what sort of weapons they were carrying, times, direction they were moving, whether they had packs on, what sort of webbing they had and I don't believe it was until a couple of years later I realised how important these patrols were. I had been told what they actually did was they substantiated agent reports, because if you had an agent and he reckons he was up in the Nui Thi Vais, the intelligence briefing officer would ask him, 'Okay, were you there on 25th of April?' or whatever and the agent would say, 'Yeah', and the intelligence officer would ask, 'What actually happened on that day?' He would then have to substantiate what we had actually seen, because we might have been 5 kilometres away on a track watching these guys go past at a certain time. It would actually give a lot of credence to what this agent was actually saying and if we could back up the agent's version of events, he would probably be telling the truth about other things. So it wasn't really only being able to identify whether they were NVA, Local Force or whatever, it was a very important part of the jigsaw of the whole intelligence picture.[7]

One day someone will write a book about these Vietnamese men and women who spent time acting as agents having infiltrated the units of the Viet Cong. It must have been a tightrope existence and one fraught with the danger, not only of exposure and certain execution, but of being killed or wounded by fire from the forces to which the agents were reporting.

PERSONAL PERSPECTIVES

What was important to these highly trained men who had spent years preparing for their job in Borneo and Viet Nam? What was their 'bottom line' when it came to their aim as a patrol member or a patrol leader? For Nev Farley,

> I guess the thing I always wanted to do was bring back the patrol. That was all I wanted to do, bring them all back and not lose anybody. That was very important to me. The old man probably put something in my mind that I heard years ago, he said to me, 'The only medal you want to win is your Returned From Active Service Badge'. I thought, yeah, that says it all. And I sort of went one further—all I want to do is bring my bloody patrol home without any scratches, and I managed that. That's one of the things that I consider to be my achievement, that's all I wanted to do.[8]

Troop commander Ron Dempsey, who also led patrols, agreed with Nev Farley:

> I think my aim as a patrol commander was to make sure that I looked after the patrol. We did what we had to and we didn't take any casualties. Bring them all back alive.[9]

Bill Hindson was a troop commander and wanted to make sure he brought his patrol back home as well. He was asked what was the most important thing to him while he was in Viet Nam:

> Looking after your men is the most important thing. It's just that it was obviously going to be a very long war, and there

A studio portrait of Bill Hindson wearing his distinctive SAS beret. Pictured in battledress with his combat ribbons including the Military Cross award, his parachute jump instructor wings and Infantry Combat Badge. Hindson was also awarded a Medal for Gallantry (MG) in the End of War List honours published in 1998 for his first tour of Viet Nam as a rifle platoon commander with 1 RAR in 1965–66. *Photo courtesy of Bill Hindson*

was just no point in trading bodies for bodies. I had seen the Americans on their first tour where they had got into fire-fights and virtually stood up and challenged the enemy to come and get them and then traded blows with them and suffered huge casualties. The way the war was going on, there was just no point in doing that. The type of operations that we were required to perform were reconnaissance patrols or ambush patrols and our intention was not to get out there and get stuck into huge fights, but to keep nibbling away at them and make them feel unsafe. To get the information on what they were doing, to be free to roam in around their territory, and you could do that quite successfully without having to put ourselves in situations of getting people injured or killed.[10]

Other patrol commanders thought that the best way to get everybody home was to carry out their job with the utmost efficiency and thereby remove the threat to their own existence, like Trevor Roderick:

Doing my job, killing the bloody enemy, simple. Or, getting information, whatever your task was, that the rest of the Task Force could use. No grand thoughts of winning war or anything like that, it was just doing our job.[11]

But there will always be casualties in war as the soldiers live and work so very close to the edge of danger. When it does happen and a mate is lost, it stays with the men for the rest of their lives:

The saddest time for me was in Borneo rather than in Viet Nam—when Paul Denehy got killed, because Paul was a particularly good friend of mine. That would have been the saddest time of my operational service. I think everyone in SAS at the time, whether you were in the squadron that was overseas or with the unit back in Australia, everyone felt it because everyone knew that it could have been them.[12]

THE DURATION OF SAS OPERATIONS IN VIET NAM

Contrary to what was taken as normal special forces doctrine which had been established by the British SAS, and despite what the Australians had learnt from their experience in Borneo against *fewer* enemy and contacts, the squadrons in Viet Nam spent twelve months on operations—with the exception of the initial squadron which was deployed for only nine months. But even the initial squadron to deploy felt the impact of arduous patrolling and operating in severe tropical environs:

Although we were young, silly and coming out of Borneo— which was a fairly physically demanding campaign with the terrain—saddling up so soon after and going off to Viet Nam, the degradation did start to take its effect after about four months. As soon as the wet season started, I started to get real crook when I was continually wet with the rains and I wasn't operating up in the Nui Thi Vais where it gets a bit cold. I was still operating down on the flat lands, but it was just the continual dampness all around started to affect me.[13]

Bill Hindson's squadron deployed believing that they would probably only do a nine-month tour like the squadron before them, but it wasn't to be and this had a big impact on the troops:

Borneo tours were six months duration. Certainly 3 Squadron on their first tour of Viet Nam did nine months, and we expected nine months. I think it was about August 1967 before we were told that our tour would be twelve months. That was a huge morale problem. About that time many of our squadron had gone back to Australia sick with various illnesses, with injuries, and we had actually been planning on the nine months. At the time the decision came through, even before there was a clear decision and we were talking about the possibility, there was a lot of anger because the patrols were really being affected—physically being run down and becoming more susceptible to colds and flu and other injuries. It did absolutely nothing for morale when we were notified that there's an extra three months. An extra three months was another five or six patrols. It really affected the morale, and it's reflected in the letters that I had written. Through the first half of the tour they were four to six pages, and the last three months they are one or two pages at best.

Physically, we were run down because our body weight was up and down, we had been exposed to all sorts of insect-borne diseases and other ailments and we were trying to cope with that. Private Geoffrey 'Rick' O'Shea died from encephalitis in October 1967 and that could have happened to anybody, I would think. Some suffered back injuries. Rick Gloede had an injured foot and had been stumbling around camp for a while and he had to go off and convalesce. So, it just ran people down, it was just too long, definitely too long.[14]

The principal reason for the twelve-month tour of duty assigned to SAS was probably a lack of trained SAS soldiers in the army precluding a greater frequency of squadron rotation and the higher echelons' ignorance of just how demanding SAS patrols really are. Ron Dempsey did a twelve-month tour and he mused that six months might have been a better option:

I thought it would have been. Certainly, the experience in Borneo with the Brits—and they reduced their tours to six months. I found that after about the six-month period, that was when you had a lot of sickness and guys coming down with bronchitis and all sorts of infections. All the patrols were hard. I think the ones we did during the wet season were worst, where it was continually wet and you got no sleep. There was no shelter, you just had to sit in the rain like a miserable dog out there and shiver and shake. A lot of the guys were just worn out at that time. Instead of having five guys ready for a patrol, you would be lucky if you could drag up three fit guys. And you would drag in a cook, and a signaller, a driver or storeman or something like that and then go out.[15]

Ron Dempsey's troop relieved B Troop led by Bill Hindson and Dempsey was able to observe just what twelve months had done to these men he had seen deploy a year earlier when he was working up to go to Viet Nam:

I think they had changed a lot. A lot skinnier. They certainly looked tired and worn out, actually. Coming to the end of their tour—they were quite looking forward to it and going home.[16]

The army ignorance of what was required of the SAS squadrons and how they should be kitted out was highly evident to those in the SAS at the time, but the rest of the foot soldiers in the conventional forces had no idea what SAS did or needed on their operations. It was frustrating for the SAS because the people who made the decisions on equipment and weaponry in Canberra had no idea what SAS did and relied on myths and legends for their knowledge. This was probably also due in part to the SAS being a bit over-zealous on security—an aura surrounded the SAS, but nobody outside the regiment knew much about what they did.

Bill Hindson complained about how they were equipped for Viet Nam:

When we arrived in Viet Nam in 1967, we had Australian gear which wasn't good for our method of operating. So we rapidly had to set about trading and wheeling and dealing to get the sort of equipment and rations and weapons that we wanted. The squadron quartermaster, Taffy Davis, used to go out on bartering trips and convert cases of Australian beer into some other commodity and then trade it for another commodity and then trade it for American packs, tiger suits, different weapons—of all sorts—to get us the sort of gear that we needed. At the end of the tour the only thing I was wearing that was Australian was my compass pouch—the only thing.

I mentioned in one of my letters home that whenever members of our squadron went anywhere we would get them to buy packs, so we were actually paying to have people on leave in Hong Kong, buy . . . Brit packs and bring them back to us.

The sort of weaponry we used, some came through the American system, because we ended up with automatic shotguns with fleschette rounds; silenced weapons; a couple of .50 cal machine-guns (only used on the Hill); GPMG M60s; 7.62 mm SLRs on automatic—sometimes with flash eliminators removed; M16s and the M203 grenade-launcher. At one stage a silenced Thompson. The Thompson is a big ugly bloody heavy thing anyway, but with a silencer on the front of it—it was just ridiculous! Absolutely incredible . . .

And the Claymores were new to us. The first patrols we had were ambush patrols and we didn't have Claymores, and when we finally got hold of them and worked out how to use them, they became a central part of our ambush patrols.

Water bottles at that stage were a problem for us. The ones that we preferred were the plastic, flexible water bladders that the Americans had, so that as we used the water they took up less space.

So, there was quite a change in gear that we went through and as our squadron members met or operated with Rangers or Long Range Reconnaissance Patrols or ultimately as they did with the SEAL teams, they were swapping Australian clothing and coming back with camouflage gear of all types. Some of our first patrols we had straight Australian gear and it was quite a change to go from that sort of stuff to ultimately the camouflage gear. Whether it was real or not, our perception was that the camouflage was better and we behaved as though the VC couldn't see us.[17]

Barry Standen's exposure to four operational tours and being a sig allowed him to take an almost detached view of the patrol members and he observed:

The squadron guys in country were very, very frazzled. I mean they were pretty stressed. After three or four months, we're talking about guys that have been in a pretty high-stress situation—continually—for three to four months . . . When you hit the five- and six-month mark, you're really starting to get ragged around the edges. And you're really starting to poke people into gaps as they appear as quickly as possible to achieve an aim, and when a Warning Order comes out and the Task Force Commander says, 'Hey, I want this done, I want your guys there,' it's pretty hard for the squadron commander to say, 'Hang on a minute', you know, 'We can't do it like that', sort of thing. 'We need a bit more notice' or 'We need a bit more warming up time' or 'We need to train for a specific job' or a specific area. Not all of the Task Force Commanders were very sympathetic to SAS, and the minute you showed a chink in your armour, they would exploit it, so that squadron commanders and troop commanders were under a lot of bloody pressure from Task Force.[18]

COMING HOME

Swanbourne Barracks, in a coastal suburb north-west of Perth city has been the home of the SAS since they were a company and grew into a regiment. They have always been a part of Perth society and are regarded as 'their own'. When the Viet Nam War was in full flight in 1968, the anti-war movement was mainly centred on the eastern seaboard and did not have much impact on the men from the SAS. That did not mean that they did not experience it when they went home to their parents, or took leave in the eastern states, or were posted on duty to places like Melbourne or Sydney or Canberra. For some it has left an aftertaste in their mouths which is still unpleasant even after 30 years.

Scum of the earth and I still think of them as scum of the earth today, principally because they didn't take the time to work out who they should aim their protests at, and they aimed their protests at the professional soldier instead of the bloody politicians. Soldiers don't declare war. Pollies declare war, the soldier implements the pollies' declaration. So it was no good throwing blood over Viet Nam veterans, for Christ's sake, during a march through Sydney and throwing horse shit at the SAS marching down St George's Terrace. It was absolutely infantile stuff. And I haven't changed my opinion in 35 years of reflection, because I think they were misguided—a bloody gang reaction. They just didn't have a mind of their own. They didn't have the sense to be objective enough to say, 'Who is at fault here?' There's some guys who have just got back from Viet Nam, and they must be at fault.[19]

Andy Nucifora came from northern Queensland and went to Borneo and then did two tours of Viet Nam. He was not impressed with the way the soldiers—especially conscripted men—were treated by protesters:

I was a regular and it didn't worry me, but I always felt sorry for the nashos that were dragged into it, without their approval in a lot of cases. A lot of other nashos that did go there, once they got in they realised they had to pull their weight like everyone else and they did. But I think that the people in Australia should have given them their support instead of putting shit on them. I think it was disgraceful.[20]

The anti-war movement grew in momentum after the National Liberation Front's militarily disastrous Tet Offensive in 1968. Politically, it was the turning point of American resolve and men like Ron Dempsey were able to observe whether the anti-war movement had an impact on the troops:

I think it did in a way. I know that at one stage there was a postal strike and I think the Diggers got very upset about that. You know, like, 'These bastards back home weren't going to send the mail' up to them because they didn't agree with the fighting, and there were big signs going up with 'Punch a Postie on Return To Australia' . . . They didn't get their mail for a week or so, and it was very upsetting for quite a lot of them.

I don't think the men got to the 'What are we doing here?' but in the opposite, saying, 'Well it's about time those bastards gave us some support' . . . Seeing the newsreels and all that sort of stuff, it wasn't 'What are we doing this for?' but, 'Why don't they come up and see it from our end?' Rather than sitting back there and mouthing off, they want .

to come up and have a look at it from this end and see what the country's like and what the enemy actually was imposing on the whole population.[21]

Arriving back at Perth airport after twelve months living in the bush, inflicting deadly and permanent grievous bodily harm on their enemies and living life on the edge from one day to the next has a cumulative effect on the persona and psyche of anyone who is normal. Bill Hindson recalled the day he touched down in Perth after a tough and dangerous tour where he was nearly killed on several occasions:

We got off the aircraft and walked into the Customs terminal. As I went through Customs I was quite calm. We did all the clearances and then the doors opened and we walked into the waiting area where our friends and relatives were waiting to greet us. I started shaking and I couldn't control it for the best part of three months. We had a very quick demob and were sent on leave. I had leave for three months from the end of February through March, April and May.

Fortunately Catherine [his fiancee] had been living down in Narrogin with her parents. So I went down to Narrogin and I got a job on a farm. Driving a tractor, mustering sheep and picking up rocks. I spent about three months on the farm doing that. Day in, day out, right through the whole of my leave. I think that's what probably helped restore my physical and mental wellbeing. I couldn't have imagined anything worse than staying somewhere in Perth in the proximity of the regiment. I wasn't in an area where I could worry about what the demonstrators were doing and who was getting ready to go to Viet Nam and what casualties were happening.[22]

ON LOOKING BACK

It is now almost three decades since the last Australian soldiers left the war zone in Viet Nam and returned to Australia to pursue a more sedate lifestyle. Some SAS men sought challenges in other war zones or areas of armed conflict like Rhodesia and South Africa. They all look back at their time in Borneo and Viet Nam with a deep sense of pride and achievement. They went, they did their job very successfully and most of them came home. At the same time they learnt much about themselves, their mates and the value of good, hard training and insistence on perfection and an ethos of excellence. They made mates who have remained so for the rest of their lives. Peter Schuman calls the SAS 'the brotherhood' and as the National President of the SAS Regiment Association until very recently has been able to observe the brotherhood binding together after disasters like the Blackhawk disaster in Townsville in June 1996. For others it is a truly Australian experience based on respect and an egalitarian approach in the regiment, the troops and the patrols. Barry Standen replied to the question about what SAS service has meant to him:

> Mateship and the fact that you had support—almost unequiv-ocal support and completely unreserved support from your counterparts of all ranks, shape and creed. I often call SAS 'the Mafia'. The SAS family is the Mafia and the longer I ponder that question, the more I support that analogy.[23]

One thing is very certain and as long as the SAS insist on the highest standards in selecting their soldiers, as long as they maintain that insistence on very high standards in training and maintain the motto of 'Who Dares Wins', then they will always be a force to be respected and admired.

NOTES

PREFACE

1 David Horner, *SAS: Phantoms of the Jungle. A History of the Australian Special Air Service*, Sydney: Allen & Unwin, 1989
2 Ian McPhedran, 'Daredevils', *Courier-Mail*, 14 February 1998
3 ibid.
4 ibid.
5 Colonel David Stirling, DSO, OBE, Memorandum on the Origins of the Special Air Service Regiment
6 Interview, Major Trevor Roderick

1 THE SAS TROOPER

1 Interview, Colonel Reg F. Beesley
2 Interview, Warrant Officer Ian Conaghan
3 Interview, Lieutenant-Colonel Peter Schuman
4 Interview, Lieutenant-Colonel Ron Dempsey
5 Interview, Major-General J. C. (Jim) Hughes
6 ibid.
7 Interview, Warrant Officer M. 'Joe' Van Droffelaar
8 ibid.
9 Interview, Lieutenant-Colonel Bill Hindson

10 Interview, Jim Hughes
11 Interview, Ian Conaghan
12 ibid.
13 Interview, Dan McDaniel, SAS officer
14 ibid.
15 Interview, Bill Hindson
16 Interview, Ian Conaghan
17 Interview, Warrant Officer Neville Farley
18 Interview, Trevor Roderick
19 Interview, Peter Schuman
20 Interview, Major Barry F. 'Muka' Standen
21 Interview, Bill Hindson

2 CUTTING THE MUSTARD

1 Interview, Neville Farley
2 Interview, Barry Standen
3 Interview, Ron Dempsey
4 Interview, Reg Beesley
5 ibid.
6 Interview, Dan McDaniel
7 ibid.
8 Interview, Ron Dempsey
9 Interview, Barry Standen
10 Interview, Bill Hindson
11 Interview, Barry Standen
12 ibid.
13 Interview, Trevor Roderick
14 Interview, Dan McDaniel
15 Interview, Bill Hindson
16 Interview, Barry Standen
17 Interview, Dan McDaniel
18 Ian McPhedran, 'Daredevils'
19 Interview, Joe Van Droffelaar
20 Interview, Sergeant Ian 'Bagza' Stiles
21 Interview, Trevor Roderick
22 Interview, Dan McDaniel
23 ibid.
24 Interview, Neville Farley
25 Interview, Dan McDaniel
26 Interview, Ian Stiles
27 Interview, Peter Schuman

28 Interview, Neville Farley
29 Interview, Dan McDaniel
30 Interview, Bill Hindson
31 Interview, Neville Farley
32 Interview, Bill Hindson
33 Interview, Ian Stiles
34 Interview, Neville Farley
35 ibid.
36 Interview, Peter Schuman
37 Interview, Dan McDaniel
38 Interview, Jim Hughes
39 Interview, Dan McDaniel
40 Interview, Bill Hindson

3 THE SAS PATROL

1 Interview, Ian Conaghan
2 Interview, Peter Schuman
3 An LUP is a Lying Up Position. It is a formation adopted by an SAS patrol to provide all-round defence and security while the patrol signaller sends a radio message, or for longer halts such as overnight stops, firm bases for closer reconnaissance by the scout and patrol commander. For further information see Chapter 10 on the routine of the patrol.
4 Interview, Joe Van Droffelaar
5 Interview, Jim Hughes
6 Interview, Bill Hindson
7 The SAS trooper is a finely honed and extremely well trained individual. Each soldier possesses a record book of the courses he has attended and shows the skills that he has when those in command have to make decisions on who next to promote and who to select for skills experience. I asked one of the troopers featured in this book to show me his AAB–83 Record of service, which shows the courses he attended during his time with the SAS Regiment.

Ian Conaghan attended and qualified on the following courses:
1965
   • A basic parachute course—which allows the member to conduct military static line parachute descent by day or by night.
   • A weapons instructors' course.
   • A regimental signallers' course, which allows the member to

operate as a signaller on an SAS patrol and includes the Morse element required for SAS patrol sigs.

1966
- The SAS medics' course at the School of Army Health, which allows the member to operate as a medic on an SAS patrol.

1968
- The officer/NCO assault pioneer course, which includes the qualification of a demolition supervisor's ticket and basic water-manship, mine warfare including improvised explosive demolition, basic field construction techniques, the operation of chainsaws, paving breakers, flame warfare using the M2A1–7 flamethrower portable.

1969
- An air portability team leaders' course, which allows the member to plan and assist in the conduct of airmobile and parachute operations.
- A stick commanders' course, which allows the member to operate as a team leader in parachute descent operations.

1971
- Air photo reading instructors' course, which allows the member to teach air photo reading essential to the planning of SAS patrols and interpretation of air photographs for intelligence gathering.
- Industrial demolitions course, which allows the member to conduct demolitions on man-made targets principally of a vertical construction nature.
- A rappelling instructors' course, which allows the member to train SAS personnel in the techniques for rappelling from aircraft and off natural and artificial features.

1972
- A military free fall parachute course which allows the member to participate in parachute operations which allow covert insertion into areas using various techniques.
- A basic roping course, which allows the member to participate in roping operations from aircraft, natural and man-made features for many types of SAS operations.
- An unconventional warfare (UW) course, which teaches the member the various SAS techniques in unconventional warfare operations including the role and tasks in such operations for SAS UW operatives.

1973
- A Special Forces intelligence course.
- A marksmanship coaching course, which allows the member to train other soldiers to attain marksman shooting qualifications

and standards. (One has to qualify as a marksman to attend the course.)

- An unconventional warfare weapons course, which exposes the member to weapons not normally held by Australian military forces and allows him to teach others on the various weaponry likely to be used in operations against and alongside SAS forces around the world.

1974

- A mortar course, which allows the member to effectively operate and conduct mortar firing with mortars provided for SAS operations.

8 Interview, Ian Stiles
9 Interview, Jim Hughes
10 ibid.
11 ibid.
12 ibid.
13 Interview, Reg Beesley
14 Interview, Bill Hindson
15 Interview, Ron Dempsey
16 Interview, Barry Standen
17 ibid.
18 Interview, Corporal Angelo 'Andy' Nucifora
19 Interview, Trevor Roderick
20 Interview, Peter Schuman
21 Interview, Ian Stiles
22 ibid.
23 Interview, Joe Van Droffelaar
24 Interview, Ian Conaghan
25 ibid.
26 Interview, Joe Van Droffelaar
27 Interview, Ian Conaghan
28 ibid.
29 Interview, Andy Nucifora
30 ibid.
31 Interview, Ron Dempsey
32 Interview, Ian Stiles
33 ibid.
34 Interview, Bill Hindson
35 Interview, Ian Conaghan
36 Interview, Ron Dempsey
37 Interview, Bill Hindson
38 ibid.
39 Interview, Barry Standen

40 Interview, Joe Van Droffelaar
41 Interview, Ian Conaghan
42 Interview, Bill Hindson

4 BORNEO—THE PROVING GROUND

1 For a more detailed account of the build-up and the formation of the SAS Regiment see David Horner, *SAS: Phantoms of the Jungle—A History of the Australian Special Air Service,* chapter 4, pp. 60–80.
2 Interview, Trevor Roderick
3 ibid.
4 Interview, Peter Schuman
5 ibid.
6 Interview, Barry Standen
7 Interview, Peter Schuman
8 ibid.
9 Interview, Trevor Roderick
10 Interview, Peter Schuman
11 ibid.
12 Interview, Jim Hughes
13 Interview, Trevor Roderick
14 ibid.
15 For a full and well documented account of this tragic episode see David Horner, *SAS: Phantoms of the Jungle,* chapter 7, pp. 110–21
16 Interview, Barry Standen
17 David Horner, *SAS: Phantoms of the Jungle,* chapter 8, p. 134
18 Interview, Jim Hughes
19 ibid.
20 Interview, Ian Conaghan
21 ibid.
22 Interview, Jim Hughes
23 Interview, Ian Conaghan
24 ibid.
25 Interview, Jim Hughes
26 ibid.
27 ibid.
28 Interview, Ian Conaghan
29 ibid.
30 ibid.
31 Interview, Jim Hughes
32 Interview, Ian Conaghan
33 Interview, Jim Hughes

34 ibid.
35 Interview, Barry Standen
36 Interview, Ian Conaghan
37 Interview, Jim Hughes
38 Interview, Ian Conaghan
39 Interview, Jim Hughes
40 ibid.
41 For a full account of the accident see David Horner, *SAS: Phantoms of the Jungle*, chapter 10, pp. 158–61
42 Interview, Jim Hughes
43 Interview, Ian Conaghan

5 PAPUA NEW GUINEA

1 Interview, Reg Beesley
2 Interview, Jim Hughes
3 ibid.
4 Interview, Ron Dempsey
5 Interview, Bill Hindson
6 Interview, Ian Stiles
7 ibid.
8 Interview, Bill Hindson
9 Interview, Ian Conaghan
10 ibid.
11 Interview, Bill Hindson
12 Interview, Ron Dempsey

6 FINE-TUNING

1 Interview, Jim Hughes
2 ibid.
3 ibid.
4 Interview, Peter Schuman
5 Interview, Reg Beesley
6 Interview, Ian Stiles
7 Sergeant Fred Roberts toured Viet Nam with 3 Squadron in 1966–67 and then again with 3 Squadron as a patrol sergeant in 1969–70. He was awarded the DCM in December 1969 for conducting two successful ambushes in one patrol.
8 Interview, Ian Stiles

9 Interview, Ian Conaghan
10 Interview, Ian Stiles
11 Interview, Peter Schuman
12 Interview, Bill Hindson
13 Interview, Terry Pinkerton
14 ibid.
15 Interview, Neville Farley

7 VIET NAM

1 Interview, Trevor Roderick
2 Interview, Ian Conaghan
3 Interview, Peter Schuman
4 Interview, Trevor Roderick
5 Interview, Peter Schuman
6 ibid.
7 Interview, Reg Beesley
8 ibid.
9 Interview, Bill Hindson
10 Interview, Ian Conaghan
11 Interview, Ian Stiles
12 Interview, Neville Farley
13 Interview, Ian Stiles
14 Interview, Peter Schuman
15 Interview, Neville Farley
16 Interview, Bill Hindson
17 Interview, Ron Dempsey
18 Interview, Barry Standen
19 ibid.
20 ibid.
21 ibid.
22 Interview, Terry Pinkerton
23 Interview, Jack Lynch
24 ibid.
25 Interview, Neville Farley

8 GETTING READY—PATROL PREPARATION

1 Interview, Peter Schuman
2 Interview, Ian Conaghan

3 Interview, Bill Hindson
4 Interview, Ian Stiles
5 Interview, Ian Conaghan
6 Interview, Terry Pinkerton
7 ibid.
8 Interview, Neville Farley
9 Interview, Joe Van Droffelaar
10 Interview, Neville Farley
11 Interview, Peter Schuman
12 Interview, Ian Conaghan
13 Interview, Bill Hindson
14 Interview, Peter Schuman
15 Interview, Terry Pinkerton
16 Interview, Trevor Roderick
17 Interview, Joe Van Droffelaar
18 Interview, Andy Nucifora
19 ibid.
20 Interview, Bill Hindson
21 Interview, Neville Farley

9 GETTING IN

1 Interview, Peter Schuman
2 ibid.
3 Interview, Ian Conaghan
4 Interview, Ian Stiles
5 The SOP was entitled 'SAS Reconnaissance Patrol Operations' and was Chapter A/8 of 9 Squadron SOPs in Viet Nam and nineteen pages in length.
6 Interview, Bill Hindson
7 Interview, Terry Pinkerton
8 Interview, Trevor Roderick
9 Interview, Neville Farley
10 Interview, Terry Pinkerton
11 Interview, Jack Lynch
12 ibid.
13 Interview, Terry Pinkerton
14 ibid.
15 Interview, Jack Lynch
16 ibid.
17 ibid.
18 ibid.

19 ibid.
20 Interview, Neville Farley
21 Interview, Andy Nucifora
22 Interview, Bill Hindson
23 Interview, Jack Lynch
24 ibid.
25 ibid.
26 Interview, Terry Pinkerton
27 Interview, Jack Lynch
28 Interview, Trevor Roderick
29 Interview, Joe Van Droffelaar
30 ibid.
31 ibid.
32 Interview, Neville Farley
33 Interview, Bill Hindson
34 Interview, Ron Dempsey
35 Interview, Bill Hindson
36 Interview, Ian Stiles
37 Interview, Ian Conaghan
38 Interview, Ian Stiles
39 Interview, Neville Farley
40 Interview, Ian Conaghan

10 THE DAILY ROUTINE

1 Interview, Joe Van Droffelaar
2 Interview, Trevor Roderick
3 Interview, Peter Schuman
4 ibid.
5 Interview, Ian Stiles
6 Interview, Bill Hindson
7 Interview, Ian Stiles
8 ibid.
9 ibid.
10 Interview, Andy Nucifora
11 Interview, Joe Van Droffelaar
12 Interview, Peter Schuman
13 ibid.
14 ibid.
15 Interview, Barry Standen
16 ibid.
17 ibid.
18 ibid.

19 Interview, Ian Conaghan
20 Interview, Barry Standen
21 Interview, Peter Schuman
22 Interview, Ian Stiles
23 Interview, Peter Schuman
24 Interview, Ian Stiles
25 Interview, Joe Van Droffelaar
26 ibid.

11 GETTING CLOSE

1   Interview, Ian Stiles
2   Interview, Ian Conaghan
3   Interview, Bill Hindson
4   Interview, Peter Schuman
5   Interview, Andy Nucifora
6   Interview, Ian Stiles
7   Interview, Ron Dempsey
8   Interview, Trevor Roderick
9   Interview, Bill Hindson
10 Interview, Peter Schuman
11 Interview, Ron Dempsey
12 Interview, Ian Conaghan
13 Interview, Trevor Roderick
14 Interview, Joe Van Droffelaar
15 Interview, Neville Farley
16 Interview, Bill Hindson
17 ibid.
18 ibid.
19 ibid.
20 ibid.
21 Interview, Joe Van Droffelaar
22 Interview, Ron Dempsey
23 Interview, Trevor Roderick
24 Interview, Ian Stiles
25 Interview, Ron Dempsey
26 Interview, Barry Standen

12 GETTING PERSONAL

1   Interview, Bill Hindson
2   Interview, Peter Schuman

3 Interview, Joe Van Droffelaar
4 Interview, Bill Hindson
5 ibid.
6 Interview, Neville Farley
7 ibid.
8 Interview, Joe Van Droffelaar
9 Interview, Trevor Roderick
10 Interview, Ian Stiles
11 ibid.
12 Interview, Neville Farley
13 Interview, Andy Nucifora
14 Interview, Neville Farley
15 The 'Bird Dog' was a Cessna or similar aircraft used by forward air controllers to coordinate and control air-to-ground or artillery fire support for ground forces. In this case it was manned by American Army pilots.
16 Interview, Andy Nucifora
17 ibid.
18 Interview, Bill Hindson
19 Interview, Trevor Roderick

13 GETTING OUT

1 Interview, Ron Dempsey
2 ibid.
3 Interview, Terry Pinkerton
4 Interview, Jack Lynch
5 Interview, Reg Beesley
6 ibid.
7 Interview, Ian Conaghan
8 Interview, Neville Farley
9 Interview, Peter Schuman
10 Interview, Terry Pinkerton
11 ibid.
12 ibid.
13 Interview, Jack Lynch
14 Interview, Terry Pinkerton
15 ibid.
16 ibid.
17 Interview, Ian Stiles
18 Interview, Reg Beesley
19 Interview, Jack Lynch
20 ibid.

21 Interview, Joe Van Droffelaar
22 Interview, Trevor Roderick
23 Interview, Terry Pinkerton
24 Interview, Barry Standen
25 Interview, Reg Beesley
26 Interview, Bill Hindson
27 ibid.
28 Interview, Terry Pinkerton
29 Interview, Reg Beesley
30 Interview, Trevor Roderick
31 Interview, Ian Stiles
32 Interview, Joe Van Droffelaar
33 ibid.
34 Interview, Jack Lynch
35 The 135th Assault Helicopter Company was based further north than Nui Dat, operated over several provinces and was manned in part by Royal Australian Navy helicopter pilots who made up the RAN Helicopter Flight Viet Nam (RANHFV).
36 Interview, Jack Lynch
37 Interview, Terry Pinkerton
38 Interview, Jack Lynch
39 ibid.
40 ibid.
41 Interview, Ian Conaghan
42 Interview, Jack Lynch
43 ibid.
44 ibid.
45 ibid.
46 ibid.
47 Interview, Joe Van Droffelaar
48 Interview, Terry Pinkerton
49 Interview, Jack Lynch
50 ibid.
51 ibid.

14 TARGETS DOWN, PATCH OUT

1 Interview, Peter Schuman
2 Interview, Reg Beesley
3 ibid.
4 Interview, Neville Farley
5 Interview, Jack Lynch
6 ibid.

7 Interview, Bill Hindson
8 Interview, Barry Standen
9 Interview, Ian Conaghan
10 Interview, Ron Dempsey
11 Interview, Barry Standen
12 Interview, Peter Schuman
13 Interview, Ron Dempsey
14 Interview, Neville Farley
15 ibid.
16 Interview, Barry Standen
17 Interview, Ron Dempsey
18 Interview, Bill Hindson
19 Interview, Barry Standen
20 Interview, Neville Farley
21 Interview, Bill Hindson
22 Interview, Jack Lynch
23 ibid.
24 ibid.
25 Interview, Ron Dempsey
26 Interview, Bill Hindson
27 Interview, Barry Standen
28 Interview, Bill Hindson
29 Interview, Barry Standen
30 Interview, Trevor Roderick
31 Interview, Barry Standen
32 Interview, Reg Beesley
33 ibid.

15 THE OPPOSITION

1 Interview, Trevor Roderick
2 Interview, Peter Schuman
3 Interview, Bill Hindson
4 Interview, Peter Schuman
5 Interview, Neville Farley
6 Interview, Andy Nucifora
7 Interview, Barry Standen
8 Interview, Peter Schuman
9 Interview, Trevor Roderick
10 Interview, Joe Van Droffelaar
11 Interview, Ian Conaghan
12 Interview, Andy Nucifora
13 Interview, Trevor Roderick

14 Interview, Neville Farley
15 Interview, Ian Stiles
16 Interview, Barry Standen
17 Interview, Bill Hindson
18 Interview, Trevor Roderick
19 Interview, Barry Standen
20 Interview, Jack Lynch

EPILOGUE

1 David Horner, *SAS: Phantoms of the Jungle*, pp. 390, 510
2 Mick Malone (ed.), *SAS, A Pictorial History of the Australian Special Air Service*
3 Interview, Ian Conaghan
4 Interview, Neville Farley
5 Interview, Barry Standen
6 Interview, Trevor Roderick
7 Interview, Ian Stiles
8 Interview, Neville Farley
9 Interview, Ron Dempsey
10 Interview, Bill Hindson
11 Interview, Trevor Roderick
12 Interview, Barry Standen
13 Interview, Peter Schuman
14 Interview, Bill Hindson
15 Interview, Ron Dempsey
16 ibid.
17 Interview, Bill Hindson
18 Interview, Barry Standen
19 ibid.
20 Interview, Andy Nucifora
21 Interview, Ron Dempsey
22 Interview, Bill Hindson
23 Interview, Barry Standen

BIBLIOGRAPHY AND SOURCES

BOOKS

David Horner, *SAS: Phantoms of the Jungle—A History of the Australian Special Air Service*, Sydney: Allen & Unwin, 1989
Mick Malone (ed.), *SAS, A Pictorial History of the Australian Special Air Service*, Northbridge, Western Australia: Access Press, 1998
9 Squadron RAAF, 'Squadron Standard Operating Procedures for Special Air Service Operations', Chapter 8

INTERVIEWS

Colonel Reg P. Beesley, AM, Scarborough, WA, 4 September 1997
Warrant Officer Ian Conaghan, Perth, WA, 6 September 1997
Lieutenant-Colonel Ron Dempsey, Canberra, ACT, 1 November 1997
Warrant Officer Neville Farley, Brisbane, Qld, 19 October 1997
Lieutenant-Colonel Bill Hindson, MC, Canberra, ACT, 1 November 1997
Major-General J. C. (Jim) Hughes, AO, DSO, MC, Melbourne, Vic., 2 September 1997
Wing Commander Jack Lynch, RAAF, Toowoomba, Qld, 23 November 1997
Lieutenant-Colonel Dan McDaniel, Perth, WA, 6 September 1977

Corporal Angelo 'Andy' Nucifora, Cairns, Qld, 7 February 1998
Sergeant Terry Pinkerton, RAAF, Karalee, Qld, 12 February 1998
Major Trevor Roderick, Lowood, Qld, 16 August 1997
Lieutenant-Colonel Peter J. Schuman, AM, MC, Fremantle, WA,
    4 September 1997
Major Barry F. 'Muka' Standen, Cairns, Qld, 7 February 1998
Sergeant Ian 'Bagza' Stiles, Perth, WA, 4 September 1997
Warrant Officer M. 'Joe' Van Droffelaar, MM, The Vines, WA,
    6 September 1997

LETTERS

Colonel R. P. Beesley, AM
Warrant Officer N. Farley
Major-General J. C. Hughes, AO, DSO, MC

INDEX